I0141399

The Father's Business
And
The Spiritual Cross

"To this end was I born,
And for this cause came I unto the world."

Second Edition 2016

Festus Enumah M.D.

The Father's Business And the Spiritual Cross
Copyright © 2016 Authored By Festus Enumah M.D.
All rights reserved.

No part of this publication may be reproduced, stored in a retrieval system or transmitted in any form or by any means-electronic, mechanical, photocopy, recording or any other-except for brief quotations in printed reviews, without the prior permission of the author.

For information regarding permission, write to:
    Festus Enumah, M.D.,
    1629 10th Avenue. Columbus, GA 31901. USA

The Library of Congress of United States in Cataloging

The Library of Congress of United States Catalog Card: TXu 1-634-756
Festus Ibeghuna Enumah. 1629 10th Avenue. Columbus, Georgia, 31901. USA
The Spiritual Cross of Jesus of Nazareth. (January 29, 2009)

Library of Congress of United States Catalog Card: TXu 1-898-431
Festus Enumah. 1629 10th Avenue. Columbus, Georgia, 31901. USA
The Father's Business and the Spiritual Cross. (January 8, 2014)

ISBN 10: 0692750029
ISBN 13: 9780692750025
Library of Congress Control Number: 2016947119
Festus Enumah, Columbus, GA

DEDICATION 1

I know not how I shall offend in dedicating my unpolished lines to your Lordship, nor how the world will censure me for choosing so strong a prop to support so weak a burden. Only if your Honor seem but pleased, I account myself highly praised and vow to take advantage of all idle hours till I have honour'd you with some graver labour... —William Shakespeare, *Venus and Adonis*

This book is dedicated to:

Jesus of Nazareth, for the completion of His Father's business and for His courage to drink of the "cup" for the accomplishment of what was "finished" at Golgotha.

The love I dedicate to your Lordship is without end: whereof this Pamphlet, without beginning, is but a superfluous moiety. The warrant I have of your honorable disposition, not the worth of my untutored lines, makes it assured of acceptance. What I have done is yours. What I have to do is yours: being part in all I have, devoted yours. Were my worth greater, my duty would show; meanwhile, it is bound to your Lordship... —William Shakespeare, *Luc*

DEDICATION 2

This dissertation is also dedicated to our parents:

Annie E. Bronersky (1920–1979) Joseph Bronersky (1917–1987)

Samuel A. Enumah, the blessed Oliaku (1908–2005) Christiana U. Enumah (1918–2012),

Other books by Festus Enumah M.D.

The Innocent Blood and Judas Iscariot
The Father's Business and the Spiritual Cross-First Edition

Coming Soon.

Complete Volume (The New Revelation Series 1-5) of the New Christianity of Christ Essentials-Made Easy

The words and the works of Jesus Christ Decoded

The New Gospel Revelations Series 1 The Naked Truth: Jesus's Kingdom of God and its Mysteries Decoded

The New Gospel Revelations Series 2 Easter Decoded: Jesus's Everlasting Miracle of the Earthly Stages of Human Creation

The New Gospel Revelations Series 3 ABC's of Eternal Life and Jesus's Role in Human Creation

The New Revelations Series 4 The Mysteries of Golgotha: Why Jesus Died

The New Revelations Series 5 An Exemplary Christian: *German Chancellor Angela Merkel.

**What makes you *NOT* a Christian.

ABOUT THE BOOK COVER

Front Cover

THE SPIRITUAL EVENTS in Jerusalem and at Golgotha carried all the divine portraits of the Father's business and placed them conspicuously in the human consciousness for everlasting remembrance. Jesus performed many healing miracles that nobody had done before. It is for these reasons that the book cover was designed, bearing with it, the Oath of Hippocrates, shaped in the form of a cross.

The image is from a 12th century Byzantine manuscript. Vatican Bibloteca Apostolica, Rome.

Back Cover

The back cover of the book portrays the footprints of the twelve ordained apostles, whose feet Jesus washed during the Last Supper in preparation for their travel to the Greco-Roman Empire and to all parts of the world, in order to spread the good news of the spiritual events at Golgotha.

CONTENTS

Acknowledgements xiii

Forewords xv

Preface: Letter to the Excellent Theophilus xvii

Introduction: The Mystery of the Satanic Temptation of Jesus xxvii

Prologue: The Prodigal Son xxxvii

Timeline xxxix

1   The Father's Business 1

2   The Father's Business and Jesus's Policy of
Secrets and Silence 10

3   What Is the Gospel? 20

4   The Predictive Metaphors of the Cross 33

5   Jesus's Last Journey to Jerusalem 40

6   The Fifth Provocative Act: The role of Judas
Iscariot 54

7   The Sixth Provocative Act: The Trials of Jesus
before the High Priest 64

8   The Seventh Provocative Act: The Trial of Jesus
before Roman Governor Pontius Pilate 68

9   The Road to the Triumphant Hill of Golgotha 72

10   Eclipse of the Great Lord and The Death of Jesus Christ 75

11   The Glorification of Jesus 85

12   Resurrection: The Manifestation of the Glorified
Spirit of Jesus Christ 90

13	Ascension of Jesus Christ	101
14	The Mystery of Jesus's Crucifixion by the Romans	105
15	The Epitome of Jesus's Life and the Cross	125
16	God and the Cross	131
17	What is the Spiritual Cross?	139
18	The Glory of the Cross	150
19	Christology of the Cross	163
20	Instructive Metaphors of the Cross	179
21	The Divine Trinity of the Human Souls	187
22	Our Colossal Task in the Father's Business	197
	Epilogue	221
	Afterwards	227
	Bibliography	235
	About The Author	241

ACKNOWLEDGEMENTS

WHAT IS IMPORTANT to me in writing this book is to share with humankind, regardless of their religious beliefs, the knowledge that I have gained by exploring the secrets of the Father's business that Jesus executed and the mysteries of the spiritual events at Golgotha. My greatest appreciation in that endeavor is to my family: my wife, Lois; my children, Tirzah, Lisette, Samuel and Zachary; our office manager, Nancy Boden and the office secretary, Sandra Beasley. I am grateful to them for their support, guidance and critical review of the manuscript. Three years ago, I had produced what I considered a good manuscript on *the Spiritual Cross* and was ready to get it published. After Lisette and Sam. edited some early pages, they told me to start all over again. They outlined the guidance I must use to transform the manuscript from good to great. I am indebted for their insights and suggestions.

The writing of this book was an endless process. Many people with whom I discussed some features in the manuscript encouraged me and contributed significantly to my work. I am grateful to them for all their efforts. I would also like to acknowledge Pastor Dora Bernal (1946-2010). Her inspirational words helped and empowered me in writing this book. May her soul join "the righteous that will shine forth as sun in the kingdom of their Father." (Matthew 13:43)

During the production of this manuscript, I read many Christian theological books. I am grateful to those authors. Their efforts inspired and prompted me to explore more of the Gospel. Those who live later often are the benefactors of the labors of their predecessors. It would be the right thing to dedicate the book to the people who labored to put in writing and proclaim to the world, what they witnessed at Golgotha. They provided the equipment I used in the production of the manuscript. My deepest thanks goes to them- the twelve ordained apostles, the physician Luke, Saint Paul and others-who labored for us.

FOREWORDS

THE FATHER'S BUSINESS and the Spiritual Cross, is the second book my husband has toiled over. His first publication, *The Innocent Blood and Judas Iscariot,* demonstrated his original thought and depth of knowledge in religious studies. In fact, it was a few years after its publication that National Geographic published *The Gospel of Judas,* which had remarkable similarity to his original ideas printed a few years earlier. I mention this because I believe it gives the reader some insight into how Festus' mind works and how deep his probing goes for understanding what really might have happened during the time of Jesus.

In this second book, Festus has again worked tirelessly toward communicating his understanding of why what transpired at Golgotha was so eminently important and unlike so many other beliefs and doctrines, has stood the test of time. It has been more than two millenniums since Jesus walked this earth. Yet the principle He preached and others wrote down for us to study and remember are still very much alive.

I observed my husband over the past several years working on this manuscript and can honestly say that he has researched this topic, spent endless hours writing out ideas and thoughts and then reconsidering and rewriting. Sometimes, we would discuss a thought or new idea and work through a concept and he would get inspired with a new or different train of thought. If you could have witnessed the exuberance, he showed as he toiled, you would then know the depth of his belief in what he writes and the import it has.

He has been baffled for years as to why the doctrine of Christ survived the ages and how many people believe in Christianity. As you will tell from reading this, he holds Jesus up as the Most High. Yet he has wanted to understand and then help others to understand why Jesus lived and died the way He did and why God allowed or rather ordained that it happen this way.

I was excited when I read the chapter at what was happening at Golgotha "behind the scenes" and believe you will find it thought provoking as well. It again demonstrates Festus brilliance with original thought and carrying a concept to its complete clarity. You, the reader will also find Festus tries to bring the reader forward and connect these ideas to current events to add relevance to this work. I hope you will think about this carefully and find some connection to what you believe and practice or are learning about for the first time and how it matters today in our world so filled with suffering, poverty and manifestations of evil.

Festus' faith has carried him his entire life to be successful as a surgeon, a husband, a father, and now a writer. I do believe his faith has helped him to persist in understanding the message of the Cross. This faith has brought him inspiration and I know you will enjoy reading it as much as he enjoyed writing it. Keep an open mind and enjoy!

Lois Bronersky-Enumah, M.D.

PREFACE

Letter to the Excellent Theophilus

The former treatise have I made, O Theophilus, of all that Jesus began both to do and teach until the day in which he was taken up, after that He through the Holy Ghost had given commandments unto the apostles whom He had chosen: To whom He showed Himself alive after His passion by many infallible proofs, being seen of them forty days, and speaking of the things pertaining to the kingdom of God.
—ACTS 1:1-3

IT SEEMED A good idea to me, based on the Gospel records of the words and deeds of Jesus of Nazareth, to write to you again, most excellent Theophilus, concerning the Father's business Jesus came here to accomplish. In the former treatise I sent to you, I discussed the authorized divine initiative of Judas Iscariot to meet the Jewish authorities. That divinely guided and authorized immortal act of Judas Iscariot, executed under the watchful eye of the invisible Father of Christ, was designed to enable Jesus to complete His work at Golgotha and keep the execution of the Father's business on the right course. In my report to you, I was certain that Judas Iscariot was innocent and did not betray Jesus. I published that report in my book, *The Innocent Blood and Judas Iscariot*. Many years after my report, the National Geographic Society reported that the Gospel of Judas was found in Egypt. That Gospel of Judas Iscariot revealed that Judas was not a betrayer of Jesus but an innocent apostle commissioned by Jesus to do what he did.

Since my report, in my insatiable quest to know who Jesus is and the Father's business He came to execute, I stayed in spirit with Him and the apostles and followed Jesus to Golgotha where He was crucified. The subject of this my treatise, is the Father's business that was carried out by Jesus Christ. What took Jesus three years to execute and how He accomplished it cannot be summarized in a few pages or be addressed in one book. The subject surveyed in this treatise is the Father's business covering the period that started with Jesus's last journey to Jerusalem and ended with the events at Golgotha. It would be an incomplete document if the resurrection of Jesus was excluded in the survey. Additionally, our colossal task in the Father's business will not be given complete treatment without reference to some of the words of Christ and events that occurred before His last trip to Jerusalem. The purposes of this treatise are to:

Reveal the objectives and the goals of the Father's business.
explore some of the secrets Jesus deployed in His works
Discuss our colossal tasks in the Father's business.
Reveal why Jesus came to this planet when
the Romans ruled the world.
Reveal some of what was "finished" at Golgotha by Jesus Christ.
Reveal the meaning of the glorifica-
tion of the Spirit of Jesus Christ.
examine how the cross revealed Jesus and His Father
Explore the promised rewards for humanity.
Reveal the long-overlooked validation of the authentic-
ity and divine origin of Jesus's words and deeds.
Reveal how human souls benefitted most from the
Father's business and the spiritual events at Golgotha.

This treatise seeks to illuminate God's plan for humanity that was designed even before Adam and Eve walked on this planet. The objective and aim of God's plan is to create humans as spiritual beings. My treatise delineates the Father's business as a process that was set in motion for the continuation of God's plan. That process is still going on even today. In doing so, I forayed to places where no one has gone before: the deep secrets of Jesus's last journey to Jerusalem and the mysteries of Golgotha where Jesus Christ erected, by the passion of His blood, God's spiritual temple of truth. In writing this treatise, I have used many spiritual quotations from the Gospel to support many of my assertions. I have allowed my imagination to blend with my spiritual insight as to penetrate into some mysteries of the events that occurred during the time covered in this treatise.

My work would have been easy if the apostles had asked Him, "Master, who are you? Tell us in a way we can understand why you came to live among us? Why did you come to Palestine at this time when we are subject to the Romans? Why did you come when the Romans rule the world and have named the sun, the moon, and other planets after their gods and goddesses? Why did you allow our leaders to arrest you, condemn you to death, and hand you over to the Romans? Why did you allow the Romans to crucify you?" The Jews always asked Jesus the wrong questions. They wanted to know if He was the expected Messiah who would expel the Romans and restore the glory to Israel or if He was the Christ, the Son of God.

Initially, my aim in writing this treatise was to enhance the under-standing of the events Jesus executed at Golgotha. However, that end-less quest was quickly pushed beyond the boundaries of Golgotha into the hidden mysteries of those spiritual events. The main source of my information is the Gospel and Jesus's own words. I meditated on the protean ramifications of the cross. I thought of what would have happened if Jesus had walked away from Gethsemane before he was arrested. What would have happened to the Father's business that Jesus executed in Jerusalem and Golgotha if Jesus did not maintain deep silence and secrets on what His Father had planned? I pondered what would have happened to the human souls that Jesus liberated from the shackles of the rulers of darkness, if Jesus had revealed Himself with heavenly signs as demanded by the Jews. I wondered if there would be any Christianity today if Jesus had disappeared and was not lifted up on that cross at Golgotha. I contemplated on the colossal task Jesus undertook in His attempt to reveal the meaning of earthly life, the truth about God, and the path to that God for the glory that awaits humanity. The stakes were high. It was not a task of questionable victory but an assignment of guaranteed victory. I found myself constantly in spirit at Golgotha, gazing at the crucified Jesus Christ who pledged His life to guarantee permanently the bondage of the human souls with Him and His father.

If we do not know why Jesus came to the world, we will not understand His mission or comprehend why He died the way He did. The spiritual events at Golgotha, where Jesus was crucified by the Romans, were the most important components of the Father's business for which Jesus was dispatched. I have tried to gain insight into those events as they related to the Father's business. In doing so, I uncovered what I considered the most important divine plan: why Jesus, without offering any physical or verbal defense, allowed the Romans to crucify Him. Why Jesus allowed Himself to be crucified has defied comprehension, and yet behind all of Jesus's words and deeds was the invisible plan God had for Jesus and for all humanity. God was relentless in His plan. His plan had to be completed the way He designed it.

Most excellent Theophilus, do you believe that God's plan was to create humans capable of reflecting His image? The spiritual image of the resurrected Jesus Christ appeared in human form as He was before His death, confirming the expectation that humankind final spiritual image, may also be in the form as we are now. I know you do believe just as I do. Have you wondered why God has not left us alone to do as we please and has followed us since our history began? The history of humanity is the history of God-human fellowship. Human life started with that bond. It is still an ongoing symbiosis. It will end with that relationship.

The Father's business Jesus came to accomplish and the kingdom of God He preached about were designed to help humans stay on the pathway of this creative evolutionary process. What is required of humans on our part is simply to do the will of God on earth as it is done in heaven, so that we may follow the path of creative development. This creative evolutionary process will continue until the glory of what the Father has created makes the entire heavenly host sing the glorious song of victory. On that day, the heavens will declare the glory of God. God mapped out the path to this end; the mission of Jesus was to make it possible and guide humanity through the narrow but straight path that leads to the final product: a completely spiritual man ready for the promised divine union with God.

As I was editing the manuscript, it became obvious to me that the events in the Gospel before Jesus's last trip to Jerusalem and the spiritual events at Golgotha where Jesus was crucified and died were not isolated events. They were interconnected, and both events formed the intrinsic part of the spiritual seed Jesus planted on this planet during the execution of the Father's business. Without either, the mission of Jesus could not have ended with triumphant victory for the Father and glory for humanity. What then is this connection? It is for this reason that I expanded my treatise to include an outline of the Father's business and an overview of what the Gospel is. I made many references to the words and works of Christ in discussing the spiritual events at Golgotha. The course Jesus took in the execution of his Father's business passed through many spiritual stations, of which Golgotha was the grand, everlasting and final spiritual station. It carried the spiritual force and the power of the kingdom of God with it to the infinite realm. In writing the first edition of this book, I thought that the mysteries of this kingdom of God are coded in many of Jesus's parables of the Kingdom. They are not coded in those parables.

Jesus was silent on why He went to Jerusalem to be arrested, condemned to death by the Jewish authorities, and crucified by the Romans. He was silent and did not discuss with anyone why He had to be crucified on the cross. The inability to discern the mysteries of the Father's business, Jesus's triumphant entry into Jerusalem, the spiritual events at Golgotha where Jesus was crucified and died, and Jesus's resurrection stem from ignorance of who we are, why we are here on this planet, and what God designed for humanity. My reconnaissance into the hidden mysteries in Jesus's Gospel evolved from my attempt to know Him, why

He came, the reason for human existence on earth, and God's holy purpose for humanity. I gained insight into the mystery of Jesus's trial before the Roman governor, Pontius Pilate, and why He allowed Himself to die by crucifixion. It opened my understanding of what Jesus meant when He said during His trial that "To this end was I born, and for this cause came I unto the world." (John 28:37

Most excellent Theophilus, my treatise is not for the theologians only. I have designed it also for the general public and for people of all religions. I believe this book will be an educational instrument and an inspiration that will fascinate and appease readers from all occupations, regardless of their religious background. It is my hope that people of all nations would also explore what is behind the spiritual door that Jesus opened, and find the truth of what was finished at Golgotha. However, I foresaw the consequences that might follow when my treatise is published. The world may censure me because I do not have formal theological training, but I cannot allow the distractions of the truth or fear of censorship to be a hindrance to the revelation of the truth as I perceive it. I am prepared for criticism, if through this treatise, the spiritual tools for human spiritual evolution are revealed. I am prepared to be chastised, if my treatise helps reveal who Jesus is and explains what the Father's business Jesus came to accomplish is. Most excellent Theophilus, I am prepared for condemnation, if I am unable to reveal why Jesus rode into Jerusalem on a colt in a New Orleans-style Mardi Gras-triumphant parade even though He knew that He was going to be killed in Jerusalem.

If we lack the knowledge of why Jesus came and what God's holy purpose for sending Him was how then can we discern why Jesus allowed Himself to be crucified and died at Golgotha? If we lack knowledge of the spiritual events at Golgotha, how can we experience the new Spirituality that Jesus introduced and harness its blessings? If we allow the dogmas and the human doctrines to blind us, how can we see the temple of the truth that was erected at Golgotha and worship God in spirit and in truth in that temple? We must not reticent from challenging the status quo as handed down to us. However, we must develop spiritual eyes and understanding trained to the ultimate goal of the Father's business.

Humanity, contrary to what we may believe, is in an early, rudimentary phase of its evolutionary spiritual development. There is one humanity, one Father in heaven, and same goal for all humanity. Humanity has yet to advance to a stage in which it can acknowledge those facts. The earthly part of the Father's business that was executed and the metaphysical drama at Golgotha, that were portrayed in a ubiquitous modus operandi, revealed the works of Jesus in bringing the knowledge of His Father and everlasting life to humankind, Jesus was confident that He would be victorious, but that victory was for His Father and for all mankind,

I believe that my treatise would add credence to the world's spirituality and redirect humanity to the path of glory as prepared by Jesus under the guide of the invisible Father, who reigns and controls all things. I hope it will spiritually awaken and excite all people who want to know why Jesus came to a small place in Palestine, where only two tribes of the Jewish people lived (ten tribes of the northern Israel had vanished), who were ruled by the mighty Roman Empire, and introduced a Spirituality that grew and expanded, "like a grain of mustard seed, which a man took and sowed in his field; which indeed is the least of all seeds; but when it is grown, it is the greatest among herbs, and became a tree, so that the birds of the air came and lodged in the branches thereof." (Matthew 13: 31-32)

Today, there is a tendency for people to seek retribution for offense committed against them. It is my hope that this treatise would help people to develop a change of heart, and not to seek revenge, but use that opportunity to seek after the Spirit of the Father that Jesus introduced to us. What joy, what jubilation, what relief from this endless work and responsibility it would be for me, if I could declare with confidence that humanity would benefit from it and that the loving Father and the Prince of peace, Jesus Christ, and His ordained apostles are pleased with my work.

Your Excellency, in executing His Father's business, Jesus Christ used it as an opportunity to do things that were dear to Him: show compassion and love for the sick and the poor. The physician Luke, in writing his Gospel, also used that opportunity to reveal what was important to him as a physician: compassion, love, and humility. He was the only one who reported on the stories of the prodigal son and the Good Samaritan. Following their examples, I have used this opportunity to make many references on issues that are important to me and blended them in many of my narratives. Such issues include but are not limited to the forgotten population in refugee camps, the late diagnosis of cancer in citizens of the developing world, the plight of the poor among us, the persistent exploitation of the natural resources of the poor nations by the modern colonial masters, the collaboration of the rulers of the poor nations with those modern colonial masters in the exploitation, the eagerness to engage in war without giving peace a chance, violence against the people by their elected rulers, the exploitation of people who trusted their religious rulers, and the refusal for humanity to recognize that we are one humanity, we serve one God, and our lifecycle and destiny is the same. In constructing this treatise, I commented on many traditions handed down to us by some authorities that became obstacles to the understanding of what was accomplished in Jerusalem and at Golgotha. They form potholes on the path of the Father's business.

The concept that Adam and Eve were created in Paradise, that God drove them away because of their sin, that we are all born in sin, that the crucifixion and death of Jesus Christ wiped away the sins of the world, and the atonement theory of salvation, are some of the human interpretations that are obstacles to the comprehension of the Father's business. Many will come after me to expand on what I have started and explore the endless hidden secrets and mysteries of the Father's business as recorded in the Gospel. I am certain they too will remove many of the obstacles, the human doctrines and dogmas, and the unwarranted religious rituals that are hindrances to the comprehension of this earthly part of the Father's business that Jesus completed.

Most excellent Theophilus, take time to read my treatise and think it over. It is my conviction and sincere hope that the topics discussed in my treatise will be read with interest. I am sure that Jesus, who was sent by

His Father and His holy angels and the twelve holy apostles, guided me in the production of this treatise. May God, the Father of Jesus Christ, bless you with His spirit.

21, January 2014
Your humble servant,
Festus Enumah, MD, FACS.

INTRODUCTION

The Mystery of the Satanic Temptation of Jesus

And immediately [after His baptism], the Spirit drove Him into the
wilderness. And He was there in the wilderness forty days, tempted of
Satan, and was with wild beasts, and the angels ministered unto Him.
—MARK 1:12-13

IT MAY SEEM odd that the introduction of this treatise on the Father's business and the Spiritual Cross is the Satan's temptation of Jesus. However, what Jesus would and would not do in the execution of the Father's business were revealed in that wilderness during His temptation. That spiritual event in the wilderness was an authentic introduction to humankind, the spiritual world of the universe that highlighted the nature of Jesus, what He planned to accomplish and the formidable powers and works of Satan. To comprehend the mystery of this temptation, you have to remove from your consciousness that Satan is the Devil. Satan is the commissioned Tempter of both the finite and infinite. The reported three scenes of the temptations, revealed how Satan explored the weaknesses and obstacles that Jesus would be confronted with, that could derail the Father's business. The satanic temptation of Jesus in the wilderness was reported in the gospel of, (Matthew 41-11; Mark 1:12-13; Luke 4:1-12).

What happened in that wilderness was a preplanned event that involved only Spirits. Jesus was in that wilderness and had fasted for forty days before Satan came to tempt Him. The inscrutable mystery of the satanic temptation of Jesus is this: why did Jesus with all His authorities and powers, allow Satan to tempt Him and subjected Himself to his authority, by allowing him to take Him from one place to another during the period of that temptation? The simple answer is that the preplanned event was in the doctrine of the Father's business and we do not know why. The full explanation is still hidden. However, it was a signal to alert us that the events in the doctrine of the Father's business are all spiritual and their executions would involve more Spirits. What was Jesus doing in that wilderness during the period that He fasted? Jesus was silent on that issue. As no human being witnessed that His encounter with Satan, Jesus must have told the story of that spiritual event to His apostles, but omitted many things. This is consistent with His policy of silence and secrets on many things that related to way He executed the Father's business.

Both Jesus and Satan knew the expectations of the Jewish people, who are waiting for the Messiah, the Son of God, to come, drive away the Romans and establish the earthly spiritual Kingdom of God for the glory of Israel. The background for all the scenes in the satanic temptations of Jesus was based on those expectations by the Jews and on the obstacles posed by those expectations on what Jesus planned to accomplish at Golgotha. Jesus knew His people very well. Jesus was in the wilderness for forty days and nights, deliberating on how to tackle the expectations of His people and be able to dispense the true bread from heaven, the manna that His father had sent through Him to humankind. Was Jesus also, during that period deliberating on what would happen to Him at Golgotha? The answer is yes. Jesus came to the world to execute what was 'finished' at Golgotha. The Jewish expectations were obstacles to that plan and must be controlled. The inscrutable mystery of the story of the satanic temptation of Jesus in the wilderness is revealed and become more comprehensible, when viewed against the background of the expectations of the Jews at the time of Christ and what Jesus planned to accomplish at Golgotha.

Jesus and Satan knew one another. Both claimed divine authorities on the works assigned to them by God. Jesus had said, "All powers are given unto me, in heaven and in earth." (Matthew 28:18) During the temptation, Satan also said to Jesus, "All this power will I give thee and the glory of them; for that is delivered unto me; and to whomsoever I will I give it." (Luke 4:6) Jesus did not refute that claim by Satan. Satan did not question the authority and power claimed by Jesus. Jesus in all His narratives did not call Satan an invisible evil agent, the evil one or identify him as the Devil.

Satan knew that Jesus was in the wilderness and followed Him there. He knew why Jesus was in the wilderness for forty days and nights. He knew why Jesus came to the world but did not discuss it with Jesus. If he did, Jesus omitted it in narrating the story to the apostles. Satan was not ignorant of what happened during the baptism of Jesus by John, the Baptist. He also heard the voice from heaven that said, "Thou art my beloved Son, and in thee I am well pleased." (Luke 3:22) Satan was waiting for Jesus to "fulfill all righteousness" following His baptism. The angels too were ready and waiting for that event. Satan, the tempter, followed Jesus even to Gethsemane and Golgotha and continued to tempt Him. The vital lesson for all mankind in this satanic temptation of Christ: we will all be tempted during our earthly life. Be ready.

After the public announcement at the age of twelve that He came for the Father's business, Jesus disappeared from the scene. I would presume He was at Nazareth, preparing for His work. Jesus's nature was modified to be like us and live among us: "In the beginning was the word, and the word was with god…And the Word became flesh and dwell among us." (John1:1–14) Jesus was ready after eighteen years of preparation to begin His earthly part of the Father's business. He had all the powers. How would He use the power? The Spirit that took Him to Golgotha wanted to know, and so Satan, the tempter, was sent to confirm it. The angels were standing by but were not allowed to witness the actual temptation. Perhaps they did. Jesus had no choice, but He knew the value of that temptation. If Jesus had failed, the Father's business would have failed. However, failure was not an option. We have given Jesus many titles, including the 'Son of God,' 'Christ,' and the 'Messiah.' Was this tempta-tion the method for Jesus to prove to the Jews that He is the Son of God or the Messiah? The answer is no. The Jews did not witness any event of the temptation.

First Temptation

Satan asked Jesus, "If you are the Son of God, command this stone to become bread," but Jesus answered him, saying, "It is written, man shall not live by bread alone, but by every word of God." (Luke 4:3–4; Matthew 3–4) If Jesus had wanted to do that, He could easily have changed the stone into bread. Jesus turned water into wine during the wedding feast at Cana. With only five loaves of bread and two fish, Jesus fed five thousand men in addition to women and children. (Matthew 14:13–21, John 6:5-14) Jesus was with Satan, all on His own, devoid of the presence of the Spirit that led Him to that wilderness. Jesus had walked on the lake in Galilee as if it was frozen. Why would He not turn stone into bread to prove He is the Son of God?

The multiple requests of the Jews to Jesus to show them signs from heaven or to come down from the cross to prove He was the Son of God were really inconsequential and a waste of time... Jesus refused to reveal that information. In the course of the execution of the Father's business, the true nature of Jesus was revealed. Message from this temptation: Jesus did not come to this world to prove to you that He is the Son of God.

The kingdom of God Jesus preached about and the spiritual events of Golgotha were the two main events in the Father's business. Perhaps we can get the answers why Jesus was sent to the world by His Father by insightful exploration of Jesus's Kingdom of God and the events at Golgotha. The second message is this: our final glory depends on the words of God and not the bread we eat. If we are to penetrate the deep frontiers of the spirit of Christianity and use the information to understand the Father's business, then we must comprehend the importance and the spiritual meanings of the words of God that Jesus brought down from heaven. Jesus had not officially launched His mission, but He used the opportunity to reassure Satan on the main theme of His work:

the preaching of the words of God that we may have life and have it abundantly.

The Second Temptation

The second temptation was as grueling as the first. Jesus was taken to the pinnacle of the temple in Jerusalem, and Satan said to Him, "If You are the Son of God, throw Yourself down from here For it is written: 'He shall give His angels charge over you, to keep you and in their hands they shall bear you up, lest you dash your foot against a stone.'" Jesus answered, "You shall not temp the Lord your God." (Matthew 4:5–7)

The successful execution of this second temptation as reported by the writers of the Gospel was an assurance to Satan that Jesus would in no way give any illustrations, miracles, or other sign that He was the Son of God. To reveal whom He was and show signs to prove it was not what He came to do. This modality of satanic temptation persisted during Jesus's mission and followed Him to Golgotha, when, again, He was asked to come down from the cross so that the people would believe He was the Son of God. But Jesus refused to come down from the cross, just as He had refused on multiple occasions to give a sign from heaven that He was the Son of God. The lack of knowledge of the nature of the Father's business and its implications for humanity have led people to persistently inquire whether Jesus was the Son of God and neglect why He came and what we must do to stay on course for the Father's business.

The hidden truth and the mysteries of who Jesus was or if He was the Son of God, manifested in the satanic temptation in the wilderness, persisted through Jesus's earthly life. The writer of the Gospel of John did not report on the temptation of Jesus in the wilderness by Satan. The writer of that Gospel was not interested in the satanic temptation because he did not need Jesus to prove that He was the Son of God. The main theme of the Gospel of John is that Jesus is the Son of God.

We must look deeper into the mysteries of the satanic temptation to harness the truth of what was revealed. Satan was not interested in Jesus proving to him that He is the Son of God. Satan knew that Jesus is the

Son of God. Jesus and Satan were alone in that wilderness. Why then did Satan ask Jesus to prove to him in that wilderness, without witnesses, that He is the Son of God? Why was it so important to Satan? Was Satan trying to disrupt the Father's business? The answer is no. Satan was not the obstacle to the Father's business that Jesus came to eliminate. If Satan were the obstacle, both would have settled it in that wilderness or even before Jesus came to the world.

In the Old Testament literature, Satan was portrayed as an agent of God whose duty was to tempt both the infinite and the finite. In the New Testament literature, Satan was portrayed as a villain, an evil spirit, and as the Devil. How can the Father allow the Devil to tempt His Son? Satan is a Tempter, given the authority to perform his duty by God. The only authority that can stop him is God. That is why Jesus instructed us to pray, "Lead us not into temptation." God has the power to command Satan to tempt or not to tempt an individual. In the cases of Jesus and Job, God authorized Satan to carry out his duty. The vilification of Satan as the Devil, the fallen angel, whose final abode would be in the bottomless pit, has cast shadow on the true meaning of his authorized temptation of Jesus in the wilderness. This second temptation allowed us to have a glimpse into the real nature of Jesus. Satan was not tempting God, the Father of Jesus, but in response to Satan, Jesus said: "You shall not temp the Lord your God." The message is this: Jesus Christ is both a Lord and a God.

The Third Temptation

Satan carefully designed the last temptation of Jesus. Even if you do not like Satan, you must acknowledge his biographical knowledge of the people Jesus would encounter and their expectations of the Messianic kingdom. You must give him credit for his knowledge of the future of humanity, our current expectations of Jesus, and the unrealistic expectation of the spiritual kingdom many are expecting Him to establish on earth when He comes again. This third temptation as recorded by Luke reveals that Satan has a kingdom. Jesus knew that, he referred to it in His Gospel. (Matthew 12:26) Satan also knew the kingdom where Jesus came from. Both had knowledge of each other, and both were not interested in any earthly kingdom.

Jesus's love and compassion for humanity is unparalleled in any recorded event in human history. His love for humanity prompted Him to come down for His mission. The question was this: would He be influenced by His love and compassion for humanity to stay on the planet Earth and even make Himself a king or accept that title of the Messiah from the Jewish people? Would He acknowledge that He came to establish an earthly, powerful kingdom that would dominate the world? Satan wanted to know. The Spirit-the Father-that led Him to the wilderness was not worried. He knew why He sent Jesus to the world. He was confident that Jesus would complete all His tasks. The angels, who were not permitted into the arena when the temptations were going on, were anxious of what the result might be but still wanted to know.

Again, the devil took him up into an exceeding high mountain, and showed him all the kingdoms of world, and the glory of them; And said unto him, "All these things will I give thee, if thou wilt fall down and worship me." Then Jesus said unto him, "Get thee hence, Satan: for it is written, Thou shall worship the Lord thy God, and him only shall thou serve." —Matthew 4:8–10

The gospel writers of Mathew and Luke reported that it was the Devil that tempted Jesus. However, Jesus directed His rebukes and utterances to Satan in all the temptations. The inscrutable mystery of this last temptation, when revealed, showed that the Kingdom of God, subsequently proclaimed by Jesus is not an earthly Kingdom. Jesus had no desire to be a king who would control the world or to demonstrate to anyone His powers. Again it revealed that Jesus is a Lord and a God. Both Jesus and Satan knew where it is written in their own spiritual world that Satan must serve Him. The successful execution of the third temptation guaranteed that Jesus would not succumb to the desires of people trying to make Him a king or declare Himself as the Messiah and accept kingship so He could rule the world. Jesus had rejected the power and wealth of our earthly world.

If we could glimpse into the mysteries of Jesus's satanic temptation or were permitted to break into the divine inner circle of Jesus Christ and His Father (who allowed that event), what you would find would surely make you breathless. To capture the imagery of this grand assemblage of Jesus as the Lord and a God, with Satan as the Tempter, you must escape from this earthly plane and transcend to the worlds of Jesus Christ and Satan. Only Satan, the tempter was allowed at the scene in that wilderness at that time. What a divine privilege! Perhaps, they must have talked of other things that Jesus did not reveal to the apostles.

During that temptation, did Jesus change as He did during His transfiguration that was witnessed by Peter, James, and John? Have you not wondered how Satan was able to take Jesus from place to place, from the top of the mountain to the pinnacle of the temple? Did Jesus leave His physical body in the wilderness and travel in spirit with Satan to those places? If you could exit this earthly world, transcend into the spiritual world of Jesus, and go to that wilderness in spirit, you would see two spiritual beings, Jesus Christ and Satan, who had known each other from the beginning of time. If by accident someone had gone to the wilderness during the temptation, saw Jesus, and made an attempt to touch Him without having transcended into the spiritual world of Christ, He would have said, "Touch me not," as He said to Mary Magdalene. You cannot touch a spirit. During the temptation, it is reasonable to assume that Jesus was in a transfigured state, as He was during His transfiguration that was witnessed by three of the apostles. (Matthew 17:2) That transformation made it possible for Him to go from one place to another during the temptation. The Father who designed it did not want any earthly witnesses. The temptation of Jesus in the wilderness was a great spiritual event, executed by the ordained Master of temptation for our benefit. That experience prepared Jesus for the works His Father sent Him to do. It was an experience that was ordained and planned by His Father. It was for this reason that Jesus subjected Himself to the authority of Satan by allowing him to take Him from one place to another. At the end of that spiritual experience, Jesus asserted His divine authority on Satan, "Thou shall worship the Lord thy God and him only shall you serve." Satan departed but would return to tempt Jesus from time to time.

The mystery of the temptation of Jesus is deeply spiritual. A review of what Jesus encountered with reference to the expectations of the Jews opened a spiritual door to the mystery of His temptation by Satan. Satan was very tactful. He knew the expectations of the Jewish people that Jesus would encounter. The three temptations covered everything. There was no need for a fourth temptation. What Satan was asking Jesus is this: in the execution of the works you were sent to do, the people you will encounter will ask you for signs from heaven and demand super miracles from you to prove you are the Son of God; how would you handle that? They will want to make you a king and declare you as the expected Messiah, who will restore the glory to Israel, establish the earthly Kingdom of God and worship you as their Savior; what would you do? Would you abandon your task from your Father and go after the power and the earthly treasures of the world? Jesus's responses revealed how He would tackle the obstacles and the key elements that He would use in the execution of the Father's business. This is the deep mystery of the temptation of Jesus by Satan.

The satanic temptation of Jesus in the wilderness was a divine initiative to what would confront Jesus in His attempt to comply with what was in the doctrines of the Father's business. It empowered Jesus and guaranteed that He would be able to execute His own earthly part of the Father's business. It was a triumphant prelude to His work. It was a divine experience, one that prepared and equipped Jesus for the journey that glorified His Father, our God, and helped humankind in our spiritual journey. It was a prologue to the proclamation of the words of His Father and the platform He would use to dispense the bread of life, that humankind may eat and live forever. It prepared and made straight Jesus's paths to Golgotha. The Lord of all Spirits-His Father-was pleased. Jesus was pleased. The earthly phase for the execution of the Father's business just started.

Prologue

The Prodigal Son

A certain man had two sons, and the younger of them said to his father: "Father, give me the portion of goods that falleth to me," and he (the father) divided unto them his living. In addition, not many days after, the younger son gathered and took his journey into a far country, and there wasted his substance with riotous living. In addition, when he spent all, there arose a mighty famine in that land; and he began to be in want and he went and joined himself to a citizen of that country; and he sent him into the fields to feed swine. In addition, he would fain have filled his belly with the husks that the swine did eat; and no man Gave unto him. In addition, when he came to himself, he said, "How many hired servants of my father's have bread enough and to spare, and I perish with hunger! "I will arise and go to my father, and will say unto him, 'Father, I have sinned against heaven, and before thee, and I am no more worthy to be called your son; make me as one of thy hired servants.'" In addition, he rose and came to his father. However, when he was a great way off, his father saw him and had compassion, and ran, and fell on his neck, and kissed him. In addition, the son said unto him; "Father, I have sinned against heaven, and in thy sight, and am no more worthy to be called thy son." But the father said to the servants, "Bring forth the best robe and put it on him, and put a ring on his hand and shoes on his feet; and bring the fattest

calf and kill it and let us eat and be merry. For this my son was dead, and he is alive again; he was lost, and is found," and they began to be merry.
—EXCERPT FROM JESUS'S PARABLE OF THE
PRODIGAL SON (LUKE 15:11–24)

There is joy in the presence of the angels of God over one sinner who repents. Jesus,
—LUKE 15:10.

TIMELINE

BC 1336 The death of Egyptian Pharaoh Akhenaten
  He was the pioneer of monotheism. (The concept of one God)
BC 900 Worship of Baal as divine god introduced in Israel and Judah
  The period of Elijah, the Prophet
BC 722 Assyria's conquest of Israel and Judah
BC 586 The Babylonians conquered Judah, destroyed the Temple in
  Jerusalem.
BC 532 Babylon defeated by Persia. Temple rebuilt in Jerusalem
BC 332 Alexander the great conquered Judah
BC 63 The birth of Emperor Augustus
BC 63 Pompey conquered Jerusalem. Judea annexed as a Roman
  province
BC 42 The birth of Emperor Tiberius
BC 27–AD 14 Emperor Augustus as first emperor of Roman Empire
BC 6 The birth of Jesus Christ; Star of Bethlehem appeared in the
  constellation
AD 6 Jesus in the temple at age twelve
AD 14–37 Emperor Tiberius as the second Roman emperor
AD 26–36 Pontius Pilate as the procurator of Judea
AD 26 Six Galileans sacrificed by the Romans to their gods in Judea
AD 30 The trials, crucifixion, death, resurrection, and ascension of
  Jesus Christ
AD 30 (fifty days after the ascension of Jesus) The day of Pentecost
AD 35 Conversion of Saint Paul on his way to Damascus

AD 36 Caiaphas deposed as high priest

AD 46 Beginning of Paul's missions to Greco-Roman Empire and Asia

AD 70 Romans destroy Jerusalem and the Temple

AD 30–100 the Apostolic age; John, the last ordained apostle, died AD 100

AD 30–313 The spread of Christianity to the Greco-Roman Empire and Asia

AD 312 Emperor Constantine became a Christian

AD 313 Emperor Constantine legalized Christianity in the Roman Empire

AD 354 Pagan temples closed in the Roman Empire

1

THE FATHER'S BUSINESS

When Jesus was twelve years old, they went up to Jerusalem after the custom of the feast. They fulfilled the days, and as they returned, the child Jesus tarried behind in Jerusalem; and Joseph and his mother knew not of it. They, supposing him to have been in the company, went a day's journey and [then] they sought him among their kinsfolk and acquaintance. When they found him not, they turned back to Jerusalem, seeking him. After three days, they found him in the temple, sitting in the midst of the doctors, both hearing them, and asking questions. All that heard him were astonished at his understanding and answers. His mother said unto him, "Son, why hast thou thus dealt with us? Behold, thy father and I have sought thee sorrowing." Jesus said unto them, "How is it that ye sought me? Don't you know that I must be about my Father's business?" And they understood not. He went down with them to Nazareth, and was subjected into them: but his mother kept all these sayings in her heart. And Jesus increased in wisdom and stature, and in favor with God and man.
—LUKE 2, 40–52

IT WAS REPORTED in the Gospel that eighteen years after the above encounter, Jesus's apostles said to Him when they were in Sychar, a city in Samaria, "Master eat." Jesus replied, "I have meat you know not of. My meat is to do the will of Him that sent me and to finish His work." (John 4:31–34) Metaphorically, this meat was the task given to Him by His Father. The earthly stages of the Father's business led Jesus to Golgotha.

The Father's business is a multiphase process that started before Abraham. What was executed two thousand years ago was the terrestrial phase of the Father's business. Jesus had knowledge of God's design even before He was sent down to earth to execute the earthly part of the plan. The Father has not abandoned that plan. It must come to its end as He has planned for all humanity. The doctrine in the Father's business is the doctrine that God delivered to us through Jesus Christ: "My doctrine is not mine, but His that sent me. If any man will do His will, he shall know of the doctrine, whether it is of God or whether I speak of myself." (John 17:16-1).

A brief outline of the Father's business:

> The Founder and the Designer: the Father, our God
> Mediator and the Executioner: Jesus Christ
> Special agents in supporting roles: the angels,
> the twelve ordained apostles,
> Objectives:
> proclaim and inaugurate the Kingdom of God
> spiritualization of human souls with the Spirit of His Father
> direct all humans to the path that leads to His Father
> provide the spiritual tool humans can use to educate and
> prepare their souls in what God, His Father planned for
> humanity: creation of spiritual beings that will live forever
> develop partnership with Jesus Christ in
> the human creative activities
> remove the obstacles to the spiritualization of human souls
> the elimination of the obstacles to the Father's Business
> silence and control the gods and goddesses of the
> Greco-Roman Empire and other Gods

reveal the nature and power of His Father
Goals:
completion of His task for His Father and for mankind
demonstration of the power of His Kingdom of God
revelation and enthronement of the
Father as the universal true God
control of the influence of other Gods
and Goddesses on human minds
revelation of Himself as a Lord and a God
completion of God's plan for humanity: eternal life for the new spiritual mankind

The end of the Father's business is unknown! "It is not for you to know the times or the seasons which the Father hath put in His own power." (Acts of the Apostles 1:7) After eighteen years of earthly preparation, Jesus commenced the Father's business with the public proclamation that, "the time is fulfilled, and the Kingdom of god is at hand; repent ye and believe in the gospel." (Mark 1:15) That utterance was an indication that the Father who planned and controlled the execution of that business had given the green light for Jesus to go ahead with the plan. The Father's business is still active today and is unstoppable, proceeding at a speed that is ordained by God. The lack of knowledge of the Father's business puts humans in utter darkness of God's plan for creation and purpose for us here on earth.

It would seem that Jesus ended His earthly portion of the Father's business at Golgotha where He was crucified and died. However, this is not so. After His resurrection, for forty days Jesus continued to preach about the kingdom of God and continued to teach His apostles the doctrines of the Father's business. Even after His ascension, Jesus kept a watchful eye on its progress. When Saint Paul, before his conversion, was interfering with the progress of the Father's business, Jesus intervened. As Paul was on his way to Damascus to persecute the disciples of Jesus Christ, suddenly a light from heaven shined around him. He fell down to the earth and heard a voice saying to him, "Saul, Saul, why persecutest thou me?" the voice from heaven asked.

"Who art thou Lord?" Paul asked.

"I am Jesus, whom thou persecuted: It is hard for you to kick against the pricks," the Lord replied. (Acts of the Apostles 9:3–6)

God, the Father that Jesus presented to us, has never looked away from any human being. "But the very hairs of your head are all numbered." (Matthew 10:30) We have never been separated from God. The invisible God is always nearby and sees everything we do. Although His Spirit lives among us, only few people recognize that Spirit. Two thousand years ago, Jesus outlined what we must do to recognize and feel the presence of God: sell all our earthly possessions, distribute the proceeds to the poor, and then follow Him to the Father. That command of yesterday is still the same today and will be in future. Our ability, in His name to, "cast out devils, speak with new tongues, take up serpents and drink any deadly thing and it shall not hurt us, and lay hands on the sick and they shall recover," (Mark 16:17-18) and be fully created as spiritual beings, depends on our obedience of that commandment. It was a commandment that penetrates the frontiers of earthly possessions, love for the poor, and the belief in Jesus and His Father that sent Him. It is a responsibility that binds us to what Jesus prescribed for us in the Father's business. Jesus encouraged us to communicate directly to the Father, who is a Spirit and who also sees and hears in secret and even knows what is in our hearts before we utter the words.

We must commit ourselves to God, the faithful Creator, in order to be participants in the Father's business for the glory that was revealed: "Who am also an elder and a witness of the suffering of Christ and also a partaker of the glory that shall be revealed." (1 Peter 5:1)

It would seem as it was reported in Genesis, the first book of Moses, that Adam and Eve were created in a perfect state in a moment. However, this is not so because, as was metaphorically also reported in the same book, they had not eaten from the tree of life to live forever. Nobody to date has told us the type of sin Adam and Eve committed. Jesus did not say anything on the original sin of Adam and Eve. The concepts of original sin and us being conceived in sin are the greatest hindrances to the appreciation and understanding of the Father's business Jesus executed. As I will reveal in this treatise, Adam and Eve were born on earth like all human beings. The earthly phase of the evolutionary process for the full creation of humans is an ongoing process. It is going on now and will transcend to the extraterrestrial phase when we die. We were not born in sin. No child was ever born in sin. We were born so that God, the Father of Christ could complete the earthly phase of human creation. This is why we are here on earth.

Jesus was sent to the world by the Father to help humanity during this earthly phase of human creation, to educate and spiritualize the souls in preparation for the next phase of God's creation. This is in essence the glory of the mission of Jesus Christ. The goals of the Father's business are the same today as it was in the past, and it will remain so in the future until the end of time. The divine team deployed by the Father has not changed. Jesus has not changed the way He operated to get the Father's business going. If Jesus were here physically, He would be saying the same thing and executing the Father's business the same way. The only difference is that instead of making references to doctrines of the scribes and the Pharisees as obstacles to the Father's business, He would be making references to the dogmas and the human doctrines of modern Christianity, to the corporate colonization of the natural resources of Africa and other developing nations, and to the deep-seated evils of human beings against one another.

Diligent search of the Holy Scriptures shows that humans must enter the pathway of the Father's business, collaborate with Jesus Christ, and abide within it for the spiritualization of our souls. We cannot do it by ourselves. The pathway leads to the union of human souls with the Father and Jesus Christ. Jesus knew He would encounter evil forces during the execution of the Father's business. He prepared Himself and was confident that His mission would succeed: "How can one enter a strong man's house and plunder his goods, unless he first binds the strong man? And then he will plunder his house." (Matthew 12:29) Jesus knew how to bind the strong man. He did it with the cross and with the epitome of His earthly life style. The ubiquitous *modus operandi* deployed by Jesus ended at Golgotha, where He was crucified.

The execution of the Father's business, which started before Abraham was born, revealed the supreme sovereignty of the Father. The Father controlled and directed all things: "For I have not spoken of myself; but the Father who sent me, He gave me a commandment what I should say and what I shall speak. And I know that His commandment is life everlasting. Therefore, whatever I speak, just as the Father has told me, so I speak." (John 12:49–5)

It is mindboggling how pervasive the Father's control was in all of Jesus's actions. All His utterances and deeds were carried out as instructed by the Father. However, while the Father directed all events in the Father's business, Jesus knew that its success depended on Him. His Father had given Him all authorities and power in heaven and on earth. In His mission, Jesus saw victory for God as well as everlasting life and glory for humans, whom He called the "blessed" of the Father.

Despite all the obstacles and hindrances, Jesus successfully executed the Father's business, allowed Himself to be humiliated, and crucified because He believed we are worth it. Jesus served the Father and worked diligently to fulfill God's plan because He loved His Father. Similarly, Jesus served humanity and became our living partner, helping—and continuing to help—us in the execution of our own task in the Father's business because He loves us.

Come, ye blessed of my Father; inherit the Kingdom prepared for you from the foundation of the world. —Matthew 25:34

We must toil and be ready to harness that gift that is freely given to us through Jesus Christ. We must be active participants and be partners with Jesus in the execution of the Father's business. We must be engaged actively in the Father's business.

Jesus made God the epitome of mercy, love, compassion, forgiveness, peace, and justice. Jesus was a trusted, loyal, and obedient Mediator for God's plan. He labored relentlessly and executed the Father's business in a systematic manner that guaranteed glory for humanity and victory for God. We too must work with Jesus so we can share the joy that was set before us and rejoice together as was written; "Behold, I say unto you, lift up your eyes and look at the fields, for they are already white for harvest! And he who reaps receives wages, and gathers fruits for eternal life, that both he who sows and he who reaps may rejoice together." (John 4:35–36)

The fields are the souls of the inhabitants of earth. Our souls are ready for spiritualization in preparation for eternal life. To "gather fruits for eternal life" is to be active participants with Jesus in the Father's business for our everlasting glory. This is the will of Jesus, which is a duplication of the will of God.

Saint Paul spoke of the race before us: "Let us lay aside every weight and the sin which so easily ensnares us, and let us run with endurance the race that is set before us, looking unto Jesus…" (Hebrew 12:1–2) This race before us is our colossal task in the Father's business. There are essential elements in the Gospel of Jesus directing us to our role in the Father's business as that will help God in His plan for the glorious end of humans. This task is for everyone: for the just and unjust, the evil and the good, the corrupt and the uncorrupt, the wicked and the compassionate, the merciful and the poor in spirit, the meek and those that thirst for righteousness, the peacemakers and the warmongers. Despite the evil and deceitful hearts of many, God our Father would not turn away from anyone. It is for this reason God sent Jesus to earth, so that no human soul would be lost in the earthly phase of His creation.

The Mediator, Jesus Christ gave us the spiritual tools we must use in the Father's business. Those spiritual tools are not numbers, emblems, or incantations one can recite. They are not found in the water or oil some people sell as holy water or anointing oil. These tools are not found in special places or in any religious institutions. These spiritual tools, which were revealed in the Gospel, demonstrated by Jesus's lifestyle, and used by His ordained apostles, are the same tools we must use today in our vital role in the Father's business. Those who do not know about the doctrines and the contents of the Father's business or the spiritual tools humans must use to accomplish our task cannot put anyone on the path of glory: "Can the blind lead the blind?" (Luke 6:39) We must learn how to use these spiritual tools to accomplish what God has assigned us to do during our earthly lives to enable Him to complete His plan of creating spiritual humans in His own image and likeness.

What manner of love the Father hath bestowed upon us, that we should be called the sons of God! Therefore, the world knoweth us not, because it knew him not. Behold, now that we are the sons of God; and it doth not yet appear what we shall be; but we know that, when He shall appear, we shall be like Him; for we shall see Him as He is. Every man that has this hope in Him purifies himself, even as He is pure. —1 John 3:1–3

This purification, for us to be like Jesus and be called the sons of His Father, can only be accomplished with the liberal use of our spiritual tools.

For what is, a man profited, if he shall gain the whole world, and lose his own soul? Or what shall a man give in exchange for his soul? For the Son of man shall come in the glory of the Father, with His angels; and then He shall reward every man according to his works. —Matthew 16:26-27

The mystery of the Father's business that Jesus executed, when revealed in any age, translated into any language, or disclosed under any religious names and symbols guides the human soul to a fuller destiny, to a life hidden in God, the Creator, through Jesus Christ. "For it pleased the Father that in Him (Jesus Christ) should all fullness dwell." (Colossians 3:19) The Father's business gave humanity access to the knowledge of Christ and His Father. It provided us with evidence of who we are, why we are her and the intrinsic value of human life. It educated the human souls so that they could develop and advance to the highest evolutionary spiritual level and be participants to what the Father is creating. It propelled the fully created human spirits to a divine union with the Father and Jesus Christ. It eliminated obstacles placed on the trajectory of the journey of human souls to this divine union. This is the glory and the blessings of the Father's business.

Blessed is He who came in the name of the Lord. —Matthew 23:39

2

THE FATHER'S BUSINESS AND
JESUS'S POLICY OF SECRETS
AND SILENCE

*If I have told you earthly things, and you believe not, how
shall you believe if I tell you of heavenly things?*
—JESUS, JOHN 3:12

*Blessed are the eyes which see the things that you see. For I tell you that many
prophets and kings have desired to see those things which you see, and have not
seen them: and to hear those things which you hear, and have not heard them.*
—LUKE 10:23–24

THE DEEP MYSTERIES and the hidden secrets of the Father and Jesus
Christ are unprecedented. The aim of this part of my treatise is to
explore some of the hidden secrets Jesus deployed in the execution of
the Father's business. I will attempt to explain why Jesus, in the execution of His Father's business, chose not to reveal the reason for many

of His actions. Jesus's Gospel of good news is indeed a book of hidden secrets and a compendium of mysteries of time and space that expanded to Golgotha and beyond. The Gospel is not just a book of morals and ethics as in the tenth commandment of Moses or in the codes of many other religions. It is a compendium of documents of a deep spirituality that centered on the Spirit of His Father, Jesus's Kingdom of God and the human souls. It forayed into the infinite realm of the spiritual universe and the divine nature of human souls that made the comprehension of the Father's business difficult to comprehend. The mysteries of Jesus's Kingdom of God and the spiritual events at Golgotha are still beyond full human understanding. Jesus completed the Father's business and walked away without revealing in plain language the real reason for many of the events He executed in Jerusalem. Jesus did not give any specific reason why He allowed the Romans to crucify Him.

How then can one break down the walls of the secrets and mysteries and pierce those coded illustrations and performances that would help one comprehend Jesus's words and deeds? How can we develop our spirituality so that we are able to project ourselves into the inscrutable insights in the Gospel and see what is in the Father's business for us and what our tasks are so that we may be benefactors of what Jesus accomplished? How can we decode Jesus's words and works? Who can understand anything about the Kingdom of God that Jesus said was hidden in three measures of meal.

Whereunto shall I liken the kingdom of God? It is like leaven, which a woman took and hid in three measures of meal, till the whole was leaven. —Luke 13:20–21

Who can comprehend Jesus's provocative acts in Jerusalem? Unfortunately, the Christians—those given the task to be the lights of the world and live like Christ, so that people would see their good works and glorify the Father in heaven for His plan—have stopped looking into the divine instructions designed for them in the Father's business. Jesus coded His messages in parables and metaphors. Jesus's miracles, the spiritual event at Golgotha, His resurrection, and His life examples, were the platforms Jesus used to illustrate what is in the Father's business. How can we understand the Gospel of Jesus or the reason why He came to the world and allowed the Romans to crucify Him without spiritual guidance? In the last days of Jesus in Jerusalem, Jesus promised His apostles that He would not leave them comfortless, that He was going to send them the Comforter: "But the Helper, the Holy ghost, whom the Father will send in my name, He will teach you all things, and bring to your remembrance all things I have said to you." (John 14:26)

Jesus revealed in private, some but not all of the hidden secrets and mysteries of His words and deeds to the apostles.

And with many such parables He spoke the words to them as they were able to hear it. But without a parable He did not speak to them. And when they (the apostles) were alone, He explained all things to His disciples. —Mark 4:33

However, He did not explain all things to them. On three occasions, when He was alone with His apostles, Jesus privately predicted His death in Jerusalem but did not explain to them why He had to die or be handed over to the Gentiles to be mocked, scourged, and crucified. The apostles "understood none of these things; this saying was hid from them, and they did not grasp what was said." (Luke 18:34) They were afraid to seek explanation from Him. Jesus allowed His body to be anointed for "His burial" at Bethany by Mary, just before He marched into Jerusalem like a victorious five-star general returning from war. Yet the deep secrets of the spiritual events at Jerusalem and Golgotha were hidden from everyone, including the apostles. At the Last Supper, Jesus told His apostles while He was washing their feet, "What I do, thou knowest not now but thou shall know hereafter." Jesus did not explain to them why He had to wash their feet. That service offered to His apostles took three centuries to manifest. However, Jesus told the apostles that the service of washing their feet was "to be part of Him." At that time, did the apostles grasp the meaning of washing their feet as to be part of Him? The answer is no. Lacking such understanding, Simon Peter wanted his whole body to be washed by Jesus.

After Jesus's resurrection but before His ascension, it was also reported that He spoke to His apostles and "opened their understanding, that they might comprehend the scriptures." (Luke 24:45) The Ethiopian eunuch, as was reported in the Acts of the Apostles, got help from the angel, who worked through the apostle Phillip to be able to understand the scripture. It would seem that without the inscrutable insight, one could not understand the Gospel of Jesus or the spiritual events at Golgotha. It is not a surprise that Jesus left something in His Gospel that would help us. However, we must, "Ask, and it shall be given you; seek, and ye shall find; knock, and it shall be opened unto you." (Matthew 7:7; Luke 11:9) What we have to seek is also reported in the Gospel: "But seek ye first the kingdom of God and His righteousness; and all these things shall be added unto you." (Matthew 6:33)

Even the spiritual tools I believe one can use for the revelations of what we need to know in His Gospel are hidden and coded in the Gospel. We must strive to acquire such knowledge with Jesus as our guide, so we can be participants in the Father's business. If the universe represented the Gospel, the special tools for decoding the hidden mysteries and secrets of the Father's business in the Gospel, if viewed as stars, they could fill up the entire sky with iridescent heavenly light. You must search for these tools yourself. When you find them, use them to find the hidden treasuries in the Gospel and share that information with mankind. I am still searching for those tools for this simple reason: they are in His Gospel.

However, how can one penetrate into the spiritual world of the Gospel literature and the mysteries of Golgotha in order to understand the meaning of what was accomplished there without help from Christ and His Father? Who opened the hearts of Cleopas and his companion on their way to Emmaus so that they could understand the scriptures concerning Jesus Himself? Jesus did. Jesus "expounded unto them in all the scriptures, the things concerning Himself." (Luke 24:27) Who revealed the mysteries of the kingdom of heaven to the apostles? Jesus did. "Because it is given unto you to know the mysteries of the Kingdom of heaven." (Matthew.13:11) After the resurrection of Jesus, who instructed the apostles in Jerusalem on how to understand the scriptures? Jesus did: "He opened their understanding that they may understand the scriptures." (Luke 24:45) Who revealed secret things about the spiritual realm to some people? God, the Father, did: "I thank thee, O Father, Lord of heaven and earth, that thou hast hid these things from the wise and prudent, and hast revealed them unto babes; even so, Father, for so it seemed good in thy sight." (Luke 10:21; Matthew. 11: 25–26) Who revealed to Peter that Jesus is Christ, the Son of God? The Father, our God did. The spiritual gifts for understanding the scriptures and the events at Golgotha can only be made possible by God, our Father and Jesus. You too can be the new recipient of this spiritual gift. You too would be blessed with spiritual eyes and spiritual ears to help you penetrate the hidden secrets of the spiritual foundation of His Gospel and the mysteries of Golgotha.

A man can receive nothing, except it be given him from heaven. —John 3:27

The more I look at what Jesus intentionally withheld and the mysteries of some of His utterances, many of which He would not reveal to the public, the more I am convinced He did it for a purpose. On many occasions, Jesus did not reveal all the truth of what He was trying to convey to the people. Jesus hid the truth in His Kingdom of God, death and resurrection and used the parables, metaphors, parabolic utterances, and even in His miracles and instructions on how to pray to the Father as to put an outer coating to the mysteries of the truth. The characteristics of hidden secrets and mysteries seemed to be the platform on which He executed the Father's business. Jesus definitely refused openly to reveal who He was and why His Father sent Him. When the chief priests and the scribes asked Jesus, "Art thou the Christ? Tell us." Jesus replied, "If I tell you, you will not believe." (Luke 22:67) What looked like a revelation of who He was at His trial before the high priest Caiaphas was actually a revelation into more mysteries of His divine nature and powers. He still withheld the revelation of the nature of the place where He came from and who He really is. To be fair to Jesus, He did reveal His Father to us.

However, would you not want to know more about His Father and the place that is beyond the brightness of the sun? Would you not want to know about the place where Jesus was all the time, before He made His appearance in Palestine? Would you not want to know what they use to monitor mankind that He knew what Paul did in the past and planned to do in Damascus? Would you not want to know about the spiritual universe and how many spiritual kingdoms that is out there? Would you not want to know how the will of His Father is done in heaven? Would you not want to know the names of the spirits who, from the period of John, the Baptist, were trying to take the kingdom of God by force? All who are spiritually awake would like to know the truth about the creation of humankind. Even the dead would wake up from their graves to hear the voice of He who would release such information.

If the hidden secrets and mysteries coded in the Gospel of Jesus are decoded and revealed, and the interpretations are written down on rolls of papyrus and spread across the surface of the planet Earth, the Earth would not be able to contain it. My aim is to point out some of those secrets and many of the things Jesus held back from the public and the spiritual elements in the Gospel that would help in our understanding of the Father's business and the spiritual events at Golgotha. Perhaps it would also aid in the comprehension of the final glory that awaits humans and our colossal task for its accomplishment. There are many hidden messages in the Holy Scripture, but some of their interpretations evolve over time. God controls the time for the revelation of any event. When the apostles, disappointed that Jesus did not proclaim Himself as the Messiah, asked Him, just before His ascension, "Lord, will you at this time restore the Kingdom to Israel?" Jesus replied, "It is not for you to know the times or seasons which the Father has put in His own authority." (Acts of the Apostles 1:6)

Perhaps the secrets and the mysteries of Jesus's words and deeds and the plan of the invisible God were not hidden from us but rather preserved for us for our own benefit, and they will be revealed when the invisible God and Christ determine that such a revelation would help us. During the mission of Jesus Christ, the revelation of who Jesus is must be held secret. It had to be so that Jesus could continue His work and move on to Golgotha and beyond and establish the everlasting final station in the pathway of the Father's business—the one that would guarantee victory for the Father and glory for humanity.

The Gospel narratives reveal in many passages where Jesus instructed people who recognized Him not to reveal who He was. "I know who thou art; the Holy One of God," the man with the unclean spirit that Jesus healed said. However, Jesus rebuked him, saying, "Be quiet." (Mark 1:24–25, Luke 4:31, 38 Matthew 4:17) When Simon Peter identified Jesus as the Christ, Jesus instructed His apostles to tell no one the secret. (Luke 9:18–21)

We have all read about the transfiguration of Jesus of Nazareth. Jesus took three of His favorite apostles—Peter, James, and John—to a high mountain and was transfigured before them. As was reported that His face shined like the sun, and His clothes were as white as the light. In addition, they saw Moses and Elias talking with Him. (Matthew 17:2–9) At the end of that episode, Jesus charged them: "Tell the vision to no man, until the Son of man be risen again from the dead." Peter kept that promise. It was only after the resurrection of Jesus that he spoke about the experience: "For he received from God the Father honor and glory, when there came such a voice to him from the excellent glory, this is my beloved Son, in whom I am well pleased. And this voice which came from heaven we heard, when we were with him in the holy mount." (2 Peter 1:17–18)

Why did Jesus instruct them to tell nobody of that incident? Why was He trying to hide His identity? Jesus refused to give a direct answer to John the Baptist, who sent two of his apostles to find out, as the Baptist put it, "Art thou He that should come or look we for another?" (Luke 7:20) Jesus was asked by the Jews, "How long do you keep us in doubt? If you are the Christ tell us plainly." (John 10:24)

Jesus replied, "The works that I do in my Father's name, they bear witness of me, but you do not believe." (John 10:25–26)

Why did Jesus maintain the silence about who He is? By maintaining silence on who He is and identifying Himself in the light of His work,

Jesus took us through the journey of seeing, hearing, and understanding things that put us on the pathway of the knowledge of the Father's business. Jesus's policy of secrecy and silence on who He is, resulted in "lifting up" the Son of man on the cross. Jesus said: "When you have lifted up (on the cross) the Son of man, you will know that I am He." That was what Jesus wanted. That was what His Father planned. The manifestations of what His Father designed in the heavenly domains and what Jesus, voluntarily executed at Golgotha, when revealed, would transcend your imagination. The successful outcome of the Father's business that was finished at Golgotha, silenced the enemies of His Father, enthroned His Father as the universally true God, revealed who Jesus is, who we are and why we are here. If Jesus had not maintained silence on His identity and why He was sent by His Father, His mission would have collapsed.

The kingdom of God, Jesus preached, is the core message in His Gospel. Yet Jesus refused to reveal what that kingdom of God is. The mystery of it was revealed only to the apostles. "Because it given unto you to know the mysteries of the kingdom of heaven, but to them it is not given." (Matthew 13:11) Jesus was indeed very secretive, even of the truth He came to reveal. What I can assure you is that some of the parts that were hidden from us will be revealed with the passage of time. They were hidden for our benefit as part of the modus operandi that guaranteed the full execution of the Father's business. I am certain that the interpretations of hidden events and the words of Jesus would evolve with time because the keys to unlock those mysteries and reveal the hidden secrets are in the same Gospel. Search the Gospels of Jesus; in them, one can find the keys to discern and interpret some of the actions and words of Jesus, comprehend God's plan, and understand why Jesus came, why He was crucified and died, and why we are here on this planet. Jesus knew we have the ability to do so, and He made every effort to modify his deeds and words to suit our understanding and intellect. He was surprised when the people of His time, even His apostles, were not able to understand many of His utterances and deeds: "Why do you not understand my speech? Even because you cannot hear my word." (John 8:43)

Jesus and His Father controlled all that happened in Jerusalem and at Golgotha and made no attempt to explain anything to anybody. Jesus's policy of silence and secrets disappointed the crowd and His disciples, who were expecting Him to declare Himself the Messiah, restore the kingdom to Israel, and bring glory to Israel. It put the Jewish authorizes in disarray. It made a mockery of the Roman government's judicial law, whose official condemned an innocent man to be crucified. This policy of silence and secrets caused much misinterpretation of the role the ordained apostle-Judas Iscariot-played in the execution of the Father's business and why Jesus allowed Himself to be humiliated, abused, and crucified. The secrets of what Jesus and His Father were doing at Golgotha shocked the apostles, and, except for John, they abandoned Him and fled. Because of the sustained secrets of what was being executed, many of the people that participated did not know what they were doing. For that same reason the crucifixion and the death of Jesus has up to this period, defied all understanding.

A guided insight into the inscrutable mysteries and secrets of Jesus's works and the spiritual events at Golgotha reveals that God was victorious in all His plans, both in heaven and on earth. Additionally, the glory of God and His deep love and joy for what He was creating were revealed. These insights and observations on the Father's business and how Jesus executed it form the foundation of my treatise. May the Spirit that guided me in writing this treatise open your heart so that you too may see the hidden light in the Father's business that Jesus executed. Live in that light, move in that light, grow spiritually in that everlasting light, be that light that you may be called the children of Light.

Believe in the light that you may be the children of the light. —John 12:36

Jesus had said, "All things are delivered unto me of my Father; and no man knowest the Son but the Father; neither knowest any man the Father save the Son and he to whom the Son will reveal Him." (Matthew 11:27) Jesus has the key to the interpretations of His words and works. To gain insight into the secrets and mysteries of His Father and His business with us and have knowledge of Jesus Christ you must have this key. The rest are details.

The Father's business is still going on and is irrepressible. The spirit of what Jesus finished at Golgotha is still evolving. The purpose of this book is to highlight the spiritual elements of what was accomplished at Golgotha that would aid in the comprehension of the Father's business and words of Christ. The commissioned metaphysical drama that was executed from the time Jesus entered Jerusalem to the time He rose from the dead was designed for multiple purposes. However, at that time nobody knew what Jesus was doing because He did not explain many of His provocative acts or the reason why He allowed Himself to be crucified by the Romans. Jesus did not reveal to anyone what happened during the three hours of darkness that occurred just before He died on the cross. Jesus spent forty days in Jerusalem before He ascended to heaven and still did not reveal what was "finished" at Golgotha. I am confident that Jesus, who is watching us, has already planned staged periodic revelations of the contents of the three measures of meal to fortify and advance the development and the progress of the Father's business.

"These things have I spoken to you in proverbs; but the time cometh when I shall no more speak unto you in proverbs." (John 16:25)

3

WHAT IS THE GOSPEL?

The words I speak to you are spirit and they are life.
—JOHN. 6:63

*I am not ashamed of the Gospel of Christ; for it is the power of God
unto salvation. For therein is the righteousness of God revealed.*
—ROMANS 1:16–17

THE INTRODUCTION OF the Gospel marked a turning point in the history
of humankind when the tools for eternal life from the Father that Jesus
revealed were placed at our disposal. It was the defining moment in history when God's design for all humanity was unfolded. The Gospel of
Jesus is the complete document containing the Father's business. The
book contains the spiritual tools Jesus used-the Spirit of His Father- to
complete His earthly part of the Father's business and describes what
He did after His ascension to guarantee the continuation of the Father's
business. The book of the Gospel of Christ contains timeless and infinite instructions and revelations what He accomplished for mankind of
all ages. Embedded in it are imprints of the spirituality that Jesus brought

down from the Father. Many of these imprints are still hidden and will be revealed to future generations according to the will of the Father. However, we have an unparalleled opportunity to search the Gospel for the spiritual elements and use the tools to advance our spirituality so that we too can perform miracles and communicate directly with the Father and Jesus Christ.

Jesus preached and gave practical demonstrations on how to use the spiritual tools that the Father used to express Himself through Him and His plan for humanity. Jesus used various parables and miracles, timeless stories and symbolic expressions, even obstacles and disappointments all became tools He used to reveal the nature and the plan of the Father. Jesus used the poor, the winebibbers, publicans, sinners, outcasts, tax collectors, fishermen, animals and plants, frozen lakes, mountains, and occupation of the people of His generation as material for His tutorials and demonstrations on how the Father expresses Himself. He presented a Father who makes His sun rise on the evil and on the good and sends rain on the just and on the unjust. (Matthew 5:45) This heavenly Father will forgive us our trespasses if we forgive those who trespass against us. (Matthew 6:14) These were some of the ways Jesus revealed the Father and gave us tutorials on how to come near the Father.

The recorded Gospel documents are a book without end—many of the events depicted in the record are still happening. It is a book in which one finds happiness, joy, peace, and the meaning and purpose of life, and its intrinsic value. It is the platform on which one must stand to find the truth and, having found it, to rejoice with friends and neighbors and share with then what you found. In seeking the truth, God is revealed and His love and glory are made manifest. The introduction of the Gospel of Jesus of Nazareth marked the epoch when God fulfilled His promise to be with us forever and manifest His love for humanity.

The Gospel is "Good News" because it is a book that guides us to our final glorious destiny. However, to give such a title to the Gospel, we must utilize its messages to take us to a high spiritual level of communication with God and with Jesus, with whom we must collaborate with in the execution of our own colossal task in the Father's business.

The partnership with Christ opens a floodgate of heavenly light that will shine into your heart, revealing the source of that light and the sparkles of the true Christian spirituality that Jesus brought down from the Father. That heavenly light is the Spirit of Christ. It will be a lamp that will guide your feet on the path of the Father's business so that you may be a participant in the glory that awaits all humanity.

As the budding plants unfold their flowering petals in spring, likewise the Gospel of Jesus of Nazareth opened the divine portals so that we could know the true God and understand whom we are, why we are here, and how we are supposed to live. Unfortunately, as was His custom, Jesus of Nazareth filled His Gospel with metaphors, parables, proverbs, figures of speech, and parabolic expressions. His intention was not to confuse humanity or hide the information but rather to protect the Gospel against dogmas and human doctrines.

With what can I compare the Gospel of Jesus of Nazareth? It is like a big, beautiful garden. In the garden, one finds many flowering and non-flowering plants of many different varieties as well as some weeds planted by the enemy. The flowering plant represents the spiritual words of Jesus of Nazareth. The non-flowering plants represent the metaphoric and symbolic expressions that protect and aid in our understanding of the Gospel. The weeds represent the false gospel, a compendium of protean misinterpretations, interpolations, and human doctrine and dogmas that have been incorporated into the true Gospel. This is well illustrated in the parable of the tares.

"The Kingdom of heaven is likened unto a man who sowed good seeds in his field. However, while men slept, his enemy came, sowed tares among the wheat, and went his way." —Matthew 13:24–29

The field is the Gospel, the good seeds are the words of God in the Gospel, and the tares are the interpolations and human misinterpretations of the Gospel that encourage humanity to act in ways that are contrary to the divine percepts of the laws and commandments of God in the Gospel. The enemy at the time of Christ was the Jewish religious leaders. Today the enemies that have planted the weeds and mounted obstacles to the Father's business are some Christian organizations and their leaders.

The Gospel is as if a super highway designed by the great Architect (God, the Father) and built by the contractor Jesus of Nazareth with the help of the twelve merchants of light that Jesus ordained as apostles. The super highway was designed for the journey of human souls to its glorious end. It leads to the Father's house. The super highway has many "relay stations" leading to one grand station. These relay stations are the educational classrooms on how to use the spiritual tools and gain knowledge of the methods Jesus used to get people ready to enter the path of that super highway. The educational instructions in the relay stations all have something in common: illustrations on how to enter into Jesus's Kingdom of God, hoe to love the Father and our fellow humans, how to repent and forgive. The final spiritual grand station was Golgotha. All who believe in Jesus Christ and seek the Spirit of the Father for eternal life must enter the grand station-death-with the Spirit of Christ. The last ship to the spiritual realm of the Father, where we can inherit the spiritual and incorruptible final glory, sails from Golgotha. Do not be left behind.

What does it profit a man if he gains the whole world and loses his soul? — *Mark 8:36*

What use are temporary, earthly wealth and powers to someone if he or she fails to be on the ship that sails to the house of imperishable righteousness, which is in heaven, where the Father will embrace and kiss him or her and put the best robe on him or her, a ring on his or her finger, and shoes on his or her feet, and kill the fattest calf in celebration, as was portrayed in the parable of the Prodigal son.

The transformers are the relay stations for electrical supply. If they are destroyed, as frequently happens in tornadoes and hurricanes, or if they are not functional, then there will be no electric light. Many households are plunged into the dark when such events happened. The lymph nodes in the human body are filtration stations against viruses, bacteria, and even cancer cells; they contain defensive T-cell lymphocytes. If they are diseased, that defense mechanism is lost, and the body may prematurely break down. Likewise, one cannot go to the Father without passing through the relay stations of repentance, love for one another, justice, peace, and obedience to the will and commandments of God.

If your heart is evil, then your journey to the Father is filled with darkness, and you will never find that narrow but straight way to Him. If your heart is like that of the Good Samaritan, or some of the real good people you have encountered in your life, then your pathway to God will be filled with light for easy access to what God planned for humanity. The Gospel of Jesus of Nazareth is the spiritual compass that helps you in finding your way to "An inheritance, incorruptible and undefiled, and that fades not away, reserved in heaven for you." (1 Peter 1:4)

Despite all the advances in science, medicine, and technology, humanity is in an era of unprecedented danger. The solution to the world's problem is not brute force or hiring mercenaries to suppress the "enemy" or the "rebels." The Gospel is one of the blueprints for world peace. If Christianity had "launched out into the deep and let down the nets for a draw" as instructed, the world would be at peace today. If the captain and crew of Christianity had collected passengers and transported them to the Father's house without stopping intermittently to hunt for treasures, there would have been many laborers in the field harvesting the good seeds Jesus sowed. The sickness of the world today stems from our inability to understand the spiritual words of Jesus of Nazareth and what was accomplished by Him in the execution of the Father's business.

John the Baptist sent two of his disciples to ask Jesus if He was the messiah. Jesus allowed them to observe his work for a while and instructed them: "Go and show John again those things which you do, hear and see; the blind receive their sight and the lame walk, the lepers are cleansed, and the deaf hear, the dead are raised up and the poor have the gospel preached to them." (Matthew 11:5) The Gospel is something that was preached to the poor in spirit to help them in their quest for spiritual growth. However, Jesus made sure that the deaf could hear so they could listen to the Gospel and the blind could see the preacher who, as predicted by John the Baptist, would baptize humanity with "the Holy Ghost and with fire."

The Gospel of Jesus of Nazareth is the most important divine directive ever given to humans that reveals the God-human interdependence and experience. Unlike the Ten Commandments that were written on the two stone tablets, the words of the Gospel of Jesus of Nazareth are written on the tablets of human hearts, which cannot be displayed in courthouses or in temples built by humankind. The true Gospel of Jesus is the divine messages and instructions that came down in the form of iridescent, heavenly light and that shines into the transcendent Christian spirituality. It is like rain and snow that came down from heaven and then returned to God after their fruitful journey, bearing a basket that ascended to God holding the spirits of His children who sought the blessing of His Spirit by obedience to His will.

The Gospel is not a biography of Jesus of Nazareth or a dissertation on "who men think I am." It is not about the second coming of Jesus of Nazareth to establish His kingdom on this earth. The Gospel is not a book of virtues, ethics, and morals. It is not about the original sin of Adam and Eve, which we inherited. It is not about the Father's choice to sacrifice Jesus on the cross to atone for the sin we inherited from Adam. To consider it as such is a hindrance to the divine truth that was revealed. It was for the Gospel that Jesus came to earth. It was for this Gospel that the Comforter, the Holy Ghost, came to help the apostles remember all that Jesus taught them: "But the Comforter, which is the Holy Ghost, whom the Father will send in my name, he shall teach you all things and bring all things to your remembrance. Whatsoever I have said to you." (John 14:26)

It was for the remembrance and the propagation of the Gospel that on the day of Pentecost, as the apostles were gathered in one place in Jerusalem, the ordained holy men were filled with the promised Holy Ghost: "And when the day of the Pentecost was fully come, they were all with one accord in one place and suddenly there came a sound from heaven as of a rushing mighty wind, and it filled all the house where they were sitting and there appeared unto them cloven tongues like as of fire, and it sat on each of them and they were filled with the Holy Ghost, and began to speak with tongues as the spirit gave them utterance." (Act 2:1–4) It was for the Gospel that Jesus of Nazareth lived and endured persecution and humiliation. It was for this Gospel that Jesus was arrested and jailed without cause. Today Jesus would be handcuffed and fingerprinted and he would be portrayed on the Internet as a criminal and imposter for claiming that God sent Him to the world.

It was for this Gospel that Jesus allowed Himself to be crucified. It was for this Gospel that Jesus of Nazareth died on the Cross. It was for this Gospel that the twelve holy men were persecuted. However, they were warned: "But the gospel must first be published among all nations, but take heed to yourselves; for they shall deliver you up to councils; and in the synagogues, you shall be beaten and you shall be brought before rulers and Kings for my sake." (Mark 13:9–10) It was for this Gospel that almost all the twelve blessed men (except John) were killed as was predicted and fulfilled: "You shall indeed, drink of that cup that I drink of; and with the baptism that I am baptized with all shall you be baptized." (Mark 10:39)

For the propagation of the Gospel, the apostles were bound, chained, imprisoned, and many were killed. They toiled and labored so that we may see the light of the Gospel. They walked in dark alleys in Judea, Galilee, Perea, and in foreign countries for all to see the light of the Gospel and use it to see the spiritual tools revealed in the Gospel; and use those tools for our spiritual evolution so that we may be the children of Light.

The Gospel of Jesus of Nazareth is the story of spiritual gift from the Father to mankind through Christ that pushes all things to its glorious end. . This glorious end is-as the Father planned-the creation of spiritual human beings. It creates the whirlwind that moves the Father-Christ-human fellowship toward its heavenly abode. It energizes and brings forth all things both new and old for edification, for remembrance, for faith, for compassion, for love, for justice, for charity, and for human glory. The Gospel brings to fruition the spiritual gifts for the development of the kingdom of God within.

Within the Gospel, one finds the tools for spiritual evolution of the human soul and the mortar that binds the God-human relationship. God so loved the world that He gave us the Gospel message and divine directives through Jesus of Nazareth so that we may all be one with the Father just as Jesus is one with the Father. Whoever obeys all the divine instructions in the Gospel will be called the merciful, the pure in heart, the peacemaker, and the child of God, and those people will be joint heirs with the angels in Paradise. "He that keeps my commandment it is he that loves me, and he that loves me shall be loved by my Father, and I will love him and will manifest myself to him, if a man loves me, he will keep my words (the words that are spirit and of life) and my Father will love him and we will come unto him, and make our abode with him." (John 14: 21–23)

The Gospel is the spiritual words of Jesus that echoes the true laws and wills of God. Eternal life lies in the lucid understanding and execution of the spiritual words. If there is any hope for universal love and world peace, if there is any hope for mercy, justice, and goodwill toward all men, women, and children of all races, it is to be found in the words that are spirit and life. Redemption from sin is a confusing phrase. Once committed, sin cannot be undone, but it can be forgiven. Repentance is what God wants. Forgiveness and repentance are the foundation of the Gospel. If there is any hope of deliverance from the evil-ridden activities of this world, it will be found in the words that are spirit and life. Whoever wishes to be saved, whoever wishes to enter into the upper chamber and see His glory, and he or she must not only do as instructed but must teach little children to do the same. "Blessed are they that hear the words of God and keep it." (Luke 11:28)

The Gospel of Jesus of Nazareth is a multifaceted phenomenon that stemmed from new concepts of God, the Father, who we are, why we are here, how we should live, and the destiny of man. It holds the keys to the mysteries of life and the way to become a member of God's family. We have always portrayed the characters of God and Jesus of

Nazareth as personalities that show love, mercy, compassion, goodness, justice, impartiality, forgiveness, righteousness, long suffering, and divinity. It never occurred to humans that all these characteristics are what they rigorously demand of us. Acceptance of that calling will advance us to real spiritual life through embracing the gift of the Spirit of God, energizing and manifesting it just as Jesus did.

Jesus's fascination with His Gospel is unparalleled. To Jesus, His Gospel is life in itself. Peter recognized it too when he said: "Lord, to whom shall we go? Thou hast the words of eternal life." Jesus associated His very personality with His Gospel. The protean terminologies—I am the Porter, I am the Good Shepherd, I am the Way, the Light, and the Truth—are all metaphoric expressions that referred to the way Jesus looked at His Gospel in reference to Himself. With the introduction of the Gospel came the light: the *magnum lux fiat*. There was indeed a great Light!

The Gospel is a universal message to all humankind irrespective of their religious orientation. Jesus came to reveal a divine truth that has never been revealed before. To claim a monopoly on the Gospel by any group is a hindrance to the Gospel's universal divine directives and a gross injustice to Jesus's personality and the Father's business that Jesus executed. Such myopic attitudes are a hindrance to the knowledge of God, His love, His righteousness, His will, and His irrevocable plan for all humankind. It prevents the Gospel from finding its target by blanketing the spirit of God in all walks of life and all forms of religious backgrounds. The Gospel of Jesus of Nazareth gave us vivid instructions on how to be participants in the Father's business and what we must do for our everlasting glory: "Seek ye first the kingdom of God and His righteousness and all these things shall be added unto you." (Matthew 6:33)

Jesus said to the people, "Whosoever (Buddhists, Christians, Muslims, Nigerians, Americans, Indians, and Chinese) will do the will of God, the same are my sister and brother." (Mark 3:35) The Gospel of Jesus of Nazareth is the guidebook of the divine principles that guide humanity to the Light, the Way, and the Truth. With what is in the Gospel, we can prepare ourselves to accept the spirit of God in order to complete the process of our creation. To attain this divine union, we can now look at the world through different spectacles. We can avoid hatred and jealousy. You must want nothing and accumulate nothing by cheating others. You can love the world and all it holds. You must hope for the hopeless. You have to open your heart to the shimmering heavenly rays, a gift from God through Christ, and allow those rays to shine into your inner consciousness to empower your soul. You have to embrace that light and manifest it for the glory of God and for the glory of what God planned for humanity. You can develop and attain the highest spiritual level because this is God's plan. In this way, you too can be with Christ in Paradise, like the thief who was crucified on His right hand. The Gospel is the *modus operandi* for the activation, realization, and manifestation of God's spirit. Let the light of the Gospel shine in your heart in its spiritual purity and be that light to others.

Some people who claim to be spreading the message of the Gospel are actually committing the greatest spiritual crime by supporting directly or indirectly all the percepts that contradict the principles of the Gospel: holy wars, slavery, racism, injustice, setting up of unjust juries, dictatorial powers, greed, tunneling wealth into their pockets, cooking of financial statements, rape, Ponzi schemes, political torture, unjustifiable executions, cannibalism, and all sorts of evil activities.

Jesus "went about all Galilee, teaching in their synagogues, and preaching the gospel of the kingdom, and healing all manner of sickness and all manner of disease among the people." (Matthew 4:23, Mark 1:35-39, Luke 4:42-44) Please, go into the world and preach the Gospel to every creature who does not know the Gospel, abiding by the principles and percepts of the true Gospel of the words and deeds of Jesus Christ, coveting neither their gold, nor silver, nor any of their natural resources. Share with them all you have learned. Teach them how to make bicycles, cars, and machinery for industrial production and farming. Help them with electricity, and if they have to have an oil refinery, help them build one. This will be good in the sight of Jesus Christ and His father. Help stop blood diamonds", "blood oil and ethnic conflicts. If their children thirst, give them water; if they hunger, give them food.

If they lack medicine, give it to them. If they lack hospitals and clinics, help them create the infrastructure for such projects. This would also be good in the sight of the Lord. If you are the judge for any conflict, local or international, be a good judge because the Lord and His angels are looking down. If you have any doubt that they are constantly looking down on all our activities, ask St. Paul what happened to him on his way to Damascus. Avoid being the unjust judge or member of the jury whose vote is influenced by racism, ethnic profiling, or religious orientation. Replace the principle of "take all you can, give back nothing" with the principle of "give all you can, take nothing." Do not participate in evil activities with the government officials of any nation. Be a true Gospelian of Jesus Christ.

For though I preach the gospel, I have nothing to glory of: for necessity is laid upon me; yea; woe is unto me, if I preach not the Gospel. —1 Corinthians 9:16

The Gospel of Jesus of Nazareth is not a race to see who will build the most impressive place of worship or erect the most mega churches and decorate them with expensive ornaments. The Gospel of Jesus of Nazareth calls for immediate plans to get rid of all the refugee camps around the world and correction of the conditions that necessitated the camps in the first place. In some parts of the world, household pets celebrate their birthdays with cakes while human beings scramble for food in competition with rats, birds, snakes, and roaches in many garbage Dumpsters all around the world. The Gospel of Jesus of Nazareth calls for you to support the poor and help one another. The Gospel of Jesus of Nazareth is a way of life with God and with all human beings. It is a way of blending our spirits with God's spirit as well as each other' spirits so that we can laugh together, sing together, cry together, and mourn together, live for each other and by each other, and prepare for the glory that awaits us.

God is not stupid; everybody who is born eventually dies. Death is not evil. If it were evil, why would God subject all He created to this evil end? Death is a process of metamorphosis and marks the moment in our evolutionary process when the spirit leaves the body that has housed it and strikes out on its own toward its ultimate goal as ordained by the Lord. If all you get from the Gospel is that Jesus is the Son of God, then Jesus died in vain. If all you can get from the Gospel is that Jesus died to wipe out your sins, then you have missed the directions to His Father's house. If all you can get from the Gospel is that the event at Golgotha was atonement for our sins, then the Gospel is not Good News.

For some individuals—and we do not know the reason—this special Spirit is bestowed on them, freely empowering them to accomplish tasks that are beyond human imagination. The majority of us must first develop our spirits with the spiritual weaponry in the Gospel, partner with Jesus, develop our spirituality in such a way that it can educate and guide us in performing our task in the Father's business. The Gospel is the touchstone in our spiritual evolution. It prepares us for our own sacrifice for mankind in this world. The sacrifice will depend on the purity of our hearts. However, the greater the purity of your heart, the greater would be the sacrifice that it demands.

The history of humanity is essentially the history of persistent God-human indwelling and experience. It is unaffected by the ever-changing scientific or cultural revolutions. It is not affected by wars or rumors of wars. It is not affected by super nationalism, super racism, or professionalism. It is irrepressible and under the directorship of the Father. Our guide in our relationship with the Father is Jesus Christ.

The Gospel provided us with the key to glimpse into who Jesus is, who His Father is the gift He brought for mankind from His Father and what awaits humanity. Perhaps it is too transcendent for many of us to fully understand it now; however, if you seek that understanding with a pure heart, you will understand it. I, myself, am still seeking to find the truth in the Gospel.

The Gospel of Jesus is a compendium of the will and the commandments of God, our Father. This will of God is summarized in the Lord's Prayer. It is not possible for me to discuss, in this introductory chapter on the Gospel, all aspects of the Gospel and comment on the spiritual tools that Jesus used in accomplishing His objectives because what in many instances looks like simple narratives and illustrations transcends far beyond human understanding and wisdom. This chapter is only an introduction to the mysteries of the Gospel that will enhance the comprehension of the Father's business that Jesus executed and how it is related to the spiritual events at Golgotha, which is the central subject of my treatise.

And this I do for the Gospel's sake that I (we) might be partakers therefore with you. —1 Corinthians 9:23

4

THE PREDICTIVE METAPHORS
OF THE CROSS

*Verily, verily, I say unto you, except a corn of wheat fall into the ground
and die, it abideth alone; but if it dies, it bringeth forth much fruit.*
—JOHN 12:24

*I have a baptism to be baptized with, and now how
am I straightened till it be accomplished.*
—LUKE 12:50, MATTHEW 20:32

The cup, which my Father gave me, shall I not drink it.
—JOHN 18:11

AS AN INTRODUCTION to the events at Golgotha, I have attempted to
explore some of the predictive metaphors Jesus used in His attempts to
explain the metaphysical drama of His death as a perfect fulfillment of
the will of His Father. Without the crucifixion and the death of Jesus,
His proclamation of the kingdom of God and His universal message

of eternal life would have been stripped of their meanings. The Jews did not have a clear vision of what Jesus was saying, and for this reason, many people rejected His deeds and messages. Who could understand what Jesus was doing without knowing the doctrines of the Father's business? What would happen at Golgotha was kept secret from the public but revealed to the apostles. Jesus resorted to metaphors, parabolic and symbolic expressions, and illustrations to tell the people about the final events in the Father's business. The images of the woman in travail, the corn of wheat, the cup, the baptism that He must be baptized with, and the lifting up of the Son of man were the metaphoric expressions in the Gospel that Jesus used to demonstrate His death and the glory of it. The entirety of the Gospel is riddled with metaphors.

The plethora of Jesus's metaphors is divine expressions that offer insight into the mysteries of the preparation, execution, and glory of the Father's business. The correct interpretation of the predictive metaphors of the cross reveals the *modus operandi* and the spiritual value of His mission, and it aids in the understanding of the Golgotha events. The complete interpretation of all of Jesus's predictive metaphors concerning the cross is not possible. As I wrote this chapter, I kept reminding myself of the Master's statement to the apostles: "Are you also without understanding?" This also applies to me.

Our inability to comprehend some of His metaphors at this evolutionary phase in human spiritual development is a problem. The metaphors form a protective barrier that hides what He did not want to reveal at that time and protects His Gospel from dogmas and other human doctrines. Jesus's metaphors are like "unto leaven, which a woman took and hid in three measures of meal, till the whole was leavened." (Matthew 13:33; Luke 13:21) Many of Jesus's metaphors act like the leaven that is hidden in His parables and in some of His parabolic expressions and illustrations in the Gospel.

Jesus's metaphors, parables, proverbs, and many of the parabolic expressions would be revealed when the time is right or, as Jesus expressed it, when "the whole is leavened." Christianity is not a stationary spirituality but one that is undergoing an evolutionary process. To comprehend that progress, we must search and explore with all the spiritual tools in the Gospel in order to discover the depths of that spirituality.

Jesus started to execute the Father's business with the utterance, "the time is fulfilled, the kingdom of God is at hand," (Mark 1:15) without revealing what time had been fulfilled or what the kingdom of God was. As the meanings of these metaphorical expressions unfold, the quest to be a true disciple of Jesus is awakened. We are inspired to search for more revelations so that we can better understand the Father's business and the truth revealed at Golgotha. Whether using spiritual eyes, wearing the angelic spectacles, tapping into our imagination and inspiration, or following a divine guide, we explore the mysteries and hidden treasures in the depository that Jesus called His Gospel. The revealed truth would help us prepare our souls for spiritualization and propel it toward God-human experience and bondage. This would be our acceptance of Jesus's invitation to come into His field and harvest the fruits even though we do not even know how the seeds were planted.

At Caesarea Philippi, Jesus tried to speak plainly about His suffering and death. Again, the disciples did not believe something like that would happen to their Master. Jesus resorted to using metaphors to reveal the spiritual events at Golgotha and the glory that would follow. The sons of Zebedee, James and John, wanted a favor from their Master and asked, "Grant unto us that we may sit, one on thy right hand and the other on thy left hand, in thy glory." Jesus replied by asking them, "...can you drink of the cup that I drink of and be baptized with the baptism that I am baptized with?" (Matthew 10:38) The sons of Zebedee replied, "We can." Then Jesus said, "Ye shall indeed drink of the cup that I drink of; and with the baptism that I am baptized withal, shall ye be baptized." (Mark 10:35–39)

That baptism and the cup referred to the events at Golgotha. Many of the apostles were subsequently murdered. Some of them were crucified. To drink from the cup that He drank from was to obey the will of God. Jesus was obedient to the will of God. He accepted what happened to Him at Golgotha for our glory, for the revelation of God, and victory for the Father. To drink our own "cup" is to learn to do the will of God like the angels in heaven. It calls for promoting justice, peace, mercy, love for humanity, forgiveness, eradication of poverty and malnutrition in all parts of the world, and reconciliation among all tribes and nations. It demands the acceptance of the concept that all humans are under one God. Most importantly, it calls for us to recognize that God reigns and controls all things; we must always pray for the kingdom of God to come and for God to give us our daily bread.

To drink from that cup, we must be humble, want nothing, ask for nothing, and surrender to the unspoken will of the invisible God. We are not in control of our destiny. We are vulnerable to predators, uncontrollable natural forces, diseases, and death. Life on earth is difficult. The wars between nations, tsunamis, hurricanes, earthquakes, malnutrition, poverty, and fear of nuclear catastrophe, flu pandemics, and multiple financial and personal problems facing families all over the world are problems we encounter frequently. As a doctor, I have seen many patients succumb to diseases of unknown origin and family members killed in accidents.

Humankind is contributing to many of these disasters. Today, the presence of evil in this world is overwhelming. We do terrible things to each other, sometimes under the guise of self-defense or protection. We make preemptive strikes even if we are not sure they will help humanity. We commit hideous crimes for money and power. We kill one another. If we continue this way, we will surely destroy ourselves and all the living things on this earth.

Since we are unable to control the devastating natural forces and are saddled with all the day-to-day problems we encounter, we must drink from the "cup" to be worthy servants of the Lord. Many people, including many Christian leaders, have looked at this self-sacrifice—giving up all worldly acquisitions of wealth, service to mankind and to Christ and His Father —and decided to pass the "cup" and chose to be baptized with holy water and not with the Spirit of Christ, even though they know that there is no water on earth that is holy.

Jesus assures us that drinking from the cup are easy and not impossible tasks only if we know learn from Him. By making sacrifices and drinking from the cup that God also gave to each one of us, we will be able to build a world in which all people will live with dignity, love, justice, and peace. A world in which all the advocates of democracy and human rights will live by their own principles as shining examples. A world in which everyone champions the eradication of endemic poverty. A world in which members of the Paris Club, World Bank, and Security Council of the United Nation refuse to drink from the cup of hypocrisy.

Ye are the salt of the earth; but if the salt has lost its flavor, wherewith shall it be salted? It is good for nothing. But to be cast out, and to be trodden under the foot of men —Jesus, Matthew 5:13

Likewise, wealth is good, but if it is not used for humanity as a gift from God, then what use is it? We must build a world in which all who collect for the poor must give all they collect to the poor; a world in which all who collect for Caesar must give all they collect to Caesar; and all who collect for God must give all they collect to God by serving humanity. We must build a world in which the principle of "take what you can, give nothing back" is replaced by "give all you can, take nothing." By making all sacrifices that benefit all of humanity, God will disclose more mysteries that will guide us to be with Him. (For every one shall be salted with fire, and every sacrifice shall be salted with salt." (Mark 9:49) Believe in the Father that sent Jesus, have compassion for the poor, "have salt in yourselves, and have peace one with another." (Mark 9:51) We must pray to Jesus Christ, asking Him to bring out one of the three measures of meal and reveal the contents to us so that we may be able to penetrate into the depths of what was accomplished at Golgotha. We are eager to know the truth so that we can use that knowledge to penetrate into the mysteries of the words and works of Christ and use the vital information to advance our intelligence, and trigger stupendous evolutional development of the spirit of Christianity, which will allow us to develop an infinite union with God and with Him. That is to be religious. In essence, this is the goal of Christianity.

Verily, verily, I say unto you, except a corn of wheat fall into the ground and die, it abideth alone; but if it dies, it bringeth forth much fruit. —John 12:24.

The corn of the wheat is Jesus Himself. The corn that "fall into the ground and die" foretold His death. The fruit are the people in all ages that believe in Him and are drawn to Him. They have opened their hearts to His glorified Spirit. The fruit will multiply as more people, today and tomorrow, will flock to Him and feel that Jesus 'abideth' with them. The metaphor of the corn of wheat also revealed the deep love of the Father and Jesus Christ for humanity: they want us to be with them. This is goal of the Father's business

When ye have lifted up the Son of man, then shall ye know that I am He. —John 8:28.

At the time Jesus talked about being lifted up, nobody knew that He was going to be crucified on the cross. Today we lift up the people that scored the winning goal in sports. We lift up men of valor who returned after victorious excursions. At the time of Jesus, the expectation for the victorious Messiah was high. Perhaps, when Jesus made that statement, the Jews associated that to the time when they would lift up Jesus after His victory against the Romans. It reinforced their expectation that Jesus may indeed be the expected Messiah. The metaphoric expression of being lifted up predicted what would happen to Him at Golgotha.

And I, if I be l be lifted up from the earth, will draw all men unto me. —John 12:32

The writer of the Gospel of John interpreted that metaphoric expression. "This He said, signifying what death He should die" (John 12:33)

A woman when she is in travail hath sorrow, but because her hour is come, but as soon as she is delivered of the child, she remembered no more the anguish, for the joy that a man is born into the world. —John 16:21

For now, we must follow Jesus to Jerusalem and to Golgotha, to see the "woman in travail." We must be in the delivery room to witness the birth of a child and participate in the joy that a child has been born into the world. We must be a witness to the everlasting event: the birth of the glorified Spirit of Jesus Christ into the world! This is the gift of the Father to humanity. The metaphor of the woman in travail was the best of all Jesus's metaphors that depicted the events at Golgotha. The woman in labor is Jesus Himself. The man that is born into the world is the glorified Spirit of Jesus Christ that manifested on Easter morning.

Greater love hath no man than this that a man lay down his life for his friends. Jesus. —John 15:13.

5

JESUS'S LAST JOURNEY TO
JERUSALEM

When ye have lifted up the Son of man, then shall ye know that I am He.
—JOHN 8:28.

*Behold, we go to Jerusalem, and the Son of man shall be deliv-
ered unto the Gentiles, and shall be mocked, and spitefully
entreated, and spitted on; And they shall scourge Him, and put
Him to death, and the third day He shall rise again.*
—LUKE 18: 31–33

WHAT WAS THOUGHT to be catastrophic and humiliating events in
Jerusalem, spontaneous utterances, unrehearsed parables, innovative
miracles, were indeed well organized provocative acts by Jesus, to antag-
onize the Jewish authorities to take action against Him. Those provocative acts led to His condemnation to death by the Jewish authorities and
crucifixion by the Romans. The ubiquitous modus operandi Jesus used
in executing the Father's business, paved the way for the revelation of

Himself and His Father and for the continuation of the Father's business to its glorious end. Jesus had to be lifted up on that cross for all His words to have any meaning and for His task from His Father to be "finished." Jesus had said; "the cup my Father gave me, must I not drink it?" The meaning is simple: Jesus must be lifted up on the cross. Without any defense during His trials, and without any resistance, Jesus allowed Himself to be crucified and died on the cross.

The plan, designed by God could not fail because many things were at stake. The victory for the Father on His plan for mankind depended on it. The spiritualization of the human souls for the completion of our creation depended on it. The control of obstacles to the Father's business depended on it. The glorification of the Spirit of Jesus, as to make permanent His control of the Father's business to the end of time depended on it. The return of Jesus to the cosmic realm where He belonged depended on it. The revelation of His Father to the world depended on it. The revelation of Jesus's nature and Godlike attributes depends on it. The knowledge of who we are and why we are here depends on it. Our journey to eternal life depends on it. It opened the portal of a spiritual world, and for the first time in its history, mankind, saw, touched and talked to a real spirit: the Spirit of the risen Christ.

Whether by imagination or spiritual insight, when you look again at all the events that were reported in the Gospel from the time Jesus entered Jerusalem riding on a colt, to the day of His resurrection, it becomes obvious that Jesus, as soon as they left Bethany, was already in another world. His countenance must have changed. His apostles were frightened.

And they were on the way going up to Jerusalem; and Jesus went before them; and they were amazed; and as they followed, they were afraid." —Mark 10:32

The Spirit of His Father guided Him. Jesus had to be on that cross before the three hours of darkness that would occur during that period. He could not abandon His Father at the final phase of God's plan. He had chosen His weapon: the cross.

Why did Jesus choose death by crucifixion in Jerusalem? Jesus's choice of the cross for the accomplishment of His objects had remained an inscrutable mystery. The Gospel narratives revealed nothing to us about the reasons behind the actions of Jesus from the time He rode triumphantly into Jerusalem to the time He ascended into heaven at Bethany. What was designed by His Father and executed by Jesus in Jerusalem and at Golgotha was the best-kept secret in the history of heavenly and earthly events. What happened during that period will never again be repeated because what Jesus executed, achieved its objectives and guaranteed successful progression of the Father's business to the end of time.

Why did Jesus refuse to give an explanation for His actions in Jerusalem and at Golgotha? The secrecy and the silence maintained by Jesus guaranteed the successful completion of what God designed. It was done to protect the truth that was revealed. It was done to protect the spirit of Christianity. It was done to protect humanity. To have revealed any information on what God planned would have not only endangered the lives of the ordained apostles but that of Jesus Himself before He was lifted up on the cross. It would have been the end of the mission and defeat for His Father.

The Father and Jesus Christ knew what was out there in the spiritual world that we do not know. The best defense and protection deployed by them in what Jesus came to accomplish was secrecy and silence.

For I tell you, that many prophets and kings have desired to see those things which ye see, and have not seen them; and to hear those things which ye hear, and have not heard them. —Jesus to His apostles. Luke 10:24

Jesus's mission was detailed and specific. In carrying out this specific plan, every utterance, every spontaneous event, every directive from Him, every silence, even blinking or the gaze of His eyes had to do with the cross. Nobody understood those events and they did not ask for explanation. The apostles did ask Him why He had to wash their feet. However, Jesus did not give them any direct answer but promised

He would explain later. But Jesus never did. The reason is simple: any explanation at that time would compromise their mission to the Roman Empire. If the Romans knew that those apostles with their tireless legs would invade the empire and silence their gods and goddesses, they would have collaborated with the Jewish authorizes to kill all of them before they took a step toward Rome and its Empire. The secrets Jesus maintained by His silence and His refusal to reveal the reasons for His actions were to protect what was executed at Golgotha and the earthly participants from demonic spirits, who may have acted through humans to disrupt the plan.

As soon as Jesus left Bethany for that last trip to Jerusalem, everything changed. What was reported in the Gospel as jubilant but unproductive events during Jesus's last days in Jerusalem were indeed lamp posts that illuminated His way to glory and the way to perfection for human souls and enabled the continuation of His Father's business.

The elucidation and interpretation of those heavenly things executed in Jerusalem and at Golgotha was meant to be revealed over time. But we must remember that cosmic time is not the same as our calendar time period handed over to us by the Greco-Roman astrologers. Do not be discouraged that we do not have all the answers now. On the heavenly time scale, two thousand earthly years is but the twinkling of an eye. One cannot gain insight into the secrets of the heavenly things that were executed in Jerusalem and at Golgotha without looking at the contents of the first part of the Father's business that Jesus executed as recorded in the Gospel before the last journey to Jerusalem. To gain insight into the mysteries of the second part of Jesus's mission, point the compass of the ship toward Golgotha but keep an eye on the Gospel, where the Master left spiritual oars to help us paddle to the holy ground of Golgotha where the truth was revealed. Jesus spent three years preaching on the Kingdom of God before His death and continued to do so after his resurrection. Jesus's kingdom of God also holds the key to the revelation of the mysteries of Golgotha.

When the mystery of Jesus's last journey to Jerusalem was revealed, it showed the absolute control the invisible Father had over all the events.

Jesus was following every step in God's plan. Jesus knew His final frontier would be at Jerusalem. Why Jerusalem and why not in Rome? The nations fighting for Jerusalem maintain that Jerusalem is a holy place. The truth is that all places on earth are holy grounds. In fact, anything made by God—humans, animals, plants, galaxies, and the universe—is a holy object. We do not know why Jerusalem was chosen. However, you will notice that Jesus was speeding things up so that he would be at Golgotha at the appointed time.

Jesus first predicted His death to His apostles at Caesarea Philippi when He told them that He "must go to Jerusalem and suffer many things at the hands of the elders, chief priests, and teachers of the law, and be killed and on the third day be raised." (Matthew 16:21) It was an admission of the secret plan the Father and Himself had worked out before Jesus's earthly birth that the final frontier would be at Jerusalem. Jesus, as was His custom, did not tell them the reason why He had to die or explain why it had to be at Jerusalem or why He had to be lifted up on a cross at Golgotha. During His last days in Jerusalem, Jesus was hastening things up for an event that He did not see as a catastrophe but as what He must do for the Father's business to be accomplished. What appeared to be tragic, humiliating, scornful events in Jerusalem were His Father's own directed spiritual events.

The First Provocative Act: *The Gala Parade on the Streets of Jerusalem*

Jesus knew that the chief priest and the Jewish authorities were planning to kill Him in Jerusalem, yet He entered Jerusalem in a New Orleans-style Mardi gras parade. The question is not why Jesus went back to Jerusalem, but why did He enter that city like a king returning from a victorious encounter with the enemy? Was it a move for popularity or was Jesus preparing to confront the Romans and restore the glory to Israel? It was reported in the Gospel that when "they heard that Jesus was coming to Jerusalem, they took branches of palm trees, and went forth to meet him and cried, 'Hosanna to the son of David: Blessed is He that cometh in the name of the Lord; Hosanna in the highest."

(Matthew 21:9) When the people saw Him riding on the back of that donkey and saw His countenance, the whole crowd cheered and hailed Him as King, the long-awaited Redeemer from the root of King David. The jubilation and the ecstasy of the people were beyond measure.

The Hosanna song erupted everywhere as people, including children, spread palm leaves on the road. Was Jesus happy? The answer is yes. He did not want the jubilation to stop. Perhaps that was also a political move for popularity. Was Jesus happy because He realized that the people had accepted Him as their King from the line of David? The answer is no. Was Jesus happy because He was about to declare to them that He is the Messiah? The answer is no. The jubilant ecstasy of His spirit manifested on His face because Jesus knew that the real work for which He had been sent from the Father had begun. Jesus was setting the stage for Him to be put on the cross.

The jealous Jewish priests noted that "all the Jerusalem is moved" and "that the whole world is gone after Him." They asked Jesus to put an end to the event: "Master, rebuke your disciples." But Jesus replied, "I tell you that, if these should hold their peace, the stones would immediately cry out." (Luke 19:39–40)

The Jews believed King David came in the name of the Lord. Likewise Jesus, who was from the line of David, also came in the name of the Lord. The Jews believed in the Divine Being, a conquer from the line of King David, who would come to defeat Israel's enemies, restore the kingdom to Israel, and establish His headquarters in Jerusalem.

If you and I were Jews in Jerusalem at that time under Roman bondage, we too would look forward to a Warrior King who would drive away the Romans and restore the kingdom of Israel. We would, like the apostles, say to Jesus when soldiers came to arrest Him, "Here are two swords," and try to put up a fight like Simon Peter did. We too, would ask Him to call down fires to consume our enemies like the apostles asked Him to do in the city of Synchar in Samaria on their way to Jerusalem. We too would ask Jesus to restore the new spiritual kingdom of Israel. We too like Cleopas and his companion on their way to Emmaus, would also hope that Jesus would bring salvation to Israel. We would surely carry palm leaves and line them on the streets and wave them as signs of support and expectation. In our jubilant expectation, out of mercy we too would like the salvation to be extended to the Gentiles. We would put on our best clothes and sing this Hosanna song. We would declare Jesus to be the expected Messiah, who would bring salvation to Israel and restore all things.

Who in his or her right mind would not fall for Jesus, who spoke with power as no man had spoken before? Who had performed so many miracles by then that even if another Christ came, would that Christ perform more miracles? Whose wisdom and power was beyond measure. How could you not fall for Him? How could you not revere Him, who raised Lazarus from the dead though he had been dead for three days? How could we not believe He was the Lord of resurrection? If you and I were in Jerusalem during that period and had also listened to all sermons and the parables of the kingdom of God, it would have been a big disappointment if Jesus did not bring forth this kingdom of God. But Jesus's Kingdom of God came already, but the people did not recognize it.

The Mardi Gras-style entry into Jerusalem had a divine purpose, and the Jewish authorities were used for its accomplishment. Jesus did not reveal anything to anybody. All He said to the apostles was that He would suffer and be killed in Jerusalem, but He hid the reason why that would happen to Him. If only you and I could get know the Father's secret document containing His plan, especially the section about the Jerusalem events, then my work would be finished.

Jesus's triumphant entry into Jerusalem was not an aspiration or an acceptance of the anticipated Jewish Messianic status. Jesus never said He was the Jewish Messiah. The stylish, royal entry into Jerusalem was not to establish the new kingdom of God with Jerusalem as the headquarters. It was true that the expectation of the kingdom of God was high. The Passover crowd and the apostles saw in Him the fulfillment of all the prophetic utterances of the expected Messiah, the Redeemer of Israel. Jesus never said He was a Redeemer of Israel. I do not blame the apostles who despite all the teaching and the revelations of the mysteries of the kingdom of God, still were thinking of an earthly kingdom and the restoration of the kingdom to Israel by their Master waging war with the Romans. They were Jews and had the same hope like other Jews.

A few days before Jesus entered into Jerusalem, the chief priests and the Pharisees, under the directorship of the High Priest Caiaphas, called a council together to plan how to put Jesus to death. An edict, a commandment from the high priest and the Pharisees in authority, was passed and circulated among the people that if anyone knew where Jesus was, he or she had to reveal it so that the authorities could arrest him. "Now both the chief priests and the Pharisees had given a commandment, that, if any man knew where he was, he should show it, that they might take him." (John 11:57) Jesus knew about the edict, yet five days before the Passover, Jesus staged the greatest victory gala as He marched into Jerusalem. What was Jesus's inner motive? Why was He fearless? There are many hidden secrets and mysteries surrounding the triumphant entry of Jesus into Jerusalem.

How do we penetrate into the deep mystery of what was going on when Jesus left Bethany and entered Jerusalem? How do we look into the document of the Father's business to decipher its contents, objectives, and aims? How do we gain insight into the spiritual world of Jesus? Without direct divine intervention, we will remain as ignorant as the people of His time. The problem is that we have carried that ignorance too far, even to the present generation. For this reason, the development of the Christian spirit has stalled. What is happening in the world today shows that the spiritual evolution of the entire human race is still in its rudimentary phase.

Jesus knew the Jews would not be able to kill Him. They had made two attempts in the past. What appeared to be a disorganized and impromptu celebration for His entry into Jerusalem was in fact a well-organized, preordained plan used to infuriate and provoke the Jewish authorities so they would act immediately to arrest Him. Jesus was acting according to the outline in the divine plan the Father designed. Human beings participated in the events at Jerusalem and at Golgotha, but they only played the role that was assigned to them. People that participated had no control over their actions. The invisible God, the Father, was in control. Jesus's secret objective, His inner aim for provoking the Jewish authorities was simply this: He must be lifted up on the cross. At that stage of His operation, only Jesus and His Father knew why He had to be lifted up on the cross.

The Second Provocative Act: *The Cleansing of the Temple*

On the same day Jesus marched into Jerusalem, He went to the temple and cleansed it. "Jesus went into the temple, began to cast out them that sold and bought in the temple, and overthrew the tables of the money changers and these of them that sold doves. And would not suffer any man should carry any vessels through the temple. And He taught and said unto them, "Is it not written, my house shall be called of all nations, the house of prayer? But ye have made it a den of thieves." (Mark 11:15–17)

Why was Jesus cleansing the temple? Jesus did not cleanse the temple to purify it in preparation for Him to be sacrificed there to atone for the sins of the Jews and the whole world at the Passover. If it was important to Him, Jesus could have made plans to preserve it forever. Was it Jesus's intention to cleanse the temple, purify it as a sanctuary for the worship of His Father? The answer is no. On His way to Jerusalem, Jesus told the Samaritan woman, "Woman, believe me, the hour cometh, when ye shall neither in this mountain, nor yet at Jerusalem worship the Father." (John 4:21) Within twenty-four hours after cleansing the temple, His apostles said unto Him, "Master, see what manner of stones and what buildings are here!" Jesus said unto them, "Seest thou these great buildings? There shall not be left one stone upon another that shall not be thrown down." (Mark 13:1-2) Jesus was not trying to cleanse and purify the temple He knew would be subsequently destroyed.

Why was Jesus angry at the traders who provided services at the outer court of the temple, where worshippers can exchange their money and buy animals for sacrifices? Such practices started in the days of

Abraham and became highly commercializes when the first temple was built. Jesus's parents took Him to the temple on many occasions during the Jewish festivals celebrated in the temple at Jerusalem. I am quite sure that they too bought something in the temple they used for sacrifice. During the last feast of the Tabernacle, Jesus was in the Temple with His brothers and sisters. Again, His siblings must have bought something from the traders that they used for sacrifice. At that time Jesus saw the traders and the money exchangers and took no action. Why then did Jesus, during the last visit to Jerusalem, went to the temple and cleansed it? By doing so, Jesus touched the very essence of the Jewish religious service. No Jew would stand for it. However, by cleansing the temple, Jesus got what He wanted. The Jewish authorities intensified their plan to kill Jesus when they heard what He did in the temple. "And the scribes and the chief priests heard it; they sought how they might destroy Him." (Mark 11:18) Jesus knew the reason for His provocative act but refused to discuss it with anyone. He knew the part the Father assigned to the Jewish authorities, but their killing Him was not in the plan.

The Third Provocative Act: *Parables of the Man with Two Sons and the Wicked Husbandmen*

Jesus returned to Bethany that evening. However, Jesus was not yet finished. He went back again to the temple the following day. Most of Jesus's discussions were centered on the Jewish authorities. His speech was no longer a sermon but inflammatory words against the Jewish authorities. What people witnessed was not a humble man who in the past spoke with goodness but Jesus of Nazareth, a man with power and authority directing all actions against the Jewish leaders. The parables of the man with two sons (Matthew 21:28–32) and of the wicked husbandmen (Matthew 21:33–45; Mark 12:1-12; Luke 20:9-19) were directed to the Jewish authorities.

The parable of the two sons depicted the story of two sons who were asked to do something by their father. One of them said he would not do it. Later, he changed his mind and did the work. The other son said that he would do it. However, he failed to do it. The interpretation is perceptible in the parable. The Jews knew that Jesus was talking about them. The son who promised the do the work, but failed to do so, depicted the Jews who promised to obey God's laws and commandments but failed to do so. The son who first refused to do the work, but later changed his mind and did the work represented those whom Jesus portrayed in the parables of the lost (the lost sheep, Matthew 18:12-14, Luke 15:3-7; the lost coin, Luke 15:8-10; the Prodigal son, Luke15:11-32) and the publicans and sinners that ate with Him. Those people believed in His words and repented. They are those who will inherit the kingdom of God.

In the parable of the wicked husbandmen, Jesus's parabolic style of concealing the true meaning of many of His parables was thrown out of the window. The interpretation of this parable was obvious and recognized by the Jewish audience. The householder who planted the vineyard is the Father. The wicked husbandmen are the Jewish people. The servants sent to the husbandmen who-beat one, and killed another, and stoned another-represented the prophets and wise men sent to the Jews. "Wherefore, behold, I send unto you prophets, and wise men, and the scribes: and some of them ye shall kill and crucify; and some of them shall ye scourge in your synagogues, and persecute them from city to city." (Matthew 23:34) When the wicked husbandmen saw the son of the householder, said among them, "This is the heir; come, let us kill him, and let us seize on his inheritance." They caught him, and cast him out of the vineyard and killed him. The son of the householder who planted the vineyard is Jesus Christ. The Jews knew immediately that the parable was directed against them. If Jesus's intention was to make the Jewish authorities angry, He succeeded. After that parable, the chief priests and the scribes sought how to lay hands on Jesus: "And the chief priests and the scribes the same hour sought to lay hands on him; and they feared the people: for they perceived that he had spoken this parable against them." (Luke 20:19)

The Forth Provocative Act: *The Proclamation of Woes against the Scribes and the Pharisee Rulers*

"But woe to you, scribes, and Pharisees, hypocrites! For ye shut up the kingdom of heaven against men; for ye neither go in yourselves, neither suffer ye them that are entering to go in." —Matthew 23:13

Why did Jesus come back to the temple? The Jewish authorities waited for Him. Who gave Jesus the authority to do what He did the previous day? As soon as Jesus showed up, the chief priest and the elders of the people asked Him, "By what authority doest thou these things and who gave you this authority?" (Matthew 21:23) Jesus refused to answer that question. Jesus resorted to parables that ridiculed the high esteem they held of themselves. Jesus had entered into the strong man's house, and he knew what to do: bind the strong man then spoil his house. Jesus had predicted this encounter and gave a metaphoric illustration of it: "how can one enter into a strong man's house, and spoil his goods, except he first bind the strong man? And then spoil his house." (Matthew 12:29) The strong man represented the scribes and the Pharisee authorities. The strong man's house was the temple.

Jesus was determined to silence them. He aggressively attacked the morals, ethics, and religious conduct of those rulers. The Jewish authorities were in disarray over what to do. Jesus did not make it easy for them. He kept up His public acts against the Jewish authorities to provoke them. Jesus's last speech in the Solomon's pouch was openly directed against the Jewish authorities. It prompted the high priest to call for an emergency meeting. "Then gathered the chief priest and the Pharisees a council, and said, what do we? For this man doeth many miracles. If we let him thus alone, all men will believe on him: and the Romans shall come and take away both our place and nation And one of them, named Caiaphas, being the high priest that same year, said unto them, Ye know nothing at all Nor consider that it is expedient for us, that one man should die for the people, and that the whole nation perish not." (John 11:47–50) At that stage and time, the Jewish authorities were not thinking of crucifixion. Getting the Romans involved never crossed their minds. All they wanted was to take Jesus secretly and kill him by stoning or throw him out of the pinnacle of the temple.

If Jesus returned today, and entered into our religious institutions and openly called the leaders hypocrites—leaders who praise God with their lips but their hearts are far from God; who, as leaders, make rules and regulations for the people that they personally fail to obey; who extract money from the poor and seek earthly things; who sell bottled water and anointing oil as holy instruments of salvation—what do you think would happen to Jesus? What happened at that temple was unimaginable. Jesus called the ruling scribes and the Pharisees fools, blind guides of the people of Israel who closed the door to the knowledge of the kingdom of heaven. Jesus described them as serpents and offspring of vipers who had killed the prophets sent to them. Jesus's condemnation of the Jewish leaders was intense and merciless. Jesus gave a practical demonstration of what would happen to those groups of leaders in His story about the fig tree on His way to Jerusalem. "And seeing a fig tree by the way side, He came to it, and found nothing on it, save leaves alone, and said to it, there shall no longer be fruit from thee forever. And the fig tree withered away immediately." (Matthew 21:19)

And so was fulfilled that which was spoken by John the Baptist: "and now also the axe is laid unto the root of the trees; therefore every tree which bringeth not forth good fruit is hewn down, and cast into the fire." (Matthew 3:10) The Jewish leaders were unable to "bring forth fruits meet for repentance." They had to be stripped of their authority over the people. The high priest Joseph Caiaphas was deposed in AD 38, and what became of him after his deposition is unknown. If Jesus walked into all our temples today, would He find similar situations with our religious leaders?

Believe nothing, no matter where you read it, or who said it or even if I have said it, unless it agrees with your own reason and common sense. —Buddha

What were recorded in the Gospel with reference to the last days of Jesus were eternal manifestations of deep spiritual events. Jesus hid His true self and His Father's plan in those spiritual events. At the end of that second day in Jerusalem, Jesus disclosed the manner of His death: the cross. "You know that after two days is the feast of the Passover, and the Son of man is betrayed to be crucified." (Matthew 26:2) That was sad news to all the apostles who heard Him but good news to Christ. That was the first time Jesus used the word "crucified" to describe His own death. On another occasion He qualified it as being lifted up. "When you shall have lifted up the Son of man, (on the cross) then shall you know that I am He." (John 8:28) Jesus was the only one talking about crucifixion. He had selected His spiritual tool for the execution of His own part of the Father's business. Jesus left enough footprints in the Gospel that we would know Him and His Father, the objectives and goals of His mission when He is lifted up on the cross.

Jesus left again for Bethany, not out of fear that the Jewish authorities would act to kill Him. He was not destined to die that day. Jesus knew the Jewish authorities were in disarray on what to do with Him. Not all members of the Sanhedrin supported the plan to arrest and kill Jesus. Jesus can discern what is in all hearts, and so He knew what was in theirs. He did not command fire from heaven to consume them for plotting against Him. When He wept for Jerusalem, He wept for all its inhabitants, including the Jewish authorities. But the will of God must be done. He knew His Father, the invisible God, was directing all things. The display of multiple provocative acts could no longer be tolerated by the Jewish authorities. But Jesus had not yet finished provoking them. His grand master plan that would help lift Him up on the cross was to send Judas Iscariot to the Jewish authorities. Jesus had crafted it well. The invisible Father knew about it and was watching.

6

THE FIFTH PROVOCATIVE ACT: THE ROLE OF JUDAS ISCARIOT

What you have to do, do quickly.
—JESUS SAID TO JUDAS AT THE LAST SUPPER

IT WAS REPORTED that, for no confirmed reason, Judas Iscariot betrayed his Master to the Jewish authorities for thirty pieces of silver. The philology of Judas Iscariot is a fascinating and eternal phenomenon. The story as it was narrated in the Gospel had a conclusion, but it is immortal. It led to Jesus being lifted up on the cross, and it formed an integral part of what was finished at Golgotha. The victory of the Father's business and the hope for everlasting life for humanity are based on the fact that God fulfilled His will through the mission of Jesus Christ. All the spiritual events were scripted and guided by the invisible Father. Judas's authorized identification of Jesus to the mob that came to arrest Him paved the way for the completion of the earthly part of the Father's business that was dictated by His Master. It was not an act of treason or a betrayal of Jesus. It was a planned ultimate provocative act that helped in lifting Jesus to the cross. If the Father's business had failed because Judas's act resulted in the crucifixion of Jesus, then Judas's act would be considered treason. The more we dig into the sanctioned act of Judas Iscariot, the more we uncover the hidden values of that divine act. God does not assign any job to a traitor. Jesus did not select and ordain a betrayer.

Overwhelmed by our inability to gain insight into the mysteries of the planned pre-Golgotha provocative demonstrations of Jesus that led Him to the cross, the act of Judas was considered a betrayal. However, humanity must not be blamed. Who can interpret all the events that happened in Jerusalem and at Golgotha without insight into the inscrutable hidden secrets of what Jesus was doing? Without exception, all the people, including the apostles, were disappointed by the way the event ended. Today, Jesus has allowed us to look at the contents of one of the three measures of the meals, where part of the leaven was hidden. We have no reason to continue to torment the spirit of an ordained blessed apostle, Judas Iscariot.

The epically ubiquitous and extraordinary drama of the last days of Jesus was performed by people who had been assigned their roles by the Father and Jesus Christ, but they had no knowledge of what they were doing. They were not allowed to ask questions or seek explanations for many of the tasks assigned to them during the last days of Jesus in Jerusalem. The Father and His Son, Jesus Christ, had not allowed anyone to know what was going on. Jesus revealed to the apostles only what He wanted them to know. They had the knowledge, as revealed to them by their Master, that He was going to Jerusalem, where "the Son of man must suffer many things; and be rejected of the elders, and of the chief priests and the scribes, and be killed; and after three days rise again." (Mark 8:31) The first time Jesus predicted His death to the apostles at Caesarea Philippi, Peter rebuked Him and said, "God forbid! This shall never happen to you." But Jesus said to Peter, "Get behind me Satan! You are a hindrance to me; for you are not on the side of God, but of men." (Matthew 16:22–23) It was an opportunity for Jesus to explain to His apostles the reason why such an event would happen to Him. However, He did not. Jesus operated on the platform of secrecy and silence. The only message one can get from that encounter is that to encourage Jesus to be killed in Jerusalem was to be on the side of God. If what Judas did led to Jesus's death on the cross, then He was on the side of God and Satan did not influence his action.

The only ones that would testify to the character of Judas Iscariot were his Master and the other apostles. Diligence, loyalty, humility, honesty, discipline, moral virtue, love of God and their Master, obedience to His instructions, and absolute silence to any revealed secret that they must keep to themselves, were the hallmarks of the ordained apostles. Jesus had said to Judas "What you have to do, do quickly." The bid question is this: what was it that Jesus instructed Judas to do?

Judas knew what Jesus had instructed him to do. Judas obeyed and said nothing to the other apostles. It was a secret mission to be executed by the most trusted apostle. His name is Judas Iscariot, the son of Simon from the tribe of Judah! When Judas left the upper chamber to carry out the Master's command, the other apostles thought, "Because Judas had the bag that Jesus had said to him, buy those things that we have need of against the feast; or that he should give something to the poor." (John 13:29) Judas could not have gone to the Jewish authorities to reveal where Jesus was. Jesus had no reason to send Judas to reveal to the Jewish authorities where He was on the day of His arrest. The Jews knew Jesus went to the garden at the Brook of Cedron many times with His apostles. The Jewish authorities needed no one to tell them where Jesus was. Jesus was not in hiding as Jesus Himself recounted to the mob that came after Him: "Then Jesus said unto the chief priests, the captain of the temple and the elders which were come to Him, Be ye come out as against a thief with swords and staves? When I was daily with you in the temple, ye stretched forth no hands against me." (Luke 22:52–53)

Some divine appointed participants, fulfilling the most important roles in the Father's business, were incapable of discussing or explaining their actions. Therefore, it was in the case of Judas Iscariot, the son of

Simon from the tribe of Judah. Judas Iscariot was an ordained apostle. He had his feet washed by Jesus and participated in the Last Supper in the upper room. He ate the bread and drank the wine that was offered to them by their Master. The gathering in the upper chamber was not to reveal to the apostles what was in God's plan that will be completed within the next two days. The Lord of secrets, Jesus Christ, with His entrenched policy of silence of many heavenly things, disclosed nothing. Such a revelation would have jeopardized the Father's business.

Judas could not know that the divine command would lead to the arrest of his Master. The outcome was hidden from him. He was not allowed to discuss where he was going. Judas, like the other apostles, had to maintain absolute secrecy on Jesus's revelations to them on the mysteries of the God's kingdom. The mysteries of the kingdom of God were revealed to the apostles, but they were to tell no one. Peter, James, and John witnessed His transfiguration, but they could not reveal it immediately. Judas was not permitted to glimpse the inscrutable truth of what the Father and His Son had designed. With no knowledge or understanding of what he was told to do quickly, when he realized his actions, Judas Iscariot, the son of Simon, cried out, "I have sinned; I have betrayed the innocent Blood." (Matthew 27:4)

Judas had no choice. The Master commanded, and in compliance with their relationship with Him, Judas obeyed. It was Jesus, His Master, who kept everything secret. Would you use Judas's statement that he had betrayed the innocent Blood against him when he saw the consequences of what Jesus had told him to do? Nay, Jesus maintained His secrecy and silence. It was not necessary to defend Judas at that time. Such defense would compromise what Jesus planned to accomplish. The reason why Jesus sent him to the Jewish authorities was hidden from him. It was for the same reason that Jesus hid from all the apostles why He had to go to Jerusalem to be killed. Judas acted on the side of God and not of men. Because Jesus did not explain the significance of the events to the apostles and kept it secret, when He was arrested, they all, except one apostle, abandoned Him and fled. On three occasions, even Peter denied that He knew Jesus. Can you blame them for such actions? No. Their actions protected the Gospel and the Father's business that continued after the death of Jesus. Their flight and denial were planned by their Master in preparation for the message they would carry to the world.

However, what was that command that Judas must go and do quickly? Why was Jesus speeding up things? It would seem that the mystery of what Jesus told Judas to do is sealed in the secret chambers of the Father and His Son, and we are not privileged enough to know it. However, if you examine the immediate reaction of the Jewish authorities when Judas delivered the message as well as the immediate reaction of the high priest Caiaphas when Jesus was tried before him, you can decipher what Judas's message was or what he was instructed to reveal to the Jewish authorities that infuriated them enough to take immediate action against Jesus. First, we have to know why the Jewish authorities had all along plotted to kill Jesus. Is it possible that Jesus sent Judas to the Jewish authorities to say something or reveal a secret that He Himself would not say or reveal to the Jewish authorities? The answer is no. Was it possible for Jesus to allow the Devil into the upper chamber during the Last Supper to "enter into Judas" as was reported? "Supper being ended, the devil having put into the heart of Judas Iscariot, Simon's son, to betray Him." (John 13:2) If we endorse that report, then we do not really know who Jesus is and we have given divine authority to the Devil over Him. Jesus has supreme authority over the Devil. When the seventy whom Jesus had sent out to preach the Gospel returned, they said to Jesus, "Lord, even the devils are subject unto us through thy name." (Luke 10:17) However, in the scene reported at last supper, Jesus did not say that the Devil entered into Judas to betray Him.

Did Satan, as was reported, tempt an ordained apostle of Christ, Judas Iscariot, who, like the other apostles, left all and followed Him for the execution of the Father's business? "And after the sop, Satan entered unto him. (Judas Iscariot) Then Jesus said unto him, what thou doest, do quickly." (John 13:27) Jesus selected the apostles. If we declare that true, then why did Jesus, ask Judas to follow Him and ordained him, then allowed him to be tempted by Satan. Alternatively, are we really missing the meaning of ordination of the apostles by Jesus and the spiritual significance of the Last Supper? If Jesus had prayed for Simon Peter for protection from satanic temptation, why did He not do the same for Judas? "And the Lord (Jesus) said, Simon, Simon, behold, Satan hath desired to have you, that he may sift you as wheat. But I have prayed for thee; that thy faith fails not, and when thou art converted, strengthen thy brethren." (Luke 22:31-32) Jesus did not pray for Judas that Satan would not "sift him like wheat."

Did Jesus reveal the same message He had instructed Judas to deliver to the Jewish authorities when He was tried before the high priest? The answer is yes.

The divine command, the fifth provocative act, to reveal who His Master was, was given to the most trusted apostle. His name was Judas Iscariot, the son of Simon. However, what did Jesus reveal about Himself to Judas alone? Definitely not that He is the Christ, the Son of the living God. That was common knowledge among all the apostles. A new revelation to Judas about Himself must have been conveyed to the Jewish authorities. Was it to reveal and prove to the Jewish authorities that Jesus was the expected Jewish Messiah who would redeem Israel? The answer is no. Jesus was not the expected Jewish Messiah. Jesus never claimed to be the Jewish Messiah. When Jesus was tried before the Jewish authorities, they did ask Him if He was the Messiah. Many had claimed to be the Messiah before Jesus, but they were not accused of blasphemy and condemned to death. Was it to reveal to them that Jesus is the King of the Jews? The answer is no. During his mission, the people wanted to make Him a King, but Jesus refused. It is most likely that the authorized divine command was the same thing Jesus revealed about Himself when He was tried before the high priest Caiaphas. They heard the same thing from Jesus's own mouth. However, it may be something more than what Jesus revealed to the Jewish authorities during His trial.

What was revealed by Judas to the Jewish authorities touched the essence and the core of their religion. They were angered beyond control. The Jewish authorities were not able to tolerate it. What Judas revealed to the Jewish authorities evoked such indignation that they immediately sent the mob with stakes and knives to arrest Jesus. Perhaps the instruction to the mob by the Jewish authorities was not really to arrest Jesus but to kill Him, to club Him to death or to murder Him with the knives. However, killing Jesus with knives and stakes by the Jews was not in the plan the Father designed. That was not the first attempt the Jews made to kill Jesus. The mob was rendered powerless in its intent when it came to arrest or kill Jesus. Jesus had asked the people, "Whom seek ye?" They replied, "Jesus of Nazareth." Jesus said to them, "I am He."

As soon as Jesus said, "I am He," they fell backward to the ground. (John 28:6) However, the plan of God had to be fulfilled. He had predicted that His people would arrest him. However, the fulfillment of God's plan at that point in did not call for the mob to kill Him. His time had not come yet.

Over the short period of their apostleship, Jesus handpicked those holy men that "are not of this world." Among them, Jesus had His favorites: Peter, James, and John. However, when the Son of man who must be "lifted up" on the cross chose the divine messenger to enact the fifth provocative act, to infuriate the Jewish authorities to act quickly, He chose Judas Iscariot, the son of Simon. Judas was obedient to his Master's command and, as he was instructed, maintained absolute secrecy of what he was told to do.

Following the completion of his role under the watchful eyes of the invisible Father and the holy angels, Judas, because of his premature death (not by suicide as was reported), was not allowed to speak anymore on the stage of the metaphysical drama being directed by His Master. The Father, who led Jesus to the cross, spoke for him with the unfolding of the impending spiritual events at Golgotha that was executed by Jesus. Jesus spoke for him by being lifted up on the cross and with a triumphant exclamation: "It is finished."

Immediately after Judas left the upper chamber to carry out His command, Jesus, in anticipation of the initiation of the process for His glorification, said, "Now is the Son of man glorified, and God is glorified in Him. If God is glorified in him, God will also glorify the Son in himself and will straightaway glorify Him." (John 31:31-32) The glorification of Jesus was initiated at Golgotha. The glory of what Judas Iscariot initiated transcended far beyond Palestine and the Greco-Roman empire. It enabled Jesus to complete His earthly part of the Father's business and prepare for His glorification.

The other apostles, who received the gift of the Holy Ghost after the death of Jesus, spoke for him and affirmed that Judas received a part of their Master's ministry: "concerning Judas, he was numbered with us and had obtained part of this ministry." (Acts of the Apostles 1:16–17) In addition, they were witnesses when their Master promised governorship to all of them in heaven: "Verily I say unto you, that ye which have followed me, in the regeneration when the Son of man shall sit in His throne of His glory, ye shall sit upon the twelve thrones, judging the twelve tribes of Israel." (Matthew 19:28)

Humanity, which did not fully understand the plot of the metaphysical drama that unfolded, spoke for him. Humanity, greatest benefactor of the acts of Judas, called him a villain, a traitor, and a betrayer of their Lord Jesus Christ and condemned him to hell. The agony and the sufferings of Jesus were heaped on Judas Iscariot. He could not be a participant in the glory the Father planned for all humanity. Jesus had prayed to His Father to grant that His apostles would be where He was going so that they could behold His glory in heaven. However, humanity, based on what it thinks it knows but really cannot comprehend, as seen with the mysteries of the acts of Judas, has enthusiastically endorsed the exclusion of Judas from the kingdom of heaven. He was called the son of perdition who must not even be allowed to behold the glory of the Son of man. However, Judas's authorized message to the Jewish authorities evoked a cascade of events that led to the glorification of Jesus, to the glory of the cross, and to the successful completion of the earthly phase of the Father's business by his Master.

By divine selection, for the earthly execution of the Father's business, the twelve holy men were summoned and ordained by their Master. Jesus said to the apostles, "Ye have not chosen me, but I have chosen you and ordained you. (John 15:16) Jesus said that the will of the Father that sent Jesus is that, "all which He hath given me; I shall lose nothing, but should raise it up again in the last day." (John 6:39) Jesus chose

Judas Iscariot for the fulfillment of His Father's holy purposes. Like the other apostles, he was raised up. Whom will the Father authorize to sit at the right of Jesus in His glory? Will it be James or John, the sons of Zebedee, will it be Simon Peter, or will it be Judas Iscariot, the son of Simon? It gives me great pleasure to think of Judas in heaven, crowned in glory and honor, being accredited the glory of all he did, and singing hallelujah with all the angelic hosts and with the great multitude in white robes forever and ever. This treatise will not reveal who sits at the right hand of Jesus Christ, but when you see who sits at the right hand of Christ when we stand before His Master during our final judgment, please control your emotions or risk being thrown out of Paradise.

They (the twelve apostles) are not of this world, just as I am not of the world.
—John 17:16

I spoke for Judas Iscariot, by making public, his role in the mission of Jesus Christ in my book: *The Innocent Blood and Judas Iscariot.* I have inserted below, a modified in memoriam from that book.

We wondered, Judas Iscariot, son of Simon.
That you went so soon without good-bye.
With the mystery of your blessed act
Sealed up in heaven.
Your Master's secret chamber.
Who can understand your role in the Father's business?
Save the Father and Jesus Christ.
Whose voice you recognized and followed at His command.
From the world's stage
To the scene of thy death in the field of blood.
Ambassador and obedient servant of the Son of man.
Chosen and ordained apostle of the Lord of eternal life.
Custodian and bearer of the purse of charity.
Advocate and champion of compassion.
Steward of the mysteries of the Kingdom of God.

Authorized initiator of what was finished at Golgotha.
For the revelation of thy Master and His Father
And for the glory of His Father and humanity.
Your holy act now complete.
As victory songs of glories and alleluias echoed.
On the four winds of heaven and on earth.
Your works yielded good fruits.
Who is the mortal that can take your glory from you?
At this fullness of time, your pious fellow.
Gives to the world, your blessed works.
Divinely guided authorized immortal act.
Immortal is your soul with your Master.
In His paradise, His Father's Kingdom.
Enjoy the divine union and the everlasting peace!

7

THE SIXTH PROVOCATIVE ACT: THE TRIALS OF JESUS BEFORE THE HIGH PRIEST

And as soon as it was day, the elders of the people and the chief
priests and the scribes came together, and led Him (Jesus) into
their council, saying, *"Art thou the Christ, tell us?"* And He said unto
them, *"If I tell you, ye will not believe: And if I also ask you, ye will not
answer Me, or let Me go. Hereafter shall the Son of man sit at the right hand
of the power of God."* Then said they all, *"Art thou then the Son of God?*
And He said unto them, *"Ye say that I am."* And they said, *"What
need us any further witness? For we ourselves have heard of His own mouth."*
—LUKE *22: 66-71*

JESUS KNEW WHY the Jewish authorities would not let Him go. The Jewish
authorities knew why they would not let Jesus go. What was it that Jesus
instructed Judas Iscariot to reveal to the Jewish authority that when he
did that, it evoked such a reaction that they immediately sent out the

mob to arrest Him? The mystery to that is revealed from what the high priest, Caiaphas did, when Jesus said to the Jewish authorizes during His trial, *"Hereafter shall the Son of man sit at the right hand of the power of God."* The Jewish authorities heard from Jesus's own mouth what Judas Iscariot revealed to them: that his Master is the Son of God who sits at the right hand of God. The confirmation of Judas's authorized divine initiative by Jesus, that they will "see the Son of man sitting at the right hand of Power, and coming in the clouds of heaven," carried with it grave consequences for his Master: "Then the high priest rent his clothes, saying, He hath spoken blasphemy; what further need have we of witnesses? Behold, now you have heard of His blasphemy. What think ye? They answered and said, He is guilty of death." (Matthew 26:65–66) It carried grave consequences for Judas also. Judas was subsequently found dead. After the death of Jesus, it carried fatal consequences for the disciple Stephen, who in his defense before the high priest said, "Behold, I see the heaven opened, and the Son of man standing at the right hand of God." (Acts of the Apostles 7:54-59) They grabbed him and stoned him to death. Repeated attempts were made by the Jewish authorities to kill all the apostles of Jesus for their unstoppable proclamation that "This Jesus hath God raised, whereof we are witnesses. Therefore, being exalted by the right hand of God, that God had made that same Jesus, whom they crucified, both Lord and Christ." (Acts of the Apostles 2:32–36)

During the trial before the high priest Caiaphas, Jesus, as recorded in the Synoptic Gospel, did not say that He was the Son of God or the Christ. Jesus was not accused of blasphemy and condemned to death because of the perceived notion that He was the Son of God or the Christ. But at the trial, He claimed to be the divine Being who sits at the right hand of God. What does "sitting at the right hand of God" mean? It was the same thing He authorized Judas Iscariot to reveal to the Jewish authorities. It was the same thing that the disciple Stephen saw that led to his murder by stoning when he verbalized it. Why did he, who sat on Moses's seat, tear his clothes? Before that trial, if you asked Jesus, "Who are you?" He would promptly reply that "I am the Good Shepherd." If you said to him, I know you, you are the Christ or you are the Son of God or the Holy one of God. Jesus would promptly ask you to tell no one and not to reveal it. On that day before the high priest in the presence of the chief priests and the elders of the Jewish people, Jesus publically revealed who He was. Who is He then? Did that statement to the Jewish authorities really reveal who Jesus is? The proclamation of being at the right hand of God did not make Jesus divine.

When I started writing this treatise, I was frustrated with the apostles because they did not ask Jesus, Master, tell us, who are you? But the almighty God who directed all things for His holy purposes made the determination that they must not ask that question. Jesus Himself held back the revelation of who He was until the trial before the Jewish authorities. If Jesus had revealed who He was at the very beginning of His work, you would have kissed the Father's business good-bye. This divine secret was endorsed by the Father and executed by Jesus for our own glory and for the revelation of the nature and the power of God. At last, the time was fulfilled; the Son of man could reveal who He was for His own glorification, for victory for the Father, and for completion of the earthly phase of what the Father designed for humanity. Timing was the essential element; the scheduled cosmic occurrence was imminent. There was no time for the formal, legal trial by the Sanhedrin. Jesus had to be "lifted up" on the cross and must be on that cross during the three hours of darkness.

Jesus identified Himself as one that "sits at the right hand of Power in heaven." The Jewish authorities knew that by this declaration, Jesus of Nazareth had put Himself far above the expected Messiah. It confirmed what Judas had revealed to them that night. Now they had it from His own mouth. Simon Peter, in his letter to the Jewish Diasporas scattered across the Greco-Roman empire and Asia, explained the meaning of the privileged position "to sit at the right hand of God." Simon Peter said that the resurrected Jesus Christ who had gone into heaven "is at the right hand of God; angels, and authorities and powers being made subject unto Him." (1 Peter 3:22) The high priest Caiaphas, having excellent knowledge of Jewish religious matters, just like Simon Peter who had been tutored by His Master, knew the significance of what Jesus said and accused Him of blasphemy against God and condemned Him to death. "When the morning was come, all the chief priests, and elders of the people took council against Jesus to put Him to death. And when they had bound Him, they led Him away and delivered Him to Pontius Pilate, the governor." (Matthew 27:1–2) Subsequently, when Paul, on his way to Damascus, affirmed that he heard the voice of the resurrected Jesus from heaven, the Jews made multiple attempts to kill him.

Everything God had designed in the Father's business was being executed by Jesus. Nobody betrayed Jesus. He was not in hiding. Jesus did not commit any offense as to be arrested. But He was arrested. Identifying Himself as one who sits at the right hand of God was not blasphemy against the Father and cause to be condemned to death. Yet Jesus was condemned to death. The Father planned that scene for specific purposes, and the Jewish authorities, without knowing what they were doing condemned Jesus to death. The Jewish authorities were not allowed to glimpse the ongoing metaphysical drama. God was fulfilling His design for humanity. Jesus was executing the earthly part of the Father's business. Some appointed active participants, fulfilling most important roles in the Father's business, did not understand what they were doing. This prompted Jesus to pray to the Father: "Father, forgive them, they know not what they do."

The Jewish authorities were under the divine influence of the Almighty God. It was Jesus who first used the term "crucify" to refer to the manner of His death. Although the Jewish authorities condemned Jesus, they did not crucify Him but handed Him over to the Romans. By handing over Jesus to the Roman governor, Pontius Pilate, Jewish authorities and the people of Israel had completed the parts assigned to them by the invisible Father in the metaphysical drama that would be executed at Golgotha.

8

The Seventh Provocative Act: The Trial of Jesus before Roman Governor Pontius Pilate

"When the morning was come, all the chief priests and elders of the people took counsel against Jesus to put him to death: And when they had bound him, they led him away, and delivered him to Pontius Pilate the governor."
—MATTHEW 27:1-2

"To this end was I born, and for this cause came I into the world, that I shall bear witness of the Truth. Every one that is of the truth heareth my voice."
—JESUS SAID TO THE GOVERNOR PONTIUS PILATE

"What is the truth?"
—PILATE ASKED JESUS, JOHN 18:37–38

THE MAIN EVENT of this earthly phase of the Father's business was not the Jewish authorities condemning Jesus to death but the delivery of Jesus to the Roman authority. The first question one must ask is why did Jesus come to the world when the Romans were the masters of the world? The Romans had enthroned their gods and goddesses and forced the people they ruled to worship them. People were even sacrificed to those gods. Why did Jesus come to Palestine when the Romans were in command? Why did Jesus allow the Romans to crucify Him? Why did the Father allow the Romans to crucify Jesus? Once the plan had been completed, the mystery of the trial of Jesus before Pontius Pilate and His crucifixion by the Romans brought to light the deep mysteries of the Father's business that Jesus performed. The revealed mystery will enhance your comprehension as to why the Father assigned death by crucifixion to the Son of man and why the Romans were used to carry out the divine command. The exploration of that mystery reveals the spiritual tool used by Jesus to enthrone His Father in the Greco-Roman empire, and complete what He had planned for humanity. By the efforts of His Son, the Father was victorious, maintaining His position as the Lord of all Lords.

The trial of Jesus before the Roman-appointed procurator Pontius Pilate, which was a prelude to the battle for Rome, was the last planned provocative act. It enabled the Son of man to be "lifted up" on the cross. Jesus used silence, arrogance, and stubbornness—the antithesis of His teachings with metaphoric expression on the truth, which confused the governor—as spiritual tools in the Father's business that involved Pontius Pilate. It was done under the influence and power of the invisible God as was reported in the Gospel: "Speaketh thou not unto me? Knowest thou not that I have the power to crucify thee, and have the power to release thee," Pilate said to Jesus. "Thou couldest have no power at all against me, except it were given unto thee from above," Jesus replied. (John 19:10–11)

During the trial, Pontius Pilate categorically stated, "I find no fault in Him," yet he delivered Jesus to the Jews to be crucified with the help of the Roman soldiers. It would seem that Pontius Pilate made a mockery of the Roman law and missed the opportunity to be seen as the great-est procurator Rome ever produced—a prefect who exhibited judicial integrity, honesty, and courage and upheld and promulgated the legal platform Rome gave the world. But what happened during the trial had been predetermined by God. Pontius Pilate had no power at all over Jesus. The power of the almighty God controlled all things. Although Pilate found no fault in Jesus, it was Caesar's appointee's fate to condemn Him to be "lifted up" and crucified for the glorification of the Son of man and for our own glory. God was also glorified.

When the true history of the trial before the Roman procurator is written, Pontius Pilate must be remembered not as one who corrupted the Roman legal system—a system that is used today all over the world. That legal system is now also plagued with corruption, injustice, pros-ecution of the innocent, plea bargains for those who did not commit the offence they were accused of, and malpractice litigations. There was no record that Tiberius Caesar rebuked Pontius Pilate for the condemnation of a man he found not guilty. The corrupt Roman legal system existed before Pontius Pilate, and it is the same crooked, bribable system that was handed over to the world. It is a system that takes into consideration testimonies from false witnesses. The Jews falsely accused Jesus: "We found this fellow perverting the nation, and forbidding to give tribute to Caesar, saying that he himself is Christ, a King."

During the trail before the high priest Caiaphas, in the presence of all the chief priests and the elders of the people, Jesus was accused of blasphemy against God and condemned to death. Jesus never said He was a King. He never told anyone not to pay tribute to the Roman gov-ernment. He paid his own tribute with the money Peter got from the belly of the fish.

Why did the Jews take Jesus to Pontius Pilate to be tried after they had condemned Him to death? Why did they not stone Him to death or kill Him in the manners used by their forefathers to kill some of the prophets? The Jewish authorities did not want the blood of that inno-cent, righteous man on their heads. So they lied to Pontius Pilate when Pilate told them, "Take ye Him, and judge Him according to your law."

"It is not lawful for us to put any man to death," the Jews replied. But a few months after the death of Jesus, the Jewish mob, in the presence of the of the high priest, the chief priests, and the elders of the people, killed Stephen by stoning. James the brother of Jesus was killed with a sword in the temple.

Pontius Pilate was not deceived. He knew that Jesus had done no evil: "Ye have brought this man unto me as one that perverteth the people; and behold, I having examined Him before you, have found no fault in this man. Touching those things whereof ye accused him. No, nor yet Herod; for I sent you to him and lo, nothing worthy of death is done unto Him. I will therefore chastise Him and release Him." (Luke 23:14–16)

But the Jews cried out all at once, saying, "Away with this man, and release unto us Barabbas." Barabbas was a Jew who, for certain sedition in the city and for murder, was cast into prison. How could Pontius Pilate understand what was happening when the Jewish authorities deliberately hid from him the main reason why they brought Jesus to him to condemn and crucify? So again, for the third time, Pontius Pilate said to the Jews, "Why, what evil had He done? I have found no cause of death in Him; I will therefore chastise Him and release Him." (Luke 23:22)

Pontius Pilate could not release Jesus of Nazareth, who claimed to be as powerful and holy as God, far above the power of their expected Messiah. All charges against Jesus before Pontius Pilate were cover-ups and false allegations. For breaking the first law of the ten commandments of Moses and teaching others to do so; for revealing another God Jesus called His Father, Jesus was a Blasphemer. He had to be crucified. The Jews would not accept any other punishment option or allow Pontius Pilate to set Him free. In their pent up fury, they all cried out: "His blood be on us, and on our children." (Matthew 27:25)

And they were instant with loud voices, requiring that He (Jesus) might be crucified. And the voices of them and of the chief priests prevailed. And Pilate gave sentence that it should be as they required...he delivered Jesus to their will. —Luke 23: 23–25

9

THE ROAD TO THE TRIUMPHANT HILL OF GOLGOTHA

Daughters of Jerusalem weep not for me…
—LUKE 23:28

If anyone desires to come after Me, let him deny him-self and take up his cross and follow Me.
—MATTHEW 16:24; LUKE 9:23

THE JOURNEY TO Golgotha was in accordance to the will of Jesus and that of His Father. Nobody could stop Him. Jesus called Simon Peter "Satan" because he tried to discourage Him from going to Jerusalem. That encounter silenced the other apostles, who then decided to go to Jerusalem to die with their Master. Jesus made no attempt to stop it. He knew why He had to die the way He did. What was planned in the heavenly domains by the Father-Son team (even before the earthly birth of Jesus) for the execution of the Father's business was executed with precision at Golgotha.

If Jesus had told the Jews that God would be with Him at Golgotha, they would have replied that God had already abandoned Him. If Jesus had told the Jews that He was going to Golgotha to reveal His Father, they would have shouted: "Blasphemer! Crucify Him." If Jesus had told the Jews that He was going to Golgotha to silence the Roman gods and goddesses, save their souls, and put an end to the murdering of some Galileans and mixing their blood with sacrificial animals' blood by the Romans, the Jews would have said, "Did we not tell you that Jesus is insane?" If you had been present at that time and Jesus told you that he was going to Golgotha to establish a temple for His Father that would be built without the aid of hands, would you have believed Him? If in addition Jesus told you He was going to accomplish all the above with the cross He was carrying to Golgotha, what would have been your reaction? The glorification of Jesus was also initiated at Golgotha. However, if you were in Jerusalem and Jesus told you God would glorify Him, would you not ask Him the meaning of glorification? Would Jesus reveal it to you? The answer is no.

When Jesus told His sympathizers not to weep for Him, He knew the reason for such instruction. Why weep for the Golgotha events if they represent a blessed memorial? Why cry for the spiritual events that were the exhibition of His majesty, power, and glory that would flourish forever? If Jesus was going to Golgotha to initiate the process for His glorification, why cry for Him? Why grieve when the foundation stone, "the stone the builders rejected," was being laid for the great spiritual temple of the truth at Golgotha, which would stand until eternity? Why agonize when Jesus was happy that He was going back to His Father. Why mourn in victory? Why lament when the greatest show on earth was staged at Golgotha by the Master of truth and authenticity? Why moan when all the essentials of Jesus's entire mission were put on display in a moment of time at Golgotha? Do we weep when a woman is in labor or do we hold her hand and comfort her in anticipation of the joy that will follow when the baby is delivered? Jesus wanted it that way. If the Lord of light was getting ready illuminate the light in our hearts that we may be the children of that Light, why not rejoice in anticipation of the impending victory of the Lord? Although Jesus was silent on what He was doing, He knew what He was doing

If you love Me, you would rejoice, because I am going to the Father, for my Father is greater than I. —John 14:28

The cup my Father gave me, must I not drink it? —Jesus

Do not let your hearts be troubled. Believe in God, believe also in Me. —John 14:1

Where I am going, you cannot follow me now, but you will follow afterwards. —John 13:36

I came from the Father, and have come into the world. Again, I am leaving the world and going to the Father. —John 16:28

The hour is come, that the Son of man should be glorified. Verily, verily, I say unto you, except a corn of wheat fall into the ground and dies, it abideth alone; but if it dies, it bringeth forth much fruit. —John 12:23–24

Verily, verily, I say unto you that ye shall weep and lament, but the world shall rejoice; and ye shall be sorrowful, but your sorrow shall be turned into joy. A woman when she is travail hath sorrow, because her hour is come; but as soon as she is delivered of the child, she remembered no more the anguish, for joy that a man is born into the world. And ye now therefore have sorrow, but I will see you again, and your heart shall rejoice, and your joy no man taketh from you. —John 16:20-22

10

ECLIPSE OF THE GREAT LORD AND THE DEATH OF JESUS CHRIST

When they came unto the place called Golgotha, they crucified Him.
—MATTHEW 27:33

When ye shall have lifted up the Son of man,
then shall ye know that I am He.
—JOHN 8:28

And I, if I be lifted up from the earth, will draw men unto me.
—JOHN 12:32

MY DREAR COMPANION the Roman soldiers have nailed Jesus on the cross and are about to lift Him up. Soon, we do not know how long it will take; the last breath of the Master will merge with all the infallible elements of the universe to bring glory to the Father and to the four winds of heaven. On earth, it will merge with the air we breathe, and we will feel the vibrations of His spiritual powers. It will carry with it the spirit of peace, mercy, forgiveness, justice, love, and righteousness. It will awaken our quest for perfection, love for our God and our fellow humans, obedience to the will of God, and the will to carry the special weaponry of Jesus. It will seek our hearts and the hearts of all humankind to deposit this spiritual power of Jesus, to illuminate and energize. In addition, it will empower our souls for eternal life so that we may have the filial experience with the Father and with Christ whom the Romans just nailed on the cross. This crucifixion of Jesus by the Romans will be the Achilles' heel of the Greco-Roman Empire.

It is now the third hour of the day (9:00 a.m.). The Roman soldiers have lifted Jesus on the cross. Jesus carried only the cross to Golgotha. However, this divine tool, constructed by His Father, which Jesus carried to Golgotha, was what Jesus wanted and today, it is at the center of the Christian spirituality. The revelation of the mysteries of Golgotha and the role the invisible God played had just begun. It was Jesus's will to leave the abode of heaven and come down to execute the Father's business. That was indeed a sacrifice.

The death of Jesus was an arranged astronomical event that caused three hours of darkness. There is no record in the history of the universe of an eclipse of the moon or sun that has lasted three hours. The Father controlled all things. "When you have lifted up the Son of man, then shall you know that I am He, and that I do nothing of myself." (John 8:28) The way Jesus acted in the last days of His earthly life would lead one to believe that He knew every part of that plan and how it would be carried out. The execution of the predetermined holy purpose of the Father at Golgotha was a perfect fulfillment of His will. Humanity can harness what was accomplished at Golgotha for the preparation of our own journey to the spiritual realm that is "above the brightness of the sun," as envisioned by Paul on his way to Damascus.

Death by scourging followed by crucifixion on a cross is the cruelest method of torture. Yet the divine plan was set during that period when the Romans used that method to kill people who had been condemned to death. Why? By divine influence, the Governor Pontius Pilate did not find any fault in Jesus, yet the governor handed Him over to be crucified on the cross. It would seem that God Himself authorized and handed over Jesus to be crucified. God's plan must be executed in accordance to His will. Jesus pointed out on many occasions that He was also subject to God's will.

The Father is greater than I. —Jesus. John 14:28.

The cup my Father gave me, must I not drink it? —Jesus. John 18:11.

The plan for what happened at Golgotha was carefully constructed in heaven. Out of His own will and for the execution of the Father's business, Jesus agreed to commit the plan. That was Good News for humanity, for Jesus Christ, and for the Father. The spiritual events at Golgotha depicted the moment in history when God Himself acted decisively to demonstrate to the world through Jesus Christ, what He had planned for humanity

The sixth hour of the day (12 Noon) is coming soon. I am certain that it was be the moment when all the spiritual evolutionary histories of human creation are gathered up into a moment in time that reveals true eternal life from God through Jesus and provide mankind with evidence for authentic life. That will be the moment in cosmic time in which the Father and legions of angelic hosts, would descend to Golgotha for the continuation of what they had planned and for the removal of obstacles to that evolutionary plan. The sixth hour of today will be Jesus's best hour for the demonstration of His power against the enemies of His Father. That too will be God's hour, when He will demonstrate to the world His divine powers and His infinite bondage with Jesus, which was never broken. Jesus was sure His Father would come down from His heavenly abode to be with Him.

Behold, the hour cometh yea, is now come, that you shall be scattered every man to his own and shall leave me alone and yet, I am not alone because the Father is with me. —John16:32

My dear companion, the hour is here! Yes, it is the sixth hour! We have been waiting for this moment. "Now from the sixth hour (noon) there was darkness over all the land unto the ninth hour (3:00 p.m.)." (Matthew 27:45; Mark 15:33) The sun went down at noon for three hours! Perhaps, the three hours of darkness, from the sixth to the ninth hour, was how God demonstrated His presence at Golgotha. Jesus was sre that His Father will come. He came!

This cross is the "cup" the Father designed, and Jesus accepted it. It became a cross of obedience to the will of God and the cross of suffering, humiliation, and scorn. In the three hours of darkness, it also became the cross of catastrophe to the eyewitnesses because they thought that God had abandoned Jesus. No, it was the moment in history when, in the presence of His Father, Jesus was executing what His Father had planned.

To this end (this event) *was I born and for this cause* (the execution of it) *came I to the world.* —Jesus

When ye shall have lifted up the Son of man, then shall ye know that I am He. —John 8:28

My friend, you can see why Jesus would not come down from the cross. Jesus was prepared to be on that cross until what He came to accomplish is finished. The three hours of darkness were the greatest of His spiritual moments. The *modus operandi* for that spiritual *magnum opus* was not revealed to the finite beings—not even to the apostles. The people who were present saw nothing. The great archangels and other angels that you've never even heard of that accompanied the Father to Golgotha were invisible to them. Jesus had said that His Father would be with Him. The Father did not come alone. If what was happening during the three hours of darkness was not revealed to anyone, how can we be sure anything happened at all? Something spectacular indeed happened during the three hours of darkness.

Are you ready to surrender yourself to the will of God if the subsequent manifestations of what happened during the three hours of darkness are revealed and you can see those events with your human eyes? Would you believe then that the invisible Father exits? If indeed Jesus built that temple for the Father in your heart, will you promise to worship His Father in truth by obeying Jesus's commandments of love that extends to the enemy? Will you be ready to express in full measures to all of humanity the spiritual gift you will receive from God through Jesus, who is now hanging on that cross in order to make it possible? Will you use that spiritual gift to help control the suffering and misery of humanity and help the poor? Will you spread the knowledge of God that will be revealed to all parts of the world trough practical demonstration of all that you have learned from Golgotha? Will you obey the will of God and His commandments as Jesus did?

For all of us, the path to the Father's business is filled in many places with potholes. However, if there is no doubt in your mind about what happened during the three hours of darkness, when all is revealed to you, will you seek to walk on the path to the Father's business for the accomplishment of our colossal duty? Will you pledge to serve God and humanity? If an opportunity is given to you to look behind the cross and see all that is hidden, will you pledge to work like the twelve ordained holy men and Paul? Will you carry your own cross and follow Jesus Christ?

In the story of the transfiguration, Peter, James, and John did not see how Jesus was transfigured, but they saw the result of that transfiguration. Likewise, those who were present did not see what was happening during the hours of darkness at Golgotha. However, the early results manifested on the third day after the death of Jesus. If we are to know if God exists, if we are to trust God, believe in on Jesus, who is still hanging on the cross, glorified by God and develop the God-Jesus experience, we too must keep our eyes on Jesus.

Jesus's willingness to obey God's will was impeccable and beyond reproach. Humiliated, spat upon, scorned, scourged, stripped almost naked, and mocked, yet He was determined to drink from the cup the Father had given Him. Jesus, without offering any resistance, allowed the Jewish authorities to condemn Him to death and the Romans to nail

Him on the cross. If we are determined to know why Jesus surrendered to the unspoken will of God absolutely and irrevocably, we must set our eyes on Jesus and watch Jesus on the cross. He is still on the cross and will not use His powers to disappear.

Let us set our eyes on Jesus, the author and perfector of our faith, who for the joy set before Him, endured the cross scorning its shame, and sat down at the right hand of God. —Hebrew 12:2

Many theologians, who had died, would turn over in their graves, if told that God intentionally sent Jesus to earth to be crucified by the Romans in order to fulfill part of His plans. Many people seeking the historical Jesus and many authors writing books on Jesus's question to Peter ("Who do men say that I am?") will surely raise an eyebrow if told that Jesus came to this world to be crucified by the Romans and that His death will reveal who He is. Many Christian theologians have given different interpretations as to why Jesus died. However, the time has come when we must put aside all rhetorical statements as to why Jesus died and look at the heavenly things that were revealed centuries ago. We must look at the priceless manifestations of the events at Golgotha that were subsequently revealed. The mystery of all those events is exciting. The cross holds many mysteries; we just have to be patient and watch.

The Death of Christ

"Now my heart is troubled and what shall I say? Father save me from this hour? No, it was for this cause came I to this hour. Father glorify your name." —John12:28

For the first time during the dark three hours, at the beginning of the ninth hour, Jesus cried out, *"Eli, Eli, Lama Sabachthani,"* (Matthew 27:46) Jesus cried out again in a loud voice soon after the above utterance. What was it that Jesus said when He cried out the second time? Was it another angelic utterance in the "original tongue" that all of us who were present could not interpret or even make out the words?

My dear companion, as a physician I have witnessed people's dying moments. They do not cry out in a loud voice just before they die. It is reasonable to assume that Jesus's last words were a jubilant doxology to His Father not just for His impending glorification but for the victory of what was "finished."

It would seem that there were eight, not seven, utterances by Jesus while on the cross. The one He loudly vocalized was a victorious assertion that marked the moment in history when what was finished at Golgotha was sealed with the divine authority of the Father. The cross became the great cathedral of Jesus's spiritual power that guaranteed the immortality of His work and the authenticity of His divine origin. The people who were present did not know what Jesus said, but they all heard His loud voice.

The Gospel of John reports that when Jesus had received the vinegar, He said, "It is finished." The demonstration and the display were over. The battle that Jesus fought without lethal weapons against the enemies of His Father was over, but it would take more than three hundred years for the results of the great battle to manifest in the Greco-Roman Empire. Perhaps it would take more than five thousand years to manifest fully in the whole world. The Father had prevailed in what He had planned and was pleased in what Jesus finished at Golgotha. His supreme authority was revealed because He had controlled all the actions of all the earthly inhabitants who participated: the authorized divine initiative of the blessed ordained apostle Judas Iscariot, the injustice of the Roman governor, the deep hatred of the Jewish authorities, the ignorance of the Jewish mob, and the unquestioned, wicked obedience of the Roman soldiers who obeyed orders and crucified Jesus.

At this ninth hour, soon after Jesus had cried out with a loud voice, He said, "Father, into Thy hands I commend my spirit." Jesus bowed His head and died. The three hours of darkness, the eclipse of the Lord, ended. A vibrant light filled Golgotha. That light was not from the sun or moon. It was the living light that is the image of God. This is the light the world needs.

That was the true Light, which lighted every man that comes into the world. —John 1:9

I am the Light of the world. —John 8:12

Believe in the light, that you may be the children of light. —John 12:36

It was reported by the people who were at the temple that the moment Jesus died, "the veil of the temple was rent in twain from the top to the bottom, and the earth did quake, and the rocks rent; and the graves were opened; and many bodies of the saints which slept arose." (Matthew 27:51–52) In victory and jubilation of the unprecedented cosmic event, the spirits of the saints that had died rose from their graves to participate in the glory and ecstasy of it.

The Father did not fail His Son. Jesus knew that the Father was there with Him. He did not commend His Spirit to a phantom God but to a God He knew existed and was right there with Him at Golgotha. Jesus did not consign His Spirit to a God who was far away from Golgotha or to a God who sat on His throne in heaven, celebrating the victory of Jesus's mission with His angels. The Father had been an active participant in Jesus's mission; that partnership continued to Golgotha and beyond. Jesus's knowledge that the God He called His Father was the special weaponry that He used in the execution of His work. You have just witnessed the initiation of the glorification of Jesus at Golgotha: the handing over of Jesus's spirit to God. The result of that process would be made manifest in few days.

My dear friend, if Jesus at this moment gave His spirit completely to God, without any hesitation and with full confidence, then He is not a hypocrite or an illusionist and that His Father is real. However, that moment in history of this grand, infinite confidence in God, His Father, transcended its demonstration. It was the epitome of the divine image of the invisible God. It revealed the existence of the God to whom Jesus commended His spirit, and the authenticity of this God was affirmed.

Jesus trusted a God that is real although you cannot see or touch Him. Jesus's obedience to the will of God was undaunted and beyond reproach. His obedience to the command of a higher vision was beyond the comprehension of all humans. This God, the Father of Jesus, who had been unknowable in the past became known and accessible at Golgotha. He controls our life and destiny too, and He is determined to accomplish what He had planned for us through Jesus. If you commend your spirit to Him, as Jesus did, you will always feel His presence. By staying with me in spirit to this final hour at the holy Golgotha, you are now a witness to some of the deep mysteries of the cross. This is your own secret spiritual weaponry, an imitation of Jesus's secret weapon: absolute trust in God of Christ as our God. Use it wisely for the spiritual journey of your soul and for the glory of what God planned for humanity.

Jesus's absolute trust and His faith in God are unparalleled in history. The crescendo of that absolute trust was a total surrender of His spirit to the will of the Father. That trust transcended far beyond the commandment to love God with all our hearts, soul, and mind. It was a quantum leap to the Father-Jesus Christ bondage and experience of the highest spiritual order that reveals God in Jesus and Jesus in God. We too recognize the limits of human knowledge and wisdom. The mysteries of God are perhaps too transcendent for us to comprehend at our rudimentary stage of the evolution of our souls.

Imagination is more important than knowledge, for knowledge is limited to all we know now and understand, while imagination embraces the entire world, all there ever will be to know and understand. —Albert Einstein

What is called knowledge in everyday parlance is only a small island in a vast sea that has not been traveled. Hence the existential question for the knower is this: Which does he love more, the small island of his so-called knowledge or the sea of infinite mystery? —Karl Rahner

Golgotha is the ocean of that infinite mystery. The events at Golgotha had an end, but the philology of the spiritual events in Golgotha is endless. Golgotha is still holding back many of the mysteries of the cross. Our spiritual journey just started.

Jesus is still on the cross. The battle is not over yet. The Roman soldiers certified that Jesus was dead after they pierced His side with a javelin and then left with Jesus's purple robe. Joseph of Arimathea, God's appointed earthly undertaker and custodian of the body of Jesus, had gone boldly to the Governor Pontius Pilate and obtained permission to take down the body of Jesus. Pontius Pilate granted Joseph of Arimathea his wish after obtaining confirmation from the centurion in charge of the execution that Jesus had died. Joseph planned to put the body in the tomb he had previously prepared for himself. Let us go with Joseph of Arimathea to the gravesite and be a witness of the burial of Jesus. Be not afraid.

As the revelation of one mystery opens the door to another, we are about to enter into the deep mystery of the glorification of the spirit of Jesus by the Father, the Lord of all Spirits and the Custodian of all souls. The initiation of this glorification was made possible by the death of Jesus. You will recall that Jesus told His apostles to rejoice because He was going back to the Father. We too must rejoice. We are also about to dive into the inscrutable mystery of He who said, "I am the Resurrection." Are you ready? I must caution you that when Paul discovered what Jesus did in the next phase, he too wanted to be crucified with Jesus. Jesus would not want you to be crucified. If Jesus asked the mob that came to arrest Him to let His apostle go, why would He want you to be crucified? There is no escape for us from our duty for what God is creating. We must be alive to execute our duty to one another and our duty to God as to harvest the fruits of what was finished at Golgotha.

Blessed is He that came in the name of the Lord. —Jesus, Matthew 21:9.

11

THE GLORIFICATION OF JESUS

*O Father, glorify thou me with thine own self with the
glory which I had with thee before the world was.*
—JOHN. 17:5

THE PRE-GLORIFICATION OF Jesus by His Father was one of the many
spiritual events at Golgotha. When Judas Iscariot left the upper chamber
to carry out the Master's will, Jesus was excited and cried out with the
triumphant assertion, "Now is the Son of man glorified, and God is
glorified in Him. If God is glorified in Him, God shall also glorify Him
in Himself, and shall straightway glorify Him." (John 13:31-32) For Jesus,
His pre-Golgotha glorification preparation was finalized when He sent
out Judas Iscariot and said to him, "What you have to do, do quickly."
That act of Judas was a part of the scripture that had to be fulfilled for
the glorification of the Son of man, and it was necessary for what was
executed at Golgotha, which guaranteed victory for the Father and the
continuation of the Father's business so we could be glorified too.

What is the meaning of "glorification" and why did Jesus keep asking the Father to glorify Him? How did God glorify Jesus and what were

the manifestations of His glorification? The quest to find the answers to those "heavenly things" remains unabated. Many of the events are part of a hidden agenda in God's plan. The people that were present when those events were executed were confused as to their purposes. Today we are in a better position than the generations before us. We stand at the threshold of revealed mysteries of the cross and have the opportunity to glimpse into the some of the heavenly things that were executed in Jerusalem and at Golgotha. The cross is the epicenter of the Christian spirituality. If we are to know Jesus and understand why He had to be lifted up on the cross to die, then we must explore the deep mysteries of the glorification of Jesus. When reveled as executed, the real Jesus was presented to the world. His power and authority in this world for the continuation of His work was guaranteed forever by His glorification. When it was revealed to Paul on his way to Damascus, he asked, "Who are you Lord?" The voice from heaven replied, "I am Jesus of Nazareth."

We know that the pre-glorification of Jesus started at Golgotha. We must find out how it happened. We must ask ourselves what that metaphysical glorification of Jesus means for humanity and what it means to Jesus and His Father? If we are to know how the glorification of Jesus was connected to the Father's business and the kingdom of God Jesus preached, then we must first explore the deep mysteries of that glorification as to understand the meaning of Jesus's Kingdom of God and the goals of the Father's business. Jesus asked God to glorify Him with "Thine own self which I had with Thee before the world was." This was a request to restore all His attributes and imagery of God that He had before the foundation of the world. It was a request to be "perfect in Godhead" again and to "be of one substance with the Father." Jesus needed all the divine powers that He had before He was sent to this world for one simple reason: He had to resurrect Himself.

Did the Father glorify Jesus? The answer is yes. The proof of it is that Jesus resurrected Himself on the third day after His Death. The initiation of the glorification of Jesus by the Father started at Golgotha when Jesus handed over His Spirit to the Father. Today, Jesus is called the effulgence of the glory of God. "Who are the brightness of His glory and the express image of His person upholding all things by the word of His power?" (Hebrew 1: 3) That effulgence of the glory of God is the manifestation of the attributes and the imagery of the Father in Jesus Christ.

If the Father glorified Him, how then did God restore Jesus's pre-existent Godlike attributes and imagery to Jesus? This is the greatest of all the mysteries. It is still hidden and will remain hidden. However, that request was made just before His crucifixion. "The hour has come," Jesus said before He carried His cross to Golgotha.

That hour was not only for us but also for initiation of His glorification by the Father. It was the hour when the cross guaranteed the victorious outcome of Jesus's task from the Father for all mankind. It was the hour when the cross promised to reveal who Jesus is. It was the hour when the cross allowed mankind to have a glimpse into the destiny of human souls. It was the hour when the cross asserted its authority that would guarantee the perpetual gift of the Spirit of Jesus Christ from God to all humans. Jesus called the gift that the Father would give the apostles the Holy Ghost or the Comforter. However, this Comforter is the Spirit of the risen Christ. Jesus had to die for this gift to be made perpetually available: "Nevertheless, I tell you the truth, it is expedient for you that I go away, for if I go not away, the Comforter will not come unto you, but if I depart, I will send Him unto you." (John 16:7) The crucifixion and the death of Jesus guaranteed that the execution of the Father's business would continue through the perpetual gift of this Holy Spirit.

Jesus had finished the work God gave Him to do. He had opened the gates of the prison for the captives to leave the Devil's enclave. Jesus allowed Himself to be crucified not for the atonement of our sins. Jesus did not allow Himself to be a human sacrifice to please God. Atonement is a Jewish tradition, celebrated when the scapegoat, without blemish, is loaded with the sins of the Jewish people and then slaughtered in the temple as a sacrifice to God for the atonement of their sins. That ceremony is a symbolic gesture and should not be taken literally. If that is a symbolic gesture, why must we take the crucifixion and the death of Jesus literally as a sacrifice to please God? Jesus was reported to have said, "I desire mercy and not sacrifice." (Matthew 9:13) The sacrifice was made when Jesus decided to leave His glory, come down to earth, live among us, and deliver the divine commandments He called His Gospel. The sacrifice was made for humanity when Jesus volunteered to do battle at Golgotha against the enemies of His Father, who by means of evil spirits were corrupting the hearts of what God is creating and directing them to the ways against righteousness. We must be very careful in labeling what happened at Golgotha as a human sacrifice to please God lest the cultists continue to slaughter innocent children and even pregnant women as sacrifices to please their gods and goddesses. The Father, like His Son, desired mercy, compassion, and love among us, not sacrifice. The sacrifice for mankind was made when Jesus, out of His own will decided to come to this world. The infinite love for mankind by His Father was made manifest when He decided to send Jesus to the world.

Jesus ate and drank like us. It was not possible to live with us in pure spiritual form. "The Word became flesh and dwelt among us" (John 1:1) Yet Jesus never lost sight of who He was and why He came. The transfiguration of Jesus, witnessed by Peter, James, and John, was esoterically a phenomenon that confirmed the interchangeability of His nature. In the story of the transfiguration, Peter, James, and John did not see how Jesus was transfigured, but they saw the result of that transfiguration. Likewise, we do not know the process by which God glorified the Spirit of Jesus that was handed over to Him at Golgotha. Jesus was sure He would be glorified. He was sure of the impending transformation and restoration of His divine nature and body, which included His full pre-earthly authoritative divine glory, privileges, and power. Paul knew what happened and said, "Who is the image of the invisible God, the firstborn of every creature for it pleased the Father that in Him shall all fullness dwell: And having made peace through the blood of His cross, by Him to reconcile all things unto Himself." (1 Colossians 15:19–20)

This mystery, which was also revealed by Paul in his letter to the Colossians, is the unspoken, unrecognized will of God to restore all His fullness (attributes) and divine imagery to Jesus. Jesus alluded to this

Father-Son bondage and filial experience during His ministry when He said that "The Father and I are one." But the Jews took up stones to kill Him for saying that. To Thomas and the other apostles Jesus said, "If you had seen me, you have seen the Father." Again, they could not understand what He was saying.

Jesus was not claiming to be God. I have used the terminology "full restoration" in discussing the glorification of Jesus because He had all the attributes of God and His imagery before He was recreated to be like one of us ("the Word was made flesh") for the accomplishment of His mission. Jesus completed His mission. He was obedient to the will of the Father, our God. He had to go back to His glory. Soon, the cross will open its doors for us to get a glimpse into the mysteries of the glorification of Christ, hidden from wise men and prophets since the foundation of the world. When that happens, you will see the power of the invisible Father and what He did with the Spirit of Jesus that was handed over to Him at Golgotha. The glorification of Jesus's Spirit is one of the deep mysteries of Golgotha.

12

RESURRECTION: THE MANIFESTATION OF THE GLORIFIED SPIRIT OF JESUS CHRIST

Therefore doth my Father love me, because I lay down my life, that I might take it again. No man taketh it (my life) from me. However, I lay it down of myself. I have the power to lay it down and I have the power to take it again. This commandment have I received of my Father.
—JOHN 10:17–18

JESUS HAD SAID that He had the power to lay down His life, and He did at Golgotha. In addition, He also said that He had the power to take it up again. Jesus did that at the hewn-rock tomb. He had promised His apostles that He would see them again. "Ye have heard how I said unto you, I go away, and come again unto you." (John 14:28) Jesus, who called Himself the Lord of Resurrection, resurrected Himself in that tomb. He first had to report to His Father. It was not the Father who resurrected Jesus. If that were the case, Jesus would not have told Mary Magdalene that He had first to present Himself to the Father before she could touch Him. When Jesus perceived that Mary was about to touch Him, said, "Touch Me not, for I am not yet ascended to my Father; and to my God, and your God." What Jesus called a command from the Father is this: He has the power to resurrect Himself.

What did the Father do with the Spirit that was handed to Him by Jesus? We do not know how the Father glorified the Spirit of Jesus Christ. However, search the Gospel narratives and you will not find any record of Jesus asking God again to glorify Him after His resurrection. It is then reasonable to assume that the Spirit of Jesus that was given to God as Custodian at Golgotha was glorified by the Father and restored to Jesus in the tomb. Jesus's original fully divine image and Godlike attributes were restored to Him by a process Jesus called glorification. It was Jesus who first asked the Father to 'glorify me.'

The resurrection of Jesus of Nazareth was the moment in history when what was initiated at Golgotha was revealed to the world. The glorified Spirit of Jesus manifested with His power in full measure. Resurrection marked the time in history when the cross revealed the mystery of what will be used for the sustenance and promulgation of the Father's business. That vehicle is the glorified Spirit of the risen Christ. The victory that was won at Golgotha on that day is celebrated as Easter today. What started with Jesus's Mardi Gras-style entry into Jerusalem and from Judas Iscariot's authorized divine initiative at Gethsemane transcended far beyond the presumed physical events at Golgotha to a deeper spiritual moment, when Jesus of Nazareth, with the glorified Spirit from His Father, our God, rose from the dead.

When you have lifted up the Son of man, you will know that I am He. —Jesus. John 8:28

The mustard seed planted at Golgotha when Jesus was lifted up on the physical cross sprouted. It will grow to be the greatest of all trees.

The spiritual force that was a result of the glorified Spirit of Jesus will materialize as iridescent divine rays of light. That light is not from the sun or the moon; it is the light of the everlasting life that will forever shine into human hearts and light the pathway of the Father's business.

I am the light of the world. —Jesus. John 8:12

Believe in the light, that ye may be the children of the light. —Jesus. John 12:36

That light will touch millions of hearts and bear with it the desire to be participants in the Father's business and become sons of God through obedience to His will. The light will guide and help our souls advance to immortality and everlasting life. Resurrection was our moment too: a guarantee for the glorification of our spirits so that we, also, not only the apostles, can see His glory and be with Him and the Father. The resurrection of Jesus was a demonstration of the transcendent moment when the earthly life of humans would ascend and complete God's plan to create man in His image and likeness. Showing us how to progress and evolve to that moment of glory was the objective of the Father's business Jesus executed.

The revelation of the Spiritual Cross by the power of what was made manifest at the resurrection must awaken and energize our efforts to look again at the Father's business and live by what is in it. God is Spirit; to bond with Him for our glory, humans must pass through the phase of resurrection. No human, at whatever spiritual level that has been achieved in this earthly life of humankind, can reach the spiritual perfection or holiness necessary to unite with God without going through resurrection. "The Spirit of truth, whom the world cannot receive, because it sees him not, neither knowest him, but you know him for he dwells with you and shall be in you, Jesus said to the apostles." (John 14:17) On the day of resurrection, that Spirit of truth was unveiled not just for the apostles but also for the world. Every individual who believes in God must allow the Spirit of truth (the Spirit of God bestowed on us through the glorified Spirit of Jesus) to touch his or her heart. Once this glorified Spirit of Jesus finds its home in your heart, you will not be the same as before. Every day, Jesus is resurrected in the hearts of those who believe in Him. The glorified Spirit of Jesus has accompanied many people in their perilous trips. Physicians silently pray to the same risen Jesus for the welfare of their patients in particular and for all patients in general.

Paul's experience of the resurrected Jesus of Nazareth is well-documented in the Acts of the Apostles. That experience brought with it, after three years of self-exile to Arabia, a complete surrender to the power of the resurrected Jesus. "Who are you Lord?" asked Paul. "I am Jesus of Nazareth whom you persecuted," replied the voice from heaven. Thereafter, everything in this world, in Paul's personal life, present and future, belonged to that risen Jesus. He found his freedom in Christ, his hope in Christ, his faith in Christ, and the truth in Christ. He found peace, love, patience, and mercy in Christ. Being led by the Spirit of that risen Jesus that he encountered en route to Damascus, Paul lived after that Spirit, walked by the Spirit, was edified by the same Spirit, and was saved by the Spirit of the risen Jesus. He was in this Spirit and the Spirit was in him: "Christ in me, I in Christ." Paul died and released his soul to that Spirit and received the crown of authentic life from the Spirit.

The mystery of all theology surrounding Paul was based on his encounter with the power of the risen Jesus that he experienced on his way to Damascus. He radiated that power of Christ and translated it into what he called "faith" in Christ. His faith in Christ is, in essence, faith in the resurrected Jesus of Nazareth and hope for his own resurrection for the promised glory. Paul's justification by faith in Christ, the central theme of Paul's theology, shows how deeply this power of the risen Christ penetrated his consciousness. What happened to Paul en route to Damascus was designed for Paul only. For Paul, it was a metamorphosis to a grand faith. Such grand faith was never seen in the history of Israel—no, not even in this world since that divine Damascus experience that only Paul can describe. That grand faith in Jesus that justified Paul in all his actions was the platform that he stood upon to preach that God glorified the Spirit and name of Jesus. He also used it as his stance to preach His gospel, challenge the Jews, destroy the religion of the great Roman Empire in order to enthrone the Father of Jesus Christ as the universal God, and argue with Peter that both circumcised and uncircumcised Gentiles must be included in the salvation. Paul labored and suffered as was predicted: "For he (Paul) is a chosen vessel unto me, to bear my name before the Gentiles, and Kings, and the children of Israel. For I will show him how great things he must suffer for my name's sake." (Acts of the Apostle 9 15–16)

Paul's justification by faith in the risen Jesus modeled all his activities. It became the trademark of his work, the hallmark of his religion, and the culture of his deep spiritualism. If Paul stayed in your house without paying a dime for rent, he would be justified because of his faith in the risen Jesus. If he claimed to be an apostle, he would be justified because of his faith in the risen Jesus. If he acclaimed Jesus as the Christ and the Lord, he would be justified by his faith. If Paul had known about the continents of Africa or the Americas, he would have insisted on sailing to those continents to spread the message of the risen Jesus. To him the long journey, suffering, or death by malaria, would be justified because of his faith in the risen Jesus whom he acknowledged as Christ.

The heavenly light from the glorified Spirit of Jesus that ignited and awakened Paul's slumbering spirit is still available to all of us. However, we too must open our hearts to feel the power of the iridescent light from heaven that glows from the crucified and risen Christ. It is this spiritual force that the Father sends through the Holy Ghost, the Comforter, to bring to our remembrance all the words and deeds of Jesus as we embark on our spiritual journey to be fully created in the Father's image and likeness. This would be our glory and our benefit from the death and resurrection of Jesus. It is our promise as also envisioned by Paul: "If the Spirit of Him (the Father) who raised up Jesus from the dead dwells in you, He that raised up Christ from the dead shall also quicken your mortal bodies by His Spirit that dwells in you." (Romans 8:11)

Resurrection was the moment in the history of both the physical and spiritual world when all the portals of the cosmic universe opened up so that we too could transcend and be with the Father, Jesus Christ, and the other inhabitants of the kingdom that was prepared for us at the beginning of the world. For this, Jesus prayed for us: "Neither pray I for these (the apostles) alone, but for them also which shall believe in me through thy word; that they all may be one; as Thou, Father art in me and I in Thee, that they also may be one in us." (John 17:20–21) For this we must rejoice and glorify the Father, Jesus Christ, and the angels in their supporting role that made all this possible.

The resurrection of Jesus did not transform Him and made Him the Christ. When you shine a light in a dark room, you see the contents of the room, but the contents were there all the time. Likewise, the resurrection of Jesus of Nazareth is the spotlight that shines on Him, revealing His divine imagery and Godlike attributes. It also revealed Jesus's impeccable and infinite trust and faith in His Father as well as Jesus as the Lord of resurrection. As I pointed out in this book, Golgotha's spiritual event is the powerhouse, the source of the perpetual light that shines on His Gospel. Likewise, the resurrection of Jesus represented the emergence of the glorified spiritual power of Jesus. The ship of Christianity must sail to all waters, bearing with it the light from both the glorified Spirit of Jesus and the divine authority of the Father in order to communicate the revelation of the words of the Father in the Gospel of Jesus Christ.

The glorified Spirit of the risen Jesus Christ became the source of unlimited and immeasurable power, radiating its heavenly rays. When this Holy Ghost comes, it will seek its abode in our hearts. It will awaken and illuminate the teachings of Jesus and our desire to do the will of God. The Holy Ghost will help us follow the light that leads to God. This is salvation. However, we must first open our hearts to absorb the power of the Spirit of Jesus and play our part in the Father's business. Failure to do so is to make our home with the Devil and his demons. Every heart that is touched by the ray of heavenly light from the glorified Spirit of Jesus is never the same. Paul's experience exemplified such an occurrence. You are my witness that after the event at Pentecost, the apostles were never the same again. They built the ship of Christianity and sailed to unchartered waters, bearing with them the news of the victory at Golgotha and the resurrection of Jesus.

By His death and resurrection, Jesus's influence increased and His spiritual powers propagated to all corners of the world. In addition, as portrayed by many who believe in Him, "the whole earth is full of His glory." Jesus felt secure in the presence of an invisible Father. Insecurity has been man's biggest problem for humanity. Only God can provide that security. If we are to trust God, we must understand God as Jesus did. If we are to be glorified by God, we must first obey God's will as Jesus did and participate in the Father's business. If we are to be sure that God is with us always, then our trust and faith in God must be impeccable and beyond reproach like that of Jesus. We must also worship Him in truth. Your life story of faith and trust in God may be like those of some of my patients. It was not the sickness that made them believe in God. The illness revealed the depth of their trust and faith in God. Many of them believed that God had been with them even when they were children, and they felt secure in His presence.

The true God, not a vindictive God, was revealed to the world by the resurrection of Jesus. The Spirit of Jesus of Nazareth that before the spiritual event at Golgotha and the subsequent resurrection resided in Palestine became a universal Spirit. This Spirit moved to all parts of the world, carrying with it the portrait of His Father and the words of His Gospel as a spiritual compass to help us. The resurrection of Jesus was a demonstration of God's love not just for Jesus but also for all, including the "enemy." We are all now beneficiaries of the blessings of the glorified Spirit of Jesus that was evidenced at His resurrection.

The resurrection events of Jesus of Nazareth had an ending, but its spiritual effect is endless, and its mysteries are overwhelming. The images it created have remained an everlasting memory in the consciousness of all, even for children. The spirit of resurrection carries with it obedience, sacrifice, empathy, humility, faith, trust, fellowship, and love. It revealed the divine authenticity of Jesus's Gospel. Resurrection is an assurance that you too can have that supernatural gift and its blessings if only you allow the mustard seed planted in your heart to grow and bear fruit, if you can get out of your house to find the great treasure hidden in the field or sell all you have to buy the pearl of great price, and if you will drink also from the "cup" of the Father. Be a participant in the Father's business.

From the sunrise services around the world to an Easter egg hunt by the children and the universal shout "He is risen," the glory of Easter is a universal joy. Resurrection is a demonstration of the knowledge and recognition of God's love, grace, and reward endowed on us, as His children, through the humility and sacrifice of His Son Jesus Christ by His obedience to God's will.

Behold, what manner of love the Father had bestowed on us, that we be called the sons of God, therefore the world knowest us not, because it knew Him not. Behold, now that we are the sons of God and it does not yet appear what we shall be, but we know that when He shall appear, we shall be like Him. —1 John 3:1–2

This is the promise of Jesus's resurrection: when we are resurrected, we shall appear like Him. This is the glory of Easter. It is a guarantee of the power of the glorified Spirit of Christ in our hearts and the certainty of our eternal life. What is not stressed during the Easter services is that the knowledge and belief in the resurrection of Jesus carries with it an enormous task for humans. By His resurrection, Jesus was not only able to imprint of His name in the hearts of humans forever, but He also has profound influence on human activities so that we may continue to be active participants in the Father's business.

The resurrection of Jesus has been portrayed as a great miracle. Indeed, it was a great miracle that revealed the truth, the reliability, and the plan of the unseen God as well as the power and nature of God. His Father became a universal God who reigns and controls all things. It revealed Jesus's unprecedented depth being one with this God. Jesus's experience of this God was the secret of His personality, His life, and the Father's business He came to accomplish.

Jesus relied absolutely on a God He called His Father. The source of Jesus's experience of God is unknown. The Gospel did not reveal when Jesus became aware that God was in Him and always heard Him. He called God His Father at the age of twelve and affirmed at that age that He came to execute the Father's business. Jesus had repeatedly said that God sent Him to this world and that He was going to be crucified and rise from the dead on the third day. The resurrection of Jesus was a fulfillment of His words. In essence, it was a proof of the existence of His Father and the revelation of the divine origin and infinite power of Jesus Christ. That power carries with it, truth, justice, harmony, love, mercy, prudence, fortitude, courage, humility, moral and ethical virtues, temperance and compassion. It is the power that propels the human soul to its final glory as fully created spiritual being.

God is a Spirit, Jesus Christ is Spirit, the Angels are spirit, the Devil is spirit, the demons are spirits, Satan the tempter is a spirit, and Lucifer is spirit. Humans must be transformed to spiritual status to associate with the spiritual world. Man must evolve spiritually in order to be fully created and be able to participate in the spiritual activities around us and in our future home. This is the goal of the Father's business that is still going on now: man must develop spiritually to become a fully created spiritual being. Spiritual evolutional process is a precondition that humans must fulfill as part of the process of our creation by the Father, the Creator. Our task is to ascend to the path of this spiritual evolution as outlined in the doctrines of the Father's business as recorded in the Gospel of Jesus.

The risen Christ is omnipresent. There are many, even today, who believe that they have seen or witnessed the presence of this crucified and risen Jesus. Paul's Damascus experience also revealed that Jesus is watching all our activities all time. The time has come when the Chinese human spirits, the Japanese human spirits, the Indian human spirits, the North American human spirits, the Asia-Pacific human spirits, the European human spirits, the African human spirits, the South American human spirits, and human spirits from the four corners of the world will band together and march to fields as laborers of the vineyard because the harvest is ready: "And he that reaped receives wages and gathered fruit unto eternal life that both he that sowed and he that reaped may rejoice together." (John 4:36)

Let the memory of the glorification and the resurrection of Jesus be the driving force that opens your heart to His Spirit. Let the divine evidence of this glorification and resurrection of Jesus be your own spiritual weaponry for building a solid foundation for God-Jesus Christ-human spirit indwelling and experience that you must develop for eternal life. How can the present or the future human life mean anything without the Father-Jesus- human experience? This experience was introduced and demonstrated by Christ two thousand years ago. Mankind relegated it in the background. That experience with the glorified Spirit of the risen Christ is what humankind lacks now. Living on this planet Earth without that experience is no life at all.

The mission of Jesus of Nazareth was accomplished. "Verily I say unto you, this generation shall not pass, till all things are fulfilled." (Matthew 24:34) The truth was revealed, but there is a greater truth we have not yet divulged, as the cross, unbelievably, is still holding some of its mysteries. We do not know all the reasons why Jesus came to earth. He spoke as nobody had spoken before. Jesus performed as nobody before Him or after Him had performed. His driving force was to reveal the true God to us, defend us, and provide us with tools we must use for our eternal life. All who understood the spiritual events at Golgotha and the subsequent glorification of His spirit by God and His resurrection have opened their hearts to God and humanity. The poor in spirit who developed and advanced their spirituality, the "blind" whose eyes were opened so they could read the words of the Gospel and comprehend them; the patients who believed their biopsies would be negative for cancer because of they believe in Jesus; the cancer patients who were cured of their malignancy because of their trust in God and His Son; the cancer patients whose diseases were found in advanced and incurable stages and still believed in Jesus Christ; the physicians who believed they could not have done all their work without the help of God, His Son, and the angels; all who believe in guardian angels; many who have forsaken the pursuit of earthly treasures and powers as to have this Father-the Spirit of the risen Jesus Christ-human soul experience; those who judge not according to appearances; those who hate evil activities and hypocrisy; those who show empathy and compassion for the enemy; all who love God with all their heart and soul, all who love all humans because it is what Jesus and His Father would like them to do; the philanthropists who considered themselves as earthly custodians and gave it all to humanity; all that mourn and are brokenhearted, the meek, all who hunger and thirst for righteousness, the merciful, the pure in heart, the judge who delivered unbiased judgment, the peacemakers, all who are persecuted for taking good care of sick people—all of these people are now properly prepared to receive the glorified spirit of Jesus Christ made manifest by His resurrection. All the Gospelians and true disciples of the Christ are those who finally turned around to see the divine power of the glorified Jesus Christ and have comprehended the glorious destiny of the human soul.

We must complete our task as outlined in the doctrines of the Father's business so that we too may be resurrected, attain our full spirituality as new creatures and rejoice together with the Father, Jesus Christ, and the holy angels. The glory of Easter is the demonstration of the assured portal we must pass through to be perfected in the image of the risen Christ. Resurrection is a grand station in our spiritual creative evolutionary process in our journey to eternal life. The resurrection of Jesus was a practical demonstration of that creative process.

I am the resurrection, and the life; he that believeth in me, though he were dead, yet shall he live. And whosoever lives and believeth in me shall never die. —John 11:25–26

13

ASCENSION OF JESUS CHRIST

Then He led them out as far as Bethany, and lifting up His hands
He blessed them. While He blessed them, he parted from them, and
was carried up into heaven. And they returned to Jerusalem with
great joy, and were continually in the temple blessing God.
—LUKE 20:50–53

BETHANY, A SMALL town near Jerusalem at the foot of the Mount of
Olives, was the home of Lazarus, whom Jesus raised from the dead,
and his sisters Martha and Mary. The present Arab name of the town
is El-Aziriyeh, derived from el-Azir, the Arabic form of Lazarus. It was
at Bethany, during supper in the house of Simon the leper, that Mary,
the sister of Lazarus, poured precious, costly ointment on the head of
Jesus from an alabaster jar. That gesture prompted Jesus to say, "Why
trouble ye the woman? For she hath wrought a good work upon me.
For in that she hath poured this ointment on my body, she did it for my
burial." (Matthew 26:6–13; Mark 14:3–9) What happened that evening
showed the deep humility of Jesus Christ. On Jesus's way from Galilee,
the rich man Zaccheus invited Him to his house for supper. Nobody

in Jerusalem invited Him to his or her house. With His apostles, Jesus quietly went to Bethany to the house of Simon, the leper, and had a simple supper with them. While in Jerusalem, nobody invited them for the Passover feast. Jesus had to make His own arrangements. He was content with that. It was again at Bethany that Jesus, having accomplished all His tasks, returned and ascended to heaven. Why Bethany? Why not at Golgotha or in Jerusalem? Why not from a mountain in Galilee where Jesus had instructed His apostles to meet with Him soon after His resurrection?

We do not know where Jesus spent all His time or where He slept during the forty days and nights from the morning of His resurrection to the day He ascended to heaven. We know that after His first appearance to Mary Magdalene, He went to present Himself to His Father: "Touch me not," Jesus said to Mary, "for I am not yet ascended to my Father; but go to my brethren, and say unto them, I ascend unto my Father, and your Father; and to my God, and your God." (John 20:17) However, the risen Jesus Christ came back that day and appeared to His apostles. The apostle Thomas was not present. However, after eight days, Jesus appeared again to all of them and allowed Thomas to touch Him. Subsequently, Jesus manifested to many people during that period. It is within the realm of possibility that Jesus must have been to Bethany after His resurrection to show Himself to Simon the leper, Lazarus, and to Mary and Martha. It is also possible that Jesus told them not to reveal to anyone that He appeared to them. The reason is simple: Jesus had planned to ascend to heaven from Bethany and did not disclose that information. He wanted only the elect followers given to Him by the Father to witness His ascension to heaven. Jesus did not want people to camp out at Bethany, waiting for Him to appear again, as they did after Lazarus was resurrected. Bethany harbored the last earthly footprints of the resurrected Jesus Christ!

O Bethany, Bethany.
The Lord cometh unto thee
To ascend to His glory.

With Him as witnesses;
The precious jewels of His kingdom.
Rejoice and sing praises to the Lord
O Bethany, Bethany.
Thou that held the secrets and the mysteries:
Of the resurrection of Lazarus,
And the anointment of His body for burial,
For this ascension of your Beloved to His Father.
Clap your hands and sing to His Father, our God.
O Bethany, Bethany.
Thou that brings good tidings of His ascension,
Get up unto the hills of Mount Olives,
Lift up your voice and sing the songs of victory.
Let the tongues of the dumb
Sing the songs of eternal life and freedom.
O Bethany, Bethany.
The Lord cometh unto you again victorious.
Let the crippled leap with joy.
Let the blind see the risenChrist of glory.
Let the children touch Him and sing again the Hosanna song.
Let the poor in spirit receive the promised Kingdom of God
O Bethany, Bethany.
Silent! Silent! Hush!
Let us hear the songs of the angels.
The song of power, glory, and victory.
Alleluia! Alleluia! Alleluia!
Holy! Holy! Holy!
Sing now with the angels and all the heavenly hosts.
O Bethany, Bethany.
Put on your wedding garment
Lift up your voice with strength.
Glory to God in the highest
And on earth, peace, goodwill and love to one another.
Blessed is He that came in the name of the Lord

Jesus said to the apostles, "All power is given unto me in heaven and on earth. Go ye therefore and teach all nations, baptizing them in the name of the Father and of the Son, and of the Holy Ghost: teaching them to observe all things whatsoever I have commanded you; and lo, I am with you always, even unto the end of the world." (Matthew 28:18-20) It was reported to us, when we met with the people who witnessed the ascension of Jesus, that while Jesus was speaking to them, He was carried into heaven.

For the memory of what happened at Bethany, are you ready to cry out against evil activities of humankind and publicize it? Are you ready to not be silenced by injustice and reject plea bargains to save yourselves, despite the fact that you know you did not commit that crime? Are you ready, as a board member of any public or private organization, to help develop policies that are beneficial to all people regardless of race or nationality? Are you ready to ask what would Jesus do in any situation and do the same? If you are able, then consider yourself a blessed disciple who is willing to serve humanity and Jesus Christ. The Father and Jesus Christ will honor you.

If any man serve me, let him follow me; and where I am, there shall also my servant be; if any man serve me, him will my Father honor. —John 12:26

Rejoice and leap for joy, for behold, your reward is in heaven. —Luke 6:23

14

THE MYSTERY OF JESUS'S CRUCIFIXION BY THE ROMANS

Ye know that after two days is the feast of the Passover,
and the Son of man is to be crucified.
—JESUS, MATTHEW 26:2

To this end was I born, and for this cause came I into the world.
—JESUS, JOHN 12:27

MANY THINGS HAVE fascinated humanity that have not been adequately explained or resolved. Why Jesus Christ came into the world as a Jew, when the Roman Empire had expanded its authority in Palestine, and with all His powers, allowed Jews to condemn Him to death and the Romans to crucify Him, is one of them. The reason for the crucifixion and the death of Jesus at Golgotha has been given many interpretations. The quest to find the answers persists even today and it is still elusive. The knowledge of why His Father sent Him to the world, who Jesus Christ is, the elucidation of the Father that Jesus revealed, and the human destiny depend on the truth of what happened at Golgotha two thousand years ago. If we do not know why Jesus came to this planet and allowed the Jews to condemn Him to death as a Blasphemer and the Romans to crucify Him, what happened at Golgotha would remain an inscrutable mystery. I have, in the epiphany on the conspiracy of the Roman governor Pontius Pilate and the High Priest Caiaphas to arrest and condemn Jesus to death, tried to answer some of those questions.

What is under review in this current epiphany is the reason why Jesus allowed the Romans to crucify Him. It was the *modus operandi* that Jesus used to accomplish the main objectives and goals of His task from His Father. In doing so He used that platform to save, protect mankind and control the influence of the Greco-Roman Gods and other Gods. There are many other reasons why Jesus allowed Himself to be crucified and died. The connecting thread in all of them is the cross

The works which the Father hath given me to finish, the same works that I do, bear witness of me, that the Father hath sent me. And the Father himself, which hath sent me, hath borne witness of me. Ye have neither heard his voice at any time, nor seen his shape. —John 5:36-37

When you have lifted up the Son of ma, then shall you know that I am He. —John 8:28

The works given to Him by His Father to finish ended at Golgotha.

On the day Jesus rode into Jerusalem, in the presence of certain Greeks who were introduced to Him by His apostle Philip, Jesus had said, "Now is my soul troubled; and what shall I say? Father, save me from this hour; but for this cause came I unto this hour." (John 12:27) No one had the power to stop Jesus from the execution of the final stage of that work at Golgotha. Jesus Himself revealed this during His trial before Pontius Pilate. Jesus knew He was going to be crucified and said to the Roman governor, "Thou couldest have no power at all against me, except it were given thee from above" (John. 19:11)

Jesus did all the works that His Father gave Him to do and provided proofs and divine origin and authenticity of the works by what He accomplished at Golgotha where He was crucified and died! The plan to be condemned to death and crucified by the Romans was designed by His Father and Jesus agreed to execute it. They had waited for that period in the history of mankind and took advantage of it when the time was fulfilled. The comprehension of the mystery of Jesus's condemnation to death and His crucifixion by the Romans will help us to understand why Jesus came to Palestine as a Jew when the Romans ruled the world and allowed them to crucify Him. On His way to Jerusalem, Jesus saw a fig tree with no fruits but leaves and said to the tree, "Let no fruit grow on thee forever." (Matthew 21:19) The fig tree did not die immediately. However, in the morning, as they passed by again, they saw the fig tree dried up from the roots. What Jesus accomplished by His crucifixion and death, did not manifest immediately. It took more than three hundred years to manifest its effects on the Roman people and their gods and goddesses. The apostles and Paul, who invaded the Greco-Roman Empire and Asia with the proclamation of the news of the crucifixion, death, and resurrection of Jesus, died before the full manifestation of what happened at Golgotha was revealed. However, do not weep for them. You know as I do that they are with Christ in His glory and have full knowledge of all that happened after their departure from the world.

If Jesus had told the Jews that He would silence the gods and goddesses of the Romans and destroy their temples, they would have said for sure that He was mad and needed treatment. On His way to Golgotha after His condemnation to be crucified by Pontius Pilate, if Jesus had told the Roman soldiers that He was going to Golgotha to wage war with the spirits that they worship as gods and goddesses, they would have told Him that, by His crucifixion, they were sacrificing Him to their gods. Piercing through that inscrutable mystery and recovering the truth and the significance of that event as to satisfy readers from all occupations looks like an impossible endeavor.

For centuries, the Christians have ignored or have not bothered to ask why Jesus, who could at His will, asks the Father to bring down twelve legions of an angelic army to fight for Him, allowed the Romans to crucify Him? Jesus's crucifixion by the Romans and His death was the crown jewel of the Father's business that Jesus executed. This information is expedient for the comprehension of why Jesus, without offering any verbal or physical resistance, allowed Himself to be crucified by the Romans. You must have sufficient knowledge of the Father's business as to gain insight into the mystery of the spiritual events at Golgotha.

The apostles, Cleopas, and his companion, as well as Jewish people who believed in Him, were disappointed that Jesus did not drive away the Romans, proclaim Himself as the Jewish Messiah, establish the kingdom of God, and bring salvation to the people of Israel. Instead, Jesus submitted Himself to a humiliating death by the Romans. A guided insight into what appeared to be an inscrutable mysteries of the spiritual events at Golgotha, revealed that what was accomplished at Golgotha, resulted in victory for the Father and glory for humanity, including the people of Israel and the Roman people that crucified Him. God ordained it for His holy purposes; Jesus accepted it and executed it with precision. For the fulfillment of the will of His Father, guided by the same Spirit of God that led Him to the desert to be tempted by Satan, Jesus allowed Himself to be humiliated, condemned to death by His own people, and crucified by the Romans. For a decisive reason and for what was in the document of the Father's business before Jesus came to earth, the Father and His Son chose the cross as the spiritual weaponry for that colossal task.

The *mysterium tremendum et fascinans* (fearful and fascinating mystery) to me is how the Spirit of someone crucified by the Romans subsequently illuminated many hearts and awakened the divine potency of human souls, including the souls of the Emperors and Roman people who sentenced Him. What will be the stage of Christian spirituality in another two thousand years? Those who lived in the past and we who live today stand at the foot of the great mountain of human spiritual evolution. We are heirs to all the spiritual gifts made available from God and handed down to us by Jesus Christ. The gifts bestowed on us would enable us to climb that great mountain to the glory that awaits all humanity. The spiritual events at Golgotha positioned Jesus Christ to lead humanity to the peak of that great mountain. The movement is irrepressible. His Father entrusted that leadership to Him.

To explore the mystery of Golgotha, we must put aside many of the explanations handed down to us, as to why Jesus was crucified and died and look again at the Gospel and other New Testament narratives. Jesus had foreknowledge of all things that would happen to Him in Jerusalem and at Golgotha. He had that knowledge even when He was twelve years old. It is therefore helpful in the understanding of the mystery to eliminate from your consciousness the picture of Jesus who suffered and was humiliated. He directed us not to weep but rather to rejoice. Jesus knew what He was doing and kept it secret. We are now left with Jesus who came to this world to execute His Father's business. In doing so, He offered no physical resistance or verbal defense and was crucified by the Romans. Jesus was not afraid of His death. Jesus knew who His was, His work, and His Father's plan for humankind.

Why did Jesus come when the Romans ruled the world and had enthroned their gods and goddesses in all their territories, including Palestine? They knew when the Assyrians conquered Israel. They witnessed the destruction of the Solomon's temple by the Babylonians who invaded Jerusalem. The omniscient Father knew what would happen to us in future. They waited until the time was fulfilled

From the days of John the Baptist until now, the kingdom of heaven suffered violence, and the violent taketh it by force. —Jesus Matthew 11:12)

That "the kingdom of heaven suffered violence and violence taketh it by force" means there was something serious happening in heaven and on earth. The 'days of John the Baptist' was not just the period when John, the son of Zacharias and Elizabeth, came baptizing in Palestine. It marked the period in the history of humankind, when the worship of the Roman gods and goddesses and other gods became serious obstacles to the revelation of the Father and His plan for humanity. Jesus did not elaborate on what type of trouble and who was making it. Perhaps the spirits who manifested through the Romans, who built temples and worship them as gods and goddesses, were waging that war against God, the Father of Christ? The battle that started in heaven spilled down to the planet Earth. That battle was to save and protect human souls. The spiritual war was fought vigorously at Golgotha and lasted for three hours during the eclipse of the great Lord. Without spiritual eyes or spiritual ears, the eyewitnesses did not see or hear what was going on.

Never before, in the history of humankind has any one group, as the Romans, collected so many idols that people worship with passion and deep devotion. The Romans attempted to make their Empire, the center of worship for all gods and goddesses of the world. For this reason, they embraced the worship of the gods of the nations they conquered. By that adaptation policy, they extended the influence of their gods and goddesses. Their god Jupiter was identified with the Greek god Zeus and with the Syrian god Baal. The Egyptian goddess Isis and the Persian god Mithras were worshipped in the Greco-Roman Empire. The Romans believed that their gods and goddesses were real spiritual beings with divine powers and had put their full trust in them. There were at least twenty-four recognized Greco-Roman gods and goddesses at the time of Christ. Jupiter, identified as the Greek Zeus, was the king of all gods; Juno, the queen; Apollo, the god of the sun; Saturn, the god of time; Diana, the goddess of the moon; Mars, the god of war; and many more. We do not know if those gods and goddesses were real. However, they had entrenched themselves and had an influence on the minds of the people of Rome and those that Rome governed.

The known planets and stars at that time were named after them. Some of the calendar months were named after the Roman Emperors and their gods and goddesses. Even today, the French named the days of the week after the Roman gods and goddesses. Most of the legal system and the government infrastructures used today are patterned after the Roman system. In astronomy, arts, architecture, literature, democracy and in philosophy, what the Romans introduced to the world is still fascinating all people. Did the Romans get the support from the spirits they worshipped as gods and goddesses? The Greeks and the Romans built the images of their gods and goddesses to look like themselves. In this respect, they were ahead of humankind. Did not Christ look like one of us? Jesus's spiritual image, after His resurrection, as was reported by the eyewitnesses, was like the shape of humankind. The spirits that were obstacles to the Father's business that Jesus came to the world to control were real and not phantom spirits.

The gods and goddesses of the Greco-Roman empire are just one group. Every culture in this world has a record of them. People build temples for them and worship them. Even as of today, sacrifices of innocent children, women, and men as well as animals are performed in some of those temples. The strong influence of the gods and the goddesses on the minds of the people of Rome and on the people they govern, are well documented in literature. Even as of today, they still have robust influence in modern art, movies, video games, and in science and technology. Today, when people think of love, the first thing that comes to their mind is the image of the cupid arrow, and not the love Jesus and His father bestowed on humanity. Cupid is the Roman god of love. On Valentine day, celebrated all over the world, Cupid is enthroned, Jesus Christ and His Father silenced. If the spiritual events at Golgotha did not happen, there would have been as of today, more than three hundred and sixty six temples, built for the Roman gods and goddesses. If the events at Golgotha did not happen, today we will be worshipping the gods and goddesses of the Roman Empire. The crafted images of Zeus and other gods and goddesses will fill our homes.

Many people think that the concept of gods and goddesses is born from imaginations based on fear of the unknown. Definitely, this is not so. Paul also hinted at the existence of these gods in his letter to the Corinthians: "For though there be that are called gods, whether in heaven or in earth, as there be gods many and lords many, but to us there is but one God, the Father." (1 Corinthians 8:5–6) Some of the Roman Emperors, like Julius Caesar and Augustus, were considered as divine and worshipped as gods. Emperor Augustus had great influence at the time when Christ was born. Of the Seven Wonders of the World, three of them relate to the Greco-Roman gods and goddess. If the "barbarians" had not destroyed the mausoleum of Emperor Augustus, there would be eight wonders of the world today.

The Christians build temples and worship one God, the Father that we had neither seen nor had His voice. The Cathedrals and the Churches are not Temples were the God of Moses is worshipped, but were God, the Father and Jesus Christ are worshipped. History of humankind showed that we have built temples and worship Gods we have never seen, but believed that they guide and protect us. A good example of this is the golden calf that Aaron made from earrings and said to the Jewish people, "These be thy gods, O Israel, which brought thee up out of the land of Egypt." (Exodus 32:1–6) There were many phantom gods and goddesses like the golden calf. Life before Abraham, after Moses, and even today reveals the worship of these gods and goddesses. The golden calf vanished. Likewise, many before it and after it, together with their temples vanished too. However, the spirits behind the worship of those gods did not evaporate from the human consciousness. If all the Christians churches and institutions are destroyed today, the Spirit of Jesus Christ will not vanish from human consciousness. Jesus was not silent on the worship of invincible spirits. "You worship what you do not know. We know what we worship.......God is Spirit, and those who worship Him must worship Him in spirit and in truth." (John 4:22, 23)

The Spirit of God and many other spirits that we all recognize as invisible influence humankind. Before the era of the great Roman Empire and after the fall of that Empire, we still build temples to worship some of those spirits. The Jewish temple in Jerusalem served that purpose. Only Moses said that He saw the back of that God. Although the temple in Jerusalem was destroyed, the Jews have synagogues all over the world constructed Synagogues for the same purpose-the worship of the invisible God. The Christians have churches build all over the world for the same purpose-the worship of the Father of Jesus that they had not seen or heard His voice. Jesus Christ whom they believed was sent from the invisible Father influenced their minds. Many other cultures did the same thing as the Jews and the Christians. Behind what they did is the concept of the all powerful invisible Spirits that they believe control their lives. The Romans did the same thing. If we as Christians and Jews believe in the invisible Spirits and worship them, then, the spirits that influenced the mind of the Romans are not phantom Spirits. The invisible God, through Moses and the prophets, influenced the mind of the Jews. The spirits that influenced the minds of the Romans acted through the Oracles of Rome and through some of their Emperors. The Romans considered those mediators divine. The Christians believe that Jesus Christ, who is their mediator, is divine. The Jews are waiting for their mediator-the Messiah. The Romans, like some other cultures, constructed images to represent the spirits of the gods and goddesses that control them.

The paramount influence of the spirits that influence the minds of the Roman people to worship them as gods and goddesses and perform human sacrifices in their temples, could no longer be tolerated. Jesus had knowledge of the spiritual realms of the universe. Those spirits were obstacles in the propagation of the Father's business and they had to be defeated and silenced. Jesus and His Father knew that if they destroy the methods used by those gods and goddess to influence their minds and replace them with their own ways and means that would enthrone them in their hearts, they will silence and destroy those gods. This is one of the deep mysteries of Golgotha.

Jesus had already surveyed the strength and the weaknesses of His enemy. The way Jesus prepared for what He accomplished can be discerned from what He said: "What king, going to make war against another king, sitteth not down first, and consulteth whether he be able with ten thousand to meet him that cometh against him with twenty thousand? Or else, while the other is yet a great way off, he sendeth an ambassage, and desireth conditions of peace." (Luke 14:31–32) "How can one enter into a strong man's house and spoil his goods, except he first bind the strong man? And then he will spoil his house." (Matthew 12:29) Jesus knew He was going to be victorious. He knew He would finish what He was sent to do. The Father orchestrated the plan in heaven for the work that Jesus had to execute. Jesus knew the path to that work was filled with obstacles, but He was determined to finish that work. "For which of you, intending to build a tower, sitteth not down first and counteth the cost, whether he has sufficient to finish it? Lest, haply, after he had laid the foundation, and is not able to finish it, all that behold it begin to mock him, saying, this man began to build, and was not able to finish." (Luke 14:28–30) Jesus armed Himself with the most potent weapon: the cross.

In his letter to the Ephesians, Paul advised them to "Put on the whole armour of God that you may be able to stand against the wiles of the devil. For we wrestle not against flesh and blood, but against principalities, against powers, against the rulers of the darkness of this world, against spiritual wickedness in high places." (Ephesians. 6:11–12) Today, those rulers of darkness are manifesting spiritual wickedness in high places through humankind.

Those spirits, manifesting as gods and goddesses of the Roman Empire, control activities directed against God. Jesus's main objective was to control the activities of those spirits. Jesus was silent on names or the nature of those spirits. The Christians adopted the names Devil and demons to represent the group. However, Jesus never used the word Devil or demons in any of His narratives. Additionally, there was no place in the Gospel that revealed that God created the Devil, who was jealous of Jesus's position in the Kingdom of Heaven. It is for these reasons that I would not identify those spirits that Jesus came to the world to silence as the Devil or demons.

Satan is the Tempter, given divine authority to tempt all. Jesus was tempted by Satan and prevailed. He protected Peter with prayer against Satan, not by allowing Himself to be crucified by the Romans. Additionally, what happened in the wilderness when Satan tempted Jesus left no clue that Jesus had to be crucified by the Romans to defeat Satan. Jesus did not come to wage war with Satan, the Temper. If Jesus controlled the anticipated influence of Satan on Peter by prayer, it would not be necessary for Him to be crucified as to control the influence of Satan on humankind.

The spirits manifesting through the Romans, were not the same group of evil spirits, Jesus encountered during His healing miracles. The terminology evil spirits is used interchangeably with devils in the Holy Scripture. The Gospel narratives revealed that Jesus believed that those evil spirits were real. Those evil spirits manipulated human spirits and subjected them to ailments such as epilepsy and psychotic illness. Jesus healed many people who were influenced mentally and physically by the evil spirits through the process of "casting out" the evil spirits with His power. (Matthew 9:32–33, Matthew 8:28–34, Mark 5:1–15, Luke 8:27–39, Matthew 17:14–21, Mark 9:17–28, Luke 9:38–43, Mark 1:21–28, Luke 4:31–37)

When some Pharisees said to Jesus, "Get out and depart hence: for Herod will kill thee." Jesus replied, "Go ye, and tell that fox, 'Behold, I cast out devils, and I do cures today and tomorrow, and the third day I shall be perfected." (Luke 13:31-32) Those evil spirits recognized Jesus's divine authority over them and, like the angels in heaven, were subject to His authority and commands. Jesus found faults with those spirits for disturbing the mental and physical welfare of humans but showed them mercy and compassion. He had the power to destroy them, but He did not. This is consistent with His teaching that we must show compassion to the enemy. With the ordination of His apostles and the power Jesus gave to them and the seventy men He sent out to preach the Gospel, these people were able to cast out devils. "Lord, even the devils are subject unto us through thy name." (Luke 10:17) It was not necessary for Jesus to allow Himself to be crucified by the Romans as to control those evil spirits. Jesus was after something bigger, more powerful than those evil spirits.

Those evil spirits knew Jesus. However, who are those evil spirits? Who controls the evil spirits? Does God plan to destroy them? Jesus did not reveal the origin of the evil spirits. However, if they were able to recognize Jesus, we can presume they were in heaven at one time in their lifecycle. Perhaps for now we can call them the prodigal spiritual sons of the earth. They are not worshipped by humans and have no temples where human and animal sacrifices are made for their services. They do not work with Satan, the Tempter. They do not work with the Devil and his demons. They have no kingdoms. Their habitation is with the humans and the animals. They may even live in our homes or on tree-tops. They are not the spirits that people worship and adore. They are not the enemies of God trying to disrupt what God is creating. Some of them were even terrified of Jesus when they saw him. God created them and they have the signature of His Spirit, the same way we do. If they were obedient to the command of Jesus to get out of the epileptic or psychotic sick people, then one can assume that if given another chance to return to heaven, they too will forever be subject to God's command and will. God is love. He is true to His nature that Jesus revealed. I am certain that the Lord of love and mercy will not destroy them. Like the prodigal sons, they will repent and return to heaven in the fullness of time.

The spiritual war at Golgotha was not directed against the evil spirits that influenced the mental and physical states of humans. Jesus did not come to wage war against the humans He came to protect and save. Although human souls benefitted most from the Father's business and the spiritual events at Golgotha, the entire operation was a battle of the Spirits of the Universe executed in the presence of humankind, who were used in the process. We must use these platforms to explore why Jesus came to this planet Earth when the Romans and their gods and goddesses were the most powerful and why, as part of His mission, Jesus allowed Himself to be crucified by the Romans.

The God and other spirits of the universe, use humans as tools to accomplish their objectives. Jesus used the Jewish authorities, the apostles (including, Judas Iscariot), the Roman governor Pontius Pilate, and the Roman soldiers to accomplish what the Father had planned. As Jesus carried His cross to Golgotha to accomplish the work that would shake the foundations of the galaxies in the universe, He knew His Father would be glorified. He knew He would be victorious. He knew that the Father would be with Him at Golgotha. He knew that the human souls in the Roman Empire inflamed and trapped in a state of lawlessness and idol worshipping, would be liberated to receive the Spirit of the Father in preparation for our final glory. This is salvation through the sacrifice of Jesus Christ enacted through the spiritual events at Golgotha. What the people saw was Jesus carrying a cross to Golgotha. However, in reality, Jesus was carrying His best spiritual weapon to Golgotha to battle for the control of human souls and enthrone His Father as the universal God who reigns and controls all things.

Jesus knew the exact day and time the great battle between Him and the spirits that influenced the Romans would transpire. Of course, the Father came down at the appointed time. The great battle was not like an earthly war that is fought with guns, missiles, tanks, or nuclear weapons. Jesus was not carrying any such weapons to Golgotha. The battle for the revelation of the Father to humanity and for salvation of our souls was not fought with such weapons. The Father designed the weapon Jesus used: the cross. The opposing spirits wanted God to remain estranged from humanity. Their hidden agenda was to stall what God had planned for humanity and entice Jesus to establish a kingdom on earth and worship them. The Father that Jesus presented to us is not interested in physical temples where we can worship Him. However, the opposing spirits like temples where people can worship them as gods. First, it was the Egyptian gods, the gods that even the Israelites worshipped in Sinai, the Babylonian gods and then the Greco-Roman gods and goddesses. We must give credit to the Egyptian Pharaoh Akhenaten, who ruled Egypt for seventeen years and died in BC 1336. He was the first to introduce the concept of one God who controls all things. He was sure that one day that God would manifest Himself to world. That prophesy was fulfilled through Jesus Christ.

Jesus must be lifted up on the cross at Golgotha at this particular time for the events that must take place during the astronomical three hours of darkness. Jesus was not speeding up things in Jerusalem so the Romans could crucify him and prove to the Jews that He was the Messiah or prove the divine origin of His work. It was reported in the Gospel literature that in the Garden of Gethsemane, some angels ministered to Jesus. It is also reasonable to assume that those angels were also at Golgotha. I can assure you that many legions of angels came down from heaven to participate as observers in that grand occasion. It was a heavenly assemblage of who is who in heaven that featured the finest of the angelic legions. When Jesus was arrested, He suggested to the mob that the apostles be allowed to go. I wish that Jesus had allowed the apostles to be participants in the great cosmic event and be living witnesses of this *magnum opus* of the Almighty God. Jesus Christ did not consider those that participated in His arrest, His trials, or His crucifixion as enemies.

The three hours of darkness was the greatest of Jesus's earthly spiritual moments. What was taking place was not revealed to the finite beings, not even to the apostles. The people that were present saw nothing. The great archangels and other unnamed angels who accompanied the Father to Golgotha were invisible to the spectators. If what was happening during the three hours of darkness was not revealed to anyone, how then can one discern what happened? How can we be sure that this narrative is true? However, what manifested three centuries in the Greco-Roman Empire after the events at Golgotha, empowered me so that I am not writing out of imagination. Jesus did not hang on the cross during the three hours of darkness and did nothing. His father, who Jesus said would be with Him, did not take a position at Golgotha and just watched His hanging on the cross.

The legions of angels that came down to Golgotha were not dressed in army uniforms or clean white linens and neither were they riding on white horses. Jesus was simply on the cross However, I must caution you that the knowledge of all the weapons used by Jesus while He was on that cross and those used by the opposing spirits carries with it colossal responsibilities on our part. In moving forward with your life, you have to decide the type of weapons you have to use to sustain what Jesus started at Golgotha.

For centuries the opposing spirits have been fighting and competing with the Christ and His Father for our human souls. Some claimed that they created us. The Father through Jesus had intervened on our behalf, against gods who used the Romans to destroy what God is creating, reaping where they did not plant, by stealing the souls of humans and forcing the humans to worship them. Under the influence of those gods and goddesses, the Romans rejoiced in human sacrifices, created a life of self-glory and artificial riches, and pursued power to suppress the people under them, glamorized stealing from the poor to feed themselves and encouraged hatred, anger, racism, discrimination, ethnic slavery, and national wars. Humanity, even today, because of its contempt for one another, does not know who is making people kill one another and many are behaving like the Romans at the time of Christ. They have not stopped to look at suffering in the refugee camps that have mushroomed because of wars.

Jesus's special weapons were Himself and the cross. Behind the cross, Jesus hid the weapons He used: compassion, forgiveness, mercy, unselfishness, love for the Father and humanity, service to humanity and to God, humility, care of the poor, tools for spiritual growth, righteousness, tools for saving the souls for what His Father is creating, tools for building the temple of His Father without human hands, spiritual tools for rich nations not to steal from the poor nations and the rulers of those poor nations not to steal from their people, tools for many religious leaders to review and stop planting weeds in His garden. Additionally, by His own examples at Golgotha, Jesus made a display of some of His weapons that the opposing spirits could also see: His commandment to love one another and even those we call the enemy, obedience to the infinite will and commandments of His Father who sees in secret and knows what is in every heart. Over the last three years during His mission, Jesus had personified and illuminated these spiritual tools by His life examples.

The gods and goddesses of the Greco-Roman Empire, that influenced the Romans, prepared themselves for what happened at Golgotha used the Romans who demanding the blood from the people of the hometown of Jesus, the Galileans, be mingled with the blood of animals and be sacrificed to them. They used as their weapons Emperor Augustus, who had claimed to be the son of a god and had occupied Palestine when Jesus was born. They used Tiberius, who was the Emperor and Pontius Pilate who was the governor, when the events at Golgotha took place. The Roman soldiers, who were all armed with the javelins they used as spears, participated. Other weapons they brought with them included brute force, arrogance, and love for power. Those gods influenced the Romans to offer human sacrifices to them as to guarantee victory as predicted by the Roman Oracles. There was a premature celebration of those spirits when Pontius Pilate, although he found no fault in Jesus, ordered His crucifixion.

At Golgotha, for the first time, the opposing spirits realized they made a mistake by putting Jesus on the cross. If only they could get Jesus to come down from the cross. They used the mob in an attempt to entice Jesus to come down from the cross. Jesus did not come down from the cross; He knew victory was at hand. Think of what would have happened to mankind if Jesus came down from that cross. The cross would be known as the cross of shame and humiliation. The triumphant hill of Golgotha will be known as the hill of dry bones. All Jesus's commandments will find their place at the bottom of the Dead Sea. The Jews will surely be crying out today that they warned that Jesus a false Messiah. Jesus knew the consequences of His rejecting to drink of the cup His Father gave Him. With the power of the Spirit of the Father in Him, Jesus was victorious. The triumphant outburst on the cross, "It is finished," by Jesus, marked the moment in history when Jesus Christ, the Liberator, accomplished God's design for humanity.

Jesus did not come to the world to be crucified by the Romans to wipe away the sins of the world or quell the wrath of God for the sins we committed against Him, including the original sin of Adam and Eve. It had nothing to do with atonement for our sins. It was a sacrifice that revealed and enthroned God, His Father, not only in the Greco-Roman Empire, but also in Asia, Africa, and all parts of the world. It was a sacrifice to liberate human souls from the spirits that influenced the Romans who built temples and worshipped them as gods and goddesses of their empire. It was a sacrifice that removed the obstacles in our journey to His Father. It was a sacrifice that guaranteed the continuation of the Father's business to the end of time. The cross became the Achilles' tendon of Rome. However, the people of the Empire benefitted from it as many of them became Christians.

The glory of the cross and what Jesus accomplished took almost three centuries to manifest. Emperor Constantine became a Christian in 312 AD. It was reported that a few days before the battle of Milvian Bridge, Emperor Constantine saw a vision of the cross in the sky with the heavenly instruction that with this sign he would conquer his enemies. Following that vision, it was also reported that Jesus appeared to him in a dream with the same cross sign. Emperor Constantine directed that the cross sign be painted on the soldiers' shields. He was victorious in that battle. Today Rome has become a holy city of God with the enclosed Vatican City as the capital of the Christian community. As the manifestations of the mysteries of Golgotha unfolded, the modus operandi used by the invisible God in the execution of His will and in dealing with the obstacles to His plan became obvious why Jesus allowed Himself to be condemned to death by the Jewish authorities and crucified by the Romans.

After the death of Jesus Christ, on the day of Pentecost, Simon Peter, first revealed the weaponry that they would use: "Therefore let all the house of Israel know assuredly that God hath made that same Jesus, whom you crucified, both Lord and Christ." (Acts of the Apostles 2:36) In his subsequent address before the Jewish authorities at Jerusalem, Peter went on to reveal that the power they used to heal a crippled man at the Beautiful Gate at the temple came from "Jesus Christ of Nazareth, whom ye crucified, whom God raised from the dead." (Acts of the Apostles4:10) In his letter to the people of Pontus, Galatia, Cappadocia, Asia, and Bithynia, Peter affirmed that the resurrected Jesus Christ had "gone into heaven, and is at the right hand of God; angels, and authorities and powers being made subject unto Him." (1 Peter 3:21–22)

At first, when Paul revealed the power of the cross, it was foolishness to the Gentiles and an obstacle to the Jews: "but we preach Christ crucified; a stumbling block to the Jews and foolishness to the Gentiles." (1 Corinthians 1:23) However, to Paul this preaching of the cross was like revealing the power of God and manifesting that power to mankind: "For the preaching of the cross is foolishness to them that perish; but unto us which are saved, it is the power of God." (1 Corinthians 1:18)

For I am determined not to know anything among you, save Jesus Christ and Him crucified. —2 Corinthians 13:4

The God that Paul presented to the Athenians and others in the Greco-Roman Empire was a God, the Father of Jesus Christ, who "made the world and all things therein, seeing that He is the Lord of heaven and earth, and dwelleth not in temples made with hands; neither is worshipped with men's hand, as though He needed anything; seeing that He giveth to all, life, and breath, and all things…We ought not to think that Godhead is like unto gold, or silver, or stone graven by art and man's device" (Acts of the Apostles 17:24, 29)

Guided by the watchful eye and the power of Christ, Peter and the apostles, together with Paul and others, invaded the Greco-Roman Empire with the message of salvation for mankind through Jesus Christ, the crucified but risen One, who now sits at the right hand of God. When it was all over, the great Roman Empire subjected itself to Christianity; their gods and goddesses were silenced and their temples destroyed. The Father's business progressed. God, the Father of Christ was glorified. The power of Jesus Christ was made manifest, and the spiritualization of human souls continued without the colossal obstacles mounted by the spirits that influenced the Romans to build temples and worship them as gods and goddesses. It was a victory for the Father and glory for humanity. It was a victory for the Roman people who were liberated from the influence of the gods and gained knowledge of the true God, the Father of Christ. The hidden mystery of Jesus's utterance was fulfilled and revealed: "Now (this) is the judgment of this world, now the ruler of this world (the Roman Emperors) shall be cast outside." (John 12:31) Today, there are no more Roman emperors. However, the time ordained for that event to happen was hidden to the apostles.

When the *mysterium tremendum et fascinans,* ordained by God and executed at Golgotha by Jesus Christ, was revealed, it showed the defeat that belonged to Caesar, was given to Caesar and the victory that belonged to God, was given to God, the Father of Christ. What the wife of Pontius Pilate saw in her dream about Jesus Christ that troubled her came true.

The Roman gods and goddesses were defeated, God and Jesus Christ enthroned. Pontius Pilate, the governor operated in an arena that was outside his control. The invisible God, the Father of Christ who reigns and controls all things, made it possible for Jesus to be lifted on the cross by the Romans as *modus operandi* to save and protect mankind.

In performing the colossal task assigned to them by their Master, the apostles and the divinely selected agents like Paul did not carry out their mission by telling people that Jesus walked on water, changed water into wine, or fed five thousand people with a few loaves of bread and a few fish. They did not propagate the Father's business by telling people about the healing miracles of their Master or the fact that He resurrected Lazarus. The story of the transfiguration of Jesus was not used in the message to the Romans. The Beatitudes were not recited. The apostles marched to Rome and to all the nations ruled by the Romans, with the proclamation of the message of the crucifixion, death and resurrection of their Master.

Jesus prepared His apostles for what they must do by washing their feet during the Last Supper in Jerusalem. As soon as supper was over, Jesus washed the feet of all His apostles with water and wiped them with a towel. Jesus did not wash their hands or clean their heads or their whole body. When Peter asked for an explanation from Jesus, Jesus replayed, "What I do, thou knowest not now; but thou shall know hereafter. Verily, verily, I say unto you, the servant is not greater than his lord; neither he that is sent greater than he that sent him. If you know these things, happy are ye if you do them." (John 13:7, 16, 17)

The inscrutable mystery of the washing of the apostles' feet is revealed when you look at the ways the apostles travelled to spread the message of what was accomplished at Golgotha and the Gospel of the kingdom of God. The apostles did not understand "these things." However, under the directorship of their Master who was crucified, died and risen from the dead; those trained agents went to all the places "sent" by Jesus and traversed the Greco-Roman Empire on foot most of the time. Their tireless feet Jesus washed, became their travelling vehicles, propelling them as they traverse the Greco-Roman world, spreading the news of Jesus's death and resurrection. . It was not necessary to ask the Father to send down twelve legions of angelic armies, when His trained apostles could accomplish the task of that large number of angelic soldiers. On his way to Damascus, St. Paul was recruited as a member of the apostolic army: "he is a chosen vessel unto me, to bear my name before the Gentiles and kings and the children of Israel." (Acts of the Apostles 9:15)

Empowered with the gift of the Spirit of the risen Christ they received on the day of Pentecost and the knowledge of what they witnessed at Golgotha and of His resurrection, the apostles became full witnesses of Jesus in Jerusalem, in all Judea, and in Samaria, and unto the uttermost part of the world. The cross of Jesus Christ became the cross of infinite love that extended to the enemies, compassion, forgiveness, mercy, obedience to the will of the Father and true light that found its home in the hearts of the people of the Greco-Roman Empire and in many parts of the world. When the cross of infinite love was coupled with the news of Jesus's resurrection that revealed Christ and His Father, was presented to the people of the Greco-Roman Empire, they abandoned their gods and goddesses and embraced God, the Father of Christ as the Creator who reigns and controls all things.

That which was from the beginning, which we have heard, which we have seen with our eyes, which we have looked upon, and our hands have handled, of the word of life; for the Life was manifested, and we have seen it, and bear witness, and show unto you that eternal life, which was with the Father, and was manifested unto us; declare us unto you, that ye may also have fellowship with us; and truly our fellowship is with the Father, and with His Son Jesus Christ. —1 John 1:1–3

Blessed is He that cometh came in the name of the Lord. —Matthew 23:39

15

THE EPITOME OF JESUS'S LIFE AND THE CROSS

Because Christ also suffered for you, leaving you an example that you should follow in his steps. When He was reviled, He did not revile in return; when He suffered, he did not threaten; but He trusted to Him who judges righteously.
—1 PETER 2:21–22

JESUS HAS NO right to ask you to obey His commandments or disseminate His message and collaborate with Him in the execution of the Father's business unless He too obeys the same commandments and follows the precepts of His Gospel. Jesus has no right to ask you to obey the will of His Father, if He cannot obey the will of that Father. If Jesus Christ, commanded us to do things that He Himself did not do, then we can call Him a hypocrite. All His instructions to us were commands. He gave us no choice, no free will. Jesus knew that humanity abused free will in the past and would do it again. It is not for us to try to be perfect; no, Jesus said that we must "be as perfect as the Father." (Matthew 5:48) and "thou shall love the Lord thy God with all thy heart, and with all your soul, and with all thy mind, and thou shall love thy neighbor as thyself."

(Matthew 22:37) The Gospel is the book of commandments of Jesus of Nazareth with instructions for us to obey the will of His Father and be participants in the Father's business. Whether you like it or not, Jesus insisted that, we must love God and obey His will or suffer the consequences. The Gospel is Good News if one can obey all its divine laws as to participate in the glory that Jesus pledged for us. Jesus insisted repeatedly that the obedience of God's law and commandments leads to everlasting life.

Jesus's ethical and moral professionalism, which is documented in the New Testament narratives and His ministry of healing support the idea that indeed He was a shining example of what He preached. However, those mission activities before the Golgotha events were just not enough for anyone to claim that Jesus gave a practical demonstration of what He had instructed us to do. "Love your enemies, bless them that curse you, do good to them that hate you, and pray for them that despitefully use you, and persecute you," (Matthew 5:44) are but a few examples of His commandments. What we witnessed at Golgotha was a practical demonstration that He too loved His enemies and prayed for those who abused Him. He was the personification of His own teachings and a demonstration of His love and trust in His Father. It would be hypocrisy for Jesus to tell us to love and trust God if He professed to love God but showed no practical demonstrations that He loved and trusted God. It would be a betrayal of trust if Jesus had instructed us to "love one another as we love ourselves" if He gave no practical demonstration of such love. You are my witness that Jesus did not call down fire from heaven to consume those who arrested Him. In addition, He did not call the Father to send down twelve legions of angelic warriors to fight the Romans.

Golgotha events revealed how Jesus complied with the precepts of His own teachings on the kingdom of God. Jesus's Golgotha experience revealed His infinite faith in God and was maintained by Him in the face of crucifixion. Jesus showed His unadulterated, unshakable bond and trust in the Father and His unfiltered love for all humanity. Jesus insisted He must go to Jerusalem and "drink of the cup" that God gave Him. Jesus's obedience to the will of God was undaunted and beyond reproach. His obedience to the command of a higher vision was beyond the comprehension of all humans. However, there was no place before Golgotha for Jesus to really give a practical demonstration of all He preached, to show His true character and His infinite trust in the Father. Jesus had preached on many occasions about obedience to the will of God: "Whosoever will do the will of God, the same are my brother, and my sister and mother." (Mark 3:35) Complete obedience to the will of God at Golgotha was proof of His infinite obedience to the Father. The Golgotha events marked the moment in history when obedience to the will of God became the cornerstone and the hallmark of Jesus's character and divine professionalism.

The revelation of what was accomplished during the crucifixion of Jesus, carries with it grave responsibilities. That you must, as instructed by the Master, "Love your enemies, do good to them who hate you, bless them that curse you and pray for them which despitefully use you and unto him that smite you on one cheek, offer also the other and he that take away thy cloke forbid not to take thy coat also." (Luke 6: 27–29) Jesus did not hate those who crucified Him. Jesus prayed for them, which was a portrayal of love and blessing for His enemies. "Father forgive them for they know not what they do." (Luke 23:36) His discourse on forgiveness is overwhelming. He instructed us to pray to the Father for forgiveness: "Forgive us our trespasses as we forgive those that trespass against us." Many of us would not be able to complete that prayer for one single reason: we have not truly forgiven all who have trespassed against us. You may have to stop if you have not settled with those who trespassed against you. God will wait for you to do that. Proceed with your prayer if you have nothing to settle with anybody. Jesus gave another illustration: if you bring your gift to the altar for offering, and you remember that you have quarreled with your brother, leave your gift on the altar and go and settle the quarrel with your brother; then go and make the offering.

Jesus forgave and prayed for His enemies at Golgotha. The reason is obvious: His infinite love for humanity. He who told us to love our enemies and forgive people when they sin against us must do the same.

If Jesus is crucified seventy times seven, He too must forgive those that crucified Him seventy times seven. It was what the Father would like Him to do, it was what He wanted to do, and it was what God would like us to do. To forgive one another is to love one another. It was reported that the apostle John, who lived to be a hundred years old and could not remember anything, kept saying "love one another." When asked why he kept saying that we must love one another, his reply was simple: "The Lord said we must do so."

Golgotha was the stage for divine demonstrations of all He had instructed us to do and believe. Golgotha was the universal classroom for both the basic and advanced fellowship instructions for all who want to do the will of the Father, our God. Within nine hours, from the time Jesus of Nazareth left the palace of the Governor Pontius Pilate to the time He gave His spirit to the Father, He gave a practical demonstration of all His instructions in the Gospel. You can now begin to understand why I said that Golgotha is the powerhouse that shed light on His Gospel and the grand station that guaranteed the continuation of the execution of the Father's business for the glory of humanity and victory for the Father. Golgotha was the great cathedral of truth.

Two thousand years ago, Jesus told His people that they do not have to go to Jerusalem to pray to the Father. Today, you do not have to go to Golgotha or Jerusalem physically for the divine instructions. The Golgotha events can be considered that great cathedral of His Father, set on that triumphant hilltop that radiates light that is not from the sun or the moon. Those events illuminated the Gospel of Jesus Christ. As instructed, if we do not have that Gospel, sell all you have and buy one.

The inability to comprehend what Jesus demonstrated at Golgotha has led to many esoteric assertions and demands. Even today, our inability to comprehend the spiritual demonstrations by Jesus of Nazareth at Golgotha has led to many unproven slogans of the crucifixion and death of Jesus. The misinterpretation of the angelic utterance, *"Eli, Eli lama sabachthani?"* as "My God, my God, why hast thou forsaken me?" is one such example. It was reported in the Gospel that "some of them that stood there when they heard that said this man calleth for Elias."

That utterance was not in Aramaic, Hebrew, Greek, or any language ever known to the human race. The witness did not understand what Jesus said. The interpreters of the Gospel reviewed the Psalms of David and found what they thought was Jesus's utterance in Psalm 22:1 as "My God, my God, why hast thou forsaken me?" Jesus knew that the Father would never forsake Him. Jesus was conscious of God at all times. His inability to function outside the Father's influence placed Him on an infinite filial relationship with God that prompted Him to say, "I and the Father are one." He did not say He was God; He always called God His Father and continued to do so to the very end at Golgotha and even after His resurrection.

Jesus loved humanity with the same intensity that He loved His Father. Scourging, abuse, and crucifixion were not barriers to that love. He was scorned, despised, buffeted, and reviled, and yet He did not open His mouth in any defense against the will of God because of His love for humanity. Golgotha is the mirror that reflected that boundless love of Jesus for humanity. We must love God and one another as Jesus loves us. Jesus of Nazareth thirsts for our souls. He wants us to come to Him. "Come unto me all you that labor and are heavy laden, and I will give you rest. Take my yoke upon you, and learn of me, for I am meek and lowly in heart: and ye shall find rest unto your souls." (Matthew 11:28) The experience of Jesus at Golgotha epitomized all His commandments and divine instructions to humankind. At Golgotha, Jesus, knowing that He had accomplished all things, said, "I thirst." Jesus does not want you to stick a sponge in vinegar and put it in His mouth as they did at Golgotha. He wants us to be meek, humble and follow Him to God. He thirsts for our souls and for us to surrender our soul to God as He has done.

What was accomplished at Golgotha was epic. It was a reflection of images of God, such as trust, forgiveness, mercy, and unconditional love for all. It was the picture of Father-human bondage. It was a reflection of the Father as the Custodian of all spirits. It was a reflection of His faithfulness in God. It was an echo of the authority of God who reigns and controls all things. It was a reflection of Jesus of Nazareth Himself and the personification of His Gospel. What Jesus demonstrated at

Golgotha showed that it is possible to obey the will of God. Every command of God must be obeyed. We too can drink from the cup of salvation, obedience, and glory. The cup of salvation is an everlasting phenomenon. If we drink from this cup, we will walk with God, not only on earth but also in heaven. What Jesus "drank" at Golgotha quickened and activated an everlasting spiritual force that carries with it a message of authority, perfection, and absolute reliance on His Father. It found its abode in imagery of the Father. God created and is still creating us in His own image. At the time of His trials and temptations, when He was humiliated and many of His friends abandoned Him, Jesus did not seek any revenge. He maintained His humility and His infinite love for God and all humanity.

The philology of the epitome of Jesus's life as depicted at Golgotha is endless. Jesus had instructed us to pray to God. You will notice that He too prayed to God at Golgotha. You have seen a practical demonstration of Jesus's mandate to pray for those who use you and persecute you. The imitation of Jesus's life calls for us also to pray to God to forgive those who persecute and abuse us. May your experience of Golgotha be the weaponry you use to pray to God during periods of trials and tribulations, when people accuse you of crimes you did not commit and bring you before judges and lawyers. The Christian spirituality Jesus introduced at Golgotha is infinite and timeless. His message and the epitome of His life are more significant today than ever. We are standing at the threshold of an exciting progression of the human spiritual evolution that is irrepressible. If we are able to learn from the epitome of Jesus's life at Golgotha, we will, as Jesus pledged, have life, and have it abundantly,

If any man serve me, let him follow me (implement my teachings and do as I do); *and where I am, there shall also my servant be, if any man serve me, him will my Father honor.* —*John 12:26*

16

GOD AND THE CROSS

GOD DESIGNED THE cross. Jesus called what His Father designed as His cup. Who is this Father? Who is the Spirit that we, "have neither heard His voice nor seen His shape"? (John 5:37) However, Jesus said, "I know Him, for I am from Him, and He hath sent me." (John 7:29) Who is this Father, who used the abominable infamous stake- the cross that the Romans used to crucify the Jews-to accomplish His holy purposes? Of all the weapons at His disposal-legions of angelic forces, His power-His Father chose the shameful *modus operandi* of crucifixion for Jesus. Crucifixion of the Jews on the cross by the Romans, was considered to be the most inhumane and loathsome act ever perpetuated by nations that had conquered them. By handing Him over to the Romans to be crucified, the Jewish authorities wanted to bring shame upon Jesus and humiliate Him. Jesus accepted it because He had the knowledge that His Father designed it. Jesus, with His omniscient attributes from His Father, knew the benefits of His action.

Jesus's experiences and His imageries of God, His Father, were unparalleled in any recorded human experience of any God. The epitome of the life of Jesus is the mirror through which we see the deeper reflections of the portraits of the Father. During His earthly life, Jesus enjoyed an enviable unbroken bondage and experience with this God,

His Father: "As the living Father had sent me, and I live by the Father." (John 6:57)

For many years, Jesus revealed to the people the tools with which God manifested Himself. Jesus used the planet Earth, nature, a person's occupation, the habits of the people, and human nature to paint the portrait of God. Jesus portrayed His Father as a merciful God: "Be therefore merciful as your Father is also merciful." (Luke 6:36) He depicted God as a perfect Spirit: "God is a Spirit and those that worship Him must worship Him in spirit and in truth." (John 4:25) "The God in heaven is perfect." (Matthew 5:48) Jesus introduced a divine Father who sees in secret and knows everything we do. "But when you give alms, let not your left hand know what you right have done. That your alms may be in secret: and thy Father who sees in secret Himself shall reward you openly." (Matthew 6:3–4) He characterized God as a good Father who loves all humankind: "there is none that is good, but one that is God." (Mark 10:18) The Father which is in heaven, makes His sun to rise on the evil and on the good, and sends rain on the just and on the unjust." (Matthew 5:45) "God is kind even to the unthankful as to the evil." (Luke 6:35) Jesus described the Father that forgives: "If you forgive men their trespasses, the heavenly Father will also forgive you: But if you forgive not men of their trespasses, neither will your Father forgive your trespasses." (Matthew 6:14–15) The finest illustration of the loving and the compassionate Father was portrayed in the events at Golgotha that manifested in the resurrection of Jesus.

All the above are only superficial images of the Father found in the Gospel. At first glance, what you see in a portrait by an artist may not be all he or she was trying to express or reveal. The artist's intention was not to hide his or her message but to prod and engage the viewer to think and view the portrait from different angles. By doing so, the viewer may discern the artist's hidden concept that would enable him or her to enjoy the beauty and message of the portrait. Poets and music composers do the same. Likewise, Jesus, as His custom was, used parables, metaphors, allegories, symbolic stories, parabolic expressions, and the regional geography known to His audience as well as their occupation and natural environment and basic human nature to paint images of the Father. His intention was not to confuse His listeners but to prod them to think and ask more questions about this God, the Father. Jesus used the Lord's Prayer as the background and the frame for all of the Father's portraits. At Golgotha, Jesus not only revealed the divine images of the Father and His presence but also a God-Jesus-human effigy.

The philology of God and the cross can be summarized as follows: God designed it for His holy purposes and Jesus, of His own free will, drank of that "cup" the Father gave Him. The quest to know who Jesus was overshadowed many things Jesus revealed about His Father. The main event in the Father's business was the revelation of His Father, our God, and not about Himself. At a church service I attended recently, I noticed that not a single word was said about God. The service was all about Jesus Christ. We speak of God. We ask, who is God, and does this God exist? Many have written books on God and where to find God. The fear of this God that Jesus revealed during His ministry and at Golgotha instantaneously earned a free ticket to Paradise for the thief crucified at His right hand.

"Have you no fear of God at all..." the thief crucified on Jesus's right side said to the one crucified on His left. "Jesus, remember me when you come into your kingdom," the good thief continued. "Today, you will be with me in Paradise," Jesus promised him.

That blessing would be bestowed on us if we believe in this God with equal enthusiasm as the blessed thief and implement the teachings of Jesus. "Anybody who receives my commandment and keeps them will be one who loves me. And anybody who loves me will be loved by my Father, and I shall love him and show myself to him. If anybody loves me he will keep my words, and my Father will love him, and we shall come to him and make our home with him." (John 14:21, 23)

Many people believe in God but cannot prove His existence simply because they have not seen Him. Many books have been written on this subject, and many Christians, without giving any explanation, have pointed to the events at Golgotha as the place to find the answer. "Where is thy God?" the Pharisees asked Jesus. The Jews, who were asking that question, believed that a God you must fear—a vindictive God that protects Israel and punishes the enemies of Israel—exists. This God makes Israel the first nation and its inhabitant's first-class citizens of this world. The God-human bondage is between this God and the Israelites. The Gentiles are excluded in that bondage, its experience, and the subsequent salvation. The Jews were taught that salvation belongs only to the Jews and that the love of God for the Jews is the only thing that never fails. Jesus revealed a universal God, the Father that blesses and loves all people and all nations.

When Jesus spoke of a God He called His Father that was quite different from the Jewish God, He sealed His fate with the Jews. However, Jesus was determined that all people and all nations must know the nature of this God who sent Him to the world. Jesus knew that what He came to the world to accomplish would result in His death. The invisible God, whose nature Jesus revealed to the world, had already made provisions for how the task must be accomplished. God constructed the spiritual weapon Jesus used. Jesus described it as the "cup" the Father gave Him: "The cup that the Father gave me, must I not drink it?" The inscrutable mystery of this cup remained hidden until the execution of the events at Golgotha. The cup became the cross Jesus carried to Golgotha! The cup that the Father gave Him was the spindle on which all things external and eternal about God rotated. Jesus used it to reveal the truth about His Father. To look into that cup, is to look into the depths of the Spirituality that Jesus introduced to the world. Therein also are the righteousness and the glory of God and Jesus Christ in the midst of the iridescent light that is not from the sun or moon.

Jesus's timeless words of wisdom, the personification of His life and His demonstrations of the power of God by His miracles, were not enough to convince the people of the existence of this God or the divine origin of His words and miracles. The Jews had demanded that Jesus give them a sign from heaven to prove the divine authenticity of His works, His person, and the existence of His Father as was reported: "the Pharisees came forth and began to question with Him seeking of Him a sign from heaven, tempting Him." (Mark 8:11) Jesus replied, "They seek a sign? Verily and there shall no sign be given to them but the sign of Jonas the prophet. For as Jonas was three days and three nights in the whales belly; so shall the Son of man be three days and three nights in the heart of the earth." (Matthew12:39–40) Inside the cave where Lazarus was raised from the dead, Jesus said, "Father, I thank thee that thou heard me. And I know that thou hearest me always, but because of the people which standby I said it; that they may believe that thou hast sent me." (John 11:41–42) However, the Jewish leaders did not believe; instead, they started the plot to kill Him

The proof of the authenticity of the divine origin of deeds and words of Jesus rests on the existence of this God, the Father. Who designed the plan that Jesus executed at Golgotha? How then did Jesus reveal this God at Golgotha? What role did His Father play in the events at Golgotha? We must first ask a few questions ourselves. How did Jesus develop His absolute and perfected trust in God, His Father? When did He develop it? What was the source of His strength that made Him a living Spirit for all who believe in Him? How is it that the Christians cannot talk of God without reference to Jesus? What was the source of power and wisdom for this tireless servant of God and of humanity? What was the origin of His noble spirit of compassion, meekness, and love for this Father that Jesus wanted us to believe in? How was it that He loved this His Father so much that He was willing to be crucified so that the Father would be revealed to the world and complete what He planned for humanity? How was it that Jesus was chastised, abused, degraded, and rejected, yet He continued to do His work, teaching people how to develop our souls and obtain the gift of spiritual power from His Father? What was His secret weapon?

Tell us, by what authority are you doing these things? Or who is he who gave you this authority? —Luke 20:2

If I do not the works of my Father, believe me not. But if I do, though you believe not me, believe the works; that you may know and believe that the Father is in me, and I in the Father. —John 10:37–38

How did the Father know that what He designed to be accomplished at Golgotha would accomplish His purpose? The answer is simple: He is the omniscient God and knew what would be the result. Why did the Father choose Jesus and not another Spirit, to do the work? The Father chose the most trustworthy Spirit, on whom He had bestowed with omnipotent attributes from the beginning of time. He chose Jesus who always obeys His will.

I always do things that please Him. —Jesus, John 8:29

The Father was unbending in His will. What He had planned, must be executed as He had designed it. There was no alternative plan. If what was designed by His Father-as claimed by Jesus-and accomplished by Him at Golgotha, manifested in His resurrection, then it was a living Spirit that Jesus called His Father that planned it. Jesus had insisted that this Father that sent Him. The resurrection of Jesus was the evidence that God, the Father exists. To glimpse into Jesus's "cup" is to look at a living true God who reigns and controls all things.

Jesus saw the face of the Father at every moment of His life. He always heard His voice. Jesus's essence of life is God, the Father. His source of authority and power is from that God. His special weaponry is His infinite and absolute knowledge of this God and the Spirit of this God He carried with Him. For the love of all human beings, the Father gave authority to Jesus to be the author and dispenser of His Spirit to humans. Jesus had knowledge of the doctrines of the Father's business and what He had to do at Golgotha. However, Jesus knew it carried with it enormous responsibilities. Jesus buckled because of the responsibilities entrusted to him. However, His Spirit never weakened, quaked, or quivered as was reflected when at Gethsemane, He said: "The body is weak, but the spirit is willing." With the knowledge of the existence of His Father, and in compliance with His Father had designed, Jesus was sure that God would be with Him at Golgotha. "Behold, the hour cometh, yea is now come, than 'ye shall be scattered, everyone to his own, and shall leave me alone, and yet I am not alone, because the

Father is with me." (John 16:32) At Golgotha, Jesus handed over His Spirit for glorification to a living Father and not a phantom God. Now that you have the knowledge of God, is your Spirit willing to work for Him as Jesus did? Are you willing, as suggested by the apostle Peter to "rid yourself of all malice, all deceit, hypocrisy, envy, slander of every kind. And like newborn babies crave pure spiritual milk, so that you may grow up in your salvation, that you have tasted that the Lord is good and real." (1 Peter 2: 1–3)

In the movie *It's a Wonderful Life*, the angel Clarence spent several hours getting acquainted with the entire life of George Bailey before he was sent down to earth to help him. Likewise, to harvest the benefits of the knowledge of the existence of God, the Father of Jesus, you too must be acquainted with His imageries and characters as they are revealed in the Gospel of Jesus. Instead of carrying only the physical cross, we must also carry Jesus's special weaponry, the Spirit of the Father and the portrait of the face of God, in our consciousness so that we too may feel His presence and see His face everywhere and in everything we do. We see the faces of the invisible God through the faces of our neighbors. The most important essence of Jesus's Gospel is that God exists and controls all things, and that it was He who designed what happened to Jesus at Golgotha for our glory. The authenticity and the divine origin of His Gospel, the God and Son bondage, and the experience would be of no value if God, His Father, did not exist.

The Spirit of the Father who was revealed by the spiritual events at Golgotha that resulted in Jesus's resurrection is in your heart. Behind the cross lays the deeper imageries of the nature and power of the Father. Behind the cross are portraits on how this Father manifests and controls all things according to His will. Behind the cross lays a demonstration of the process of what humans must pass through for what God is creating. Behind the cross, the counsel of God and its purpose was revealed. Behind the cross, the permanent delivery channel for the gift of the Spirit of God through the Spirit of Christ was established. The cross was the template the apostles, Paul, and others used to invade the Greco-Roman Empires, Asia, and all parts of the world, to proclaim the imageries of the nature of God, the Father of Jesus and enthrone Him as the universal God. Jesus's experience of the cross and its subsequent manifestations in Palestine, in Greco-Roman Empire and in all parts of the world, revealed the living Father that Jesus worships and obeys.

Ye worship you know not what: we know what we worship. —Jesus. John 4:22

The greatest accomplishment of the cross that manifested in Jesus's resurrection and the subsequent gift of His glorified risen Spirit as the Holy Ghost validate the existence of His Father and the divine origin of Jesus's words and deeds. "I am not come of myself, but He that sent me is true, whom ye know not." (John 7:28) The Father that people worshipped in ignorance was revealed by the spiritual events at Golgotha.

Blessed is He that came in the name of the Lord. —Jesus, Matthew 23:39

17

WHAT IS THE SPIRITUAL CROSS?

THE CONCEPTION OF the cross Jesus carried to Golgotha was spiritual. The execution of events when Jesus was lifted on that cross was spiritual. The series of events following the death of Jesus on the cross were all spiritual. We can label anything Jesus said and did as spiritual without blinking an eye. We can touch His body before His resurrection and say we have touched a spirit. We can eat on the table with Him, as Cleopas and his companion did at Emmaus, and our hearts will burn with excitement because we ate with a divine Being. We have watched exciting movies on the cup Jesus used to serve His apostles at the Last Supper.

If the technology had been available at the time Jesus was crucified to freeze drops of His blood that were shed at Golgotha, the droplets would carry the highest price tag today. We have made movies on the robe the Romans took when they crucified Him. That robe was portrayed as a sacred item in those movies. The reason is simple: the words and deeds of Jesus were spiritual. The plan enacted by Jesus at Golgotha was spiritual.

It was even a miracle that Jesus allowed Simon the Cyrene to touch the physical cross He was carrying to Golgotha. He kept constant watch on it. If for any reason somebody had attempted to take that cross away from Him, Jesus would have called down the twelve legions of the angelic army to prevent such an act. Jesus knew what He was doing and did not explain it to anyone.

Some of Jesus's utterances concerning the deep secrets surrounding all the heavenly things that He did confused the people. Whenever the inscrutable mystery of Golgotha is revealed, the physical cross vanishes and is replaced with imperceptible events that are all spiritual. It is for this reason that I have used Spiritual Cross to represent the spiritual events that related to the crucifixion and death of Jesus.

The metaphysical drama at Golgotha, portrayed in a ubiquitous way, were temporal manifestations of a deeply spiritual order. "We look not at things which are seen, but at things which are not seen: for the things which are seen are temporal; but the things which are not seen are eternal." (2 Corinthians 4:18) Jesus knew the infinite human benefits and the glory of behind His crucifixion. Jesus's tolerance of shame and humility, the unrelenting obedience to the will of His Father, and His own formidable will to present Himself at Golgotha were features of the deep spiritual order that must be comprehended in order to see the path to truth that was revealed and harness the fruits and the blessings of the cross. Without the Golgotha events, there would be no Christianity as we know it today. Golgotha events are like the sails of the merchant ship without which the ship would not sail. The ship of Christianity, as it sails from one port to another spreading the Gospel messages, is powered by the events at Golgotha. Without the Golgotha events, the spirits that Jesus silenced and defeated at Golgotha would have sunk Christianity. Without the Golgotha events to spearhead the Christian movement, the messages of the apostles would have been ineffective.

The physical cross reminds the Christians of the events at Golgotha, but the spiritual component of what happened at Golgotha is what helps us educate our souls in preparation for our final glory. We must use the spiritual force from the glorified Spirit of risen Jesus Christ that was made available to us through His crucifixion at Golgotha in order to find our way to the Father, our God. With this spiritual force, a gift from God to us through Jesus Christ, we can read His Gospel with understanding, collaborate with Him in the execution of our own colossal task in the Father's business, and follow its light to our greatest destiny. The activation of our inherited uneducated souls from God depends on this spiritual force.

Pinning a cross to the clothes of a priest or hanging it around his or her neck does not make that individual a priest. There is more to true priesthood than the cross in his or her possession. It is something spiritual that fills his or her heart with a sacred duty to love and serve God and all humanity. True priesthood must reflect the knowledge of all the divine laws and the willingness not only to obey them with perfect obedience but also to teach humanity the ways to God. The priest's life examples must epitomize his instruction to the congregation-an imitation of the life of Jesus Christ. A wedding band identifies an individual as married, but there is more to marriage than a wedding band. The wedding band can be lost or disfigured, but it does not mean the person is not married. The spiritual significance and purpose of marriage has nothing to do with the wedding band. The physical body is what one looks at to affirm that the individual is a human being, but a human being is more than the physical body. The physical cross in our possessions identifies us as members of the Christian group. Many religions have distinctive identifying symbols. The Jews have the Star of David (a six-pointed star), the Muslims have the Ay-yildiz (a star and the crescent moon), and the Buddhists the dharmachakra (a wheel with eight spokes). Today the Christian symbol of the cross is found in buildings where Christians worship and in their homes, and it is considered a part of their earthly possessions. The cross symbols are also widely used in various Christian arts and architecture.

For many generations the cross has been at the center of the Christian faith and piety. Many Christians associate the cross of Jesus of Nazareth with His crucifixion and death at Golgotha. Many Christians believe that Jesus had to die on the cross to please God; God would then forgive our sins and accept us as His children. Some believe that Jesus bore the wrath of God on the cross to pay the penalty for our sins and to purchase with His innocent blood a place for us in heaven. The universal expressions in Christian literatures—"redeemed by the blood of Jesus," "saved by the blood of Jesus," "washed clean by the blood of Jesus," "purified by the blood of Jesus," "Jesus died for me"—are some of the phrases Christians use to express their interpretation of the Golgotha events and their belief in Jesus Christ.

True understanding of what happened at Golgotha is attained by looking beyond the universal superfluous expressions used by the Christians to a deeper spirituality of those inscrutable spiritual events. If we are to perceive the real meaning of the cross of Jesus of Nazareth, we must understand what happened at Golgotha not just as events in history but also as a cascade of well-orchestrated spiritual events that were executed for divine purposes. The spiritual events at Golgotha have endless revelations.

The metaphoric expressions of Jesus of Nazareth and His request for the Father to glorify Him are better understood when viewed through the Father's business that Jesus was performing. All the expressive language used to portray the events of the cross —"atonement by the blood of Jesus," "redemption, salvation," "sacrifice"—can only be analyzed through expository documentation of why Jesus came to earth and allowed Himself to be condemned by His own people and crucified by the Romans. The conception of the cross and the vernacular used to express its significance must be applicable to all humans irrespective of their religious orientations—Muslims, Buddhist, Hindus, Confucians, Taoists, Shintoists, and so on. It must give guidance regarding who we are, why we are here, how we are to live, how we are to develop our spirituality, and how we relate to God.

Every religion has a spiritual door to the truth that its prophet revealed. For the Christians, the spiritual door as portrayed in this treatise is the cross. All believers must pass through a spiritual door to a class-room set up for instruction on how to develop and advance the spiritual status of our souls. Golgotha is the classroom for the Christians, where we can learn God's plan for humanity and use that knowledge to guide into the spiritual realm where God, Jesus Christ and His angels reside. There is absolutely nothing in that classroom that suggested that the spiritual events at Golgotha washed humanity clean of sin. There is no poster with inscription that what happened at Golgotha was atonement. The Spiritual Cross is the polar star that orients and gives guidance to all who seek eternal life. It brings to every heart a sacred duty in the quest for spiritual evolution and seeking the righteousness of God. It opens the door to the infinite instructions and to the cosmic, infinite purity that humans can stand on to reach the revelation of who we are, why we are here, how we are to live, and how to go about finding the true answer to God's plan for humans.

The metaphysical drama at Golgotha brings eternal life only if the transcendental events open our hearts to the Gospel message, illuminating the divine spirits in human souls that are willing to obey the will of God, the Father of Christ. However, eternal life cannot be achieved by putting the cross under your pillow, wearing it around your neck, or displaying it on a physical building. To follow Jesus of Nazareth, to love Him, to believe in Him, to be born again, to have faith in Him, to believe that the events at Golgotha were ordained spiritual events is to allow the iridescent rays of Christ's spiritual forces that were released at Golgotha to penetrate into your heart and activate the inherited spirit of God in you, catapulting it to the next spiritual abode: the Father-Christ-human bondage and experience.

The Gospel of Jesus of Nazareth is the everlasting echoes of His voice. "Everyone that is of the truth hears my voice." (John 18:37) It is the voice designed for every generation to hear. Jesus of Nazareth knew that His voice would be silenced if he failed to provide the essential tools with which all humans could listen to His voice. The tools were collected at Gethsemane, assembled at Golgotha, and made available to us by His glorified risen Spirit that manifested its power on the day of Pentecost.

Many people, including children, who lack knowledge of Jesus of Nazareth, remember that He was crucified. What was assembled at Golgotha was not a wooden object or a decorative item for cathedrals or religious institutions to display. It is not an inert object that drives away evil spirits or performs miracles. It is not an object you put in your home, schools, or workplaces to fight against secularization. It is not something you can decorate with precious stones. It is not something you pin on your clothes or hang around your neck like a surgeon hoping for guidance during surgical procedures.

Destroy the physical cross, burn it, or melt it down, yet you have not touched that living Spiritual Cross. The secret influence of the Spiritual Cross is the awakening of our consciousness to what was finished at Golgotha, enabling us to reveal and manifest our true spiritual nature and preparing us for the next phase of spiritual life. Those who are broadened by the power of the Jesus Christ-human spirit effulgence initiated at Golgotha have not only worshipped God in spirit but also in the actions of their own lives—actions that stood firmly on the side of truth, justice, righteousness, love that extended to the enemy, mercy, compassion and obedience of the divine laws in the Gospel. The Spiritual Cross is still playing the music of its master's voice. It played it in the past, but it is guaranteed to play in the future without metaphors and parables, proverbs, or parabolic and figurative expressions. At that time, the mysteries and the glory of the crucifixion of Jesus of Nazareth will be completely revealed, and the wisdom and plan of God, for all humans, will be made manifest.

Humanity has been busy accumulating wealth and weapons of mass destruction. Today the world is lamenting over and distrusts the global economic crisis. They are frightened that it may be protracted and eventually lead to a depression. The truth is that we are in a global, evolutionary, spiritual crisis and if we fail to do something, it may lead us to global refugee camps; make permanent, the eternal loss of the God-human indwelling and experience; and miss what God had planned for us. The time has come for all Christians to transcend to the world of Jesus of Nazareth and march again to Golgotha to open their hearts to the lyrics of the music of His voice and feel the heavenly rays of the spiritual powers of His glorified Spirit. We must start with the basic, divine instructions of repentance and "seek after the kingdom of God and his righteousness." (Matthew 6:33) Jesus's music brings to heart the messages of forgiveness, unselfishness, righteousness, charity, love for all humanity, and all that God wants us to do as revealed in His Gospel. The lyrics also remind us of Golgotha, where Jesus made available every device that helps us listen to the music.

If Christianity is to "feed my lamb,"(John 21:15), then Christianity must play the music of His voice, which originated from Golgotha in its spiritual form, loud enough that every creature in heaven, on earth, and in the sea will hear it. Christianity must play the music in its pure form, removing all human notes that were added in the past. The voice of Christ is the greatest spiritual melody ever recorded. The spiritual melody is the voice of the glorified Spirit of Jesus Christ radiating iridescent rays of eternal life, revealing the way that leads to the truth.

I am the way, the life, and the truth. —John 14:6

Many who have allowed the vibrations of the melody of His music, the divine arrow, known as the spiritual force of the spirit of Christ, to pierce their hearts, have found peace, serenity, purity, gentleness, love, compassion for humanity, and obedience to the will of God. They are eager to be participants in the Father's business. To them, we are all one humanity, under the same Father, who is in heaven. They are carrying the Spiritual Cross in their hearts, and unaware that they are doing so. They do not even have a physical cross in their homes or in any of their personal belongings. They opened their hearts to the music of His voice that illuminated their inherited spirit of God. They are constantly developing their spirituality, manifesting it and playing this music to all humanity. Likewise, there are many who display the physical cross in a grandiose manner and decorate it with precious jewels, but they have completely closed their hearts to the melody of the music of the Spiritual Cross. They have, directly or indirectly, subjected humanity to misery, destroyed the environment we live in and, introduced many human doctrines and dogmas in the doctrines of the Father's business. Many people are now confused.

Christianity is not ignorant of how to play the music the Master composed at Golgotha, but the care of the world, the vanity of human activities, and the deceitfulness of the rich have prevented many from doing so. The world needs to advance to a greatness of a higher stage of spiritual evolution in order to help it in coping with the multifaceted evolutionary changes and the spiritual crisis of today. The time has come, and now is when we must look again to the mandate from Jesus of Nazareth and open our hearts to the glorified spirit of Jesus Christ. To embrace that spiritual force in your heart is to believe in God and in Jesus and live under the will of God.

The Spirit of Jesus Christ does not see color or boundaries between nations. It sees no Chinese, no American, no African or Indian, no Italian, no black or whites, no Native Americans or Mexicans, no Catholics or Protestants, no Muslims or Christians, no liberals or conservatives as enemies. It sees all as one humanity. It stands on the divine platform observing the universe, of which the Earth is just one planet and the human species is one among many seen and unseen species. It seeks to establish its abode within the human soul in preparation for what God had planned. Eternal life and fellowship with God are accomplished by obeying God's divine laws, living under the influence of the spiritual force of Jesus Christ, practicing what was revealed at Golgotha, and being an active participant in the Father's business. It opens the heart, enabling it to explore the vast mysteries of the Gospel, which reveals the truth and the true meaning of the kingdom of God, why Jesus was sent to this world by His Father and why He died on the cross.

The great events at Golgotha led to the great spiritual movement we today call Christianity. Christianity is a spiritual process through which the human spirit is liberated from the shackles of evil forces and progresses to great moments in its spiritual evolution. It looks for both the good and the bad, planting in their hearts Christ's spiritual forces for the restoration and manifestation of the Father-Jesus Christ-human indwelling and experience. It also seeks, in essence, the celestial origin and destiny of the human divine imagery.

The spiritual events at Golgotha defined and reshaped the history of humanity and opened the path of authentic life. If Christianity and the teachings of the Gospel are to spread to all nations, then Christianity has no other option than to continue the great spiritual movement, planting without violence Christ's spiritual forces in the hearts of humans who are looking, longing, and silently working toward great moments of new experiences with the Father-Jesus Christ-human spirit association that would enable God to complete His business in creating humans in His image and likeness. This is in essence what Christianity is. If Christianity is to "drink of the cup" that Jesus drank from and be "baptized with" the baptism (Mark 10:39) its Master was baptized with, then Christianity has no other option than to reveal to humanity what was "finished" at Golgotha and why Jesus insisted He must go to Golgotha to be crucified and die. Christianity must instruct all its members to participate actively in all of Jesus's divine instructions and commandments, or, as John the Baptist addressed it, be baptized with fire, lest we make mockery of all that Jesus accomplished at Golgotha.

At Golgotha, the cloud that shrouded the mystery of how Jesus and His Father concealed the divine imagery and the Godlike attributes of Jesus and the divine authenticity of His words and works were removed by His death and His resurrection that followed. The victory of the Father and Jesus Christ over the gods and goddesses of the universe removed the smokescreen that enveloped and prevented the development of the Father-human experience and indwelling. The immortal human soul regained its freedom for unity with the Spirit of Christ for the execution of our own colossal task in the Father's business in preparation for our own glory. What looked like a completely disorganized set of events leading to Golgotha was actually a cohesive plan of well-organized spiritual events that revealed not only the nature and power of God and His plan for all living things on this planet Earth but also allowed humankind to look at the spiritual force of the glorified Jesus of Nazareth and His Gospel of the kingdom of God that He introduced to the world. It was also the divine method for Jesus to reveal the Father and return to Him for the fulfillment of the promise that guaranteed the gift of His risen Spirit, the Holy Spirit, that would guide us on the correct course of the Father's business for our own glorification and victory for God, our Father.

The story of the Spiritual Cross is now our own story. We do not have to go to Jerusalem to be scourged, buffeted, and crucified at Golgotha. As I was writing this section, a patient came to see my wife, who is a family physician. As they discussed the economic crisis facing the world and America in particular, she told my wife that although her pension had been whacked by the Wall Street meltdown and wasn't worth much, she took money out of it to give to poor families to buy Christmas presents for their children. Since that global economic meltdown, the person who has benefitted most is my wife's patient. The moment she took out money from her savings to serve the poor without thinking of her financial future, a bell rang in heaven and all the angels looked down to observe what happened. You can finish writing her story.

May the everlasting Lord, the Father of Jesus Christ, our God, give everyone a pure and humble heart so that we may obey His will on earth as it is done in heaven; a heart of love so that we may love one another and extend that love to our enemies and those that abuse us; a humble heart so that we may serve with compassion; a courageous heart for forgiveness and for the experience and sacrifice necessary for that service; an open heart that we may continue to strive, whenever possible, with all our might to be a multicultural, united family of nations of integrity, honesty, and incorruptible, God-dependent humanity that seeks nothing but the love of God and the progress and the stability of all His children.

The touchstone of the truth of God's plan for humanity and the glory of the cross were all made possible by the will of Jesus Christ to finish His own part of the Father's business and the will of God to glorify Him. The philology of the cross presented in this dissertation is only an attempt to make comprehensible the deeply spiritual events executed at Golgotha. The commissioned *magnum opus* that was executed by Jesus of Nazareth at Golgotha, the protean parables that touched on both heavenly and earthly activities, the metaphors and the comparable expressions of the kingdom of God, the symbolic and the parabolic expressions used by Him are mind boggling.

In our attempts to be participants in the Father's business, may all our endeavors be directed toward the increase in the level of our spiritual evolution and the goodwill of others. May the iridescent rays of divine light from the glorified Spirit of risen Jesus Christ illuminate your heart in the revelation of all the hidden secrets and the mysteries of Jesus Christ and His Father. May the glorified spirit of Christ give you the peace and the purity of mind in your earthly phase of spiritual evolution and guide you as you transcend to the next spiritual realm as a full-fledged spiritual being with the image and likeness of Christ.

18

THE GLORY OF THE CROSS

Let us set our eyes on Jesus, the author and finisher of our
faith; who, for the joy set before Him endured the cross, scorn-
ing its shame, and sat down at the right hand of God.
—HEBREW 12:2

THE VICTORY, THE ecstasy, and the glory of the cross is the revelation of God, the Father, to humanity, the glorification of the Spirit of Jesus Christ, and the erection of the spiritual temple of God that was built without the aid of hands by Jesus at Golgotha for the glory of human souls. It paved the way for the elimination of the obstacles to the Father's business and the continuation of that business with the promised gift of the Holy Spirit (the glorified Spirit of risen Jesus Christ). As a reward for what Jesus "finished" at Golgotha, His Father blessed Him with the greatest of all gifts that had never been bestowed on anyone, not in heaven or on earth. That gift enthroned Jesus as the exclusive divine authority for the perpetual dissemination of the Spirit of His Father for the spiritualization of human souls. The gift also guaranteed the continuation of the Father's business to the end of time, under the directive of Jesus Christ. Fifty days after the ascension of Jesus, the apostles received the gift of the glorified Spirit of risen Christ on the day of Pentecost. The fulfillment of that promised gift to humanity from His Father through the Spirit of the risen Christ was the greatest blessing of the cross for humanity. What was revealed in the form of human events at Golgotha was the presence of the divine will that directed all things toward one goal: eternal life. This divine goal is for all humanity. Those events guaranteed the continuation of God's design for humanity: the creation of perfected spiritual humans. It is for this purpose that Jesus allowed Himself to be crucified. What God planned and executed at Golgotha with precision through Jesus, paved the way for the revelation of Himself and Jesus Christ and for the perpetual spiritualization of with human souls with the glorified Spirit of risen Jesus Christ until all God's purpose are fulfilled. All these are in essence, the glory of the cross.

For centuries many have made many unsubstantiated assumptions about the cosmic events at Golgotha. What some people two thousand years ago in Palestine witnessed at Golgotha was what they saw with their eyes, touched with their hands, and heard with their ears; some of it they did not understand, but all were external manifestations of the cross. The spiritual force of the events that were accomplished is still dazzling the world today. Its radiant heavenly light is still spiritualizing and protecting human souls in preparation of what God planned for humanity.

True Christianity is alive, active, and vibrant today because of what was "finished" at Golgotha: the culmination of a plan that had been in place even before Abraham was. Abraham, Adam, and Eve were all benefactors of that plan that the Father designed. The conception of the Golgotha events was based on the saving and protecting of human souls as part of the creation process for humans to become spiritual beings. Some of the objectives of what was "finished" were summarized in the passage Jesus read from the book of the Prophet Esaias on a Sabbath day in a synagogue at Nazareth: "The Spirit of the Lord is upon me, because he had anointed me to preach the gospel to the poor; he had sent me to heal the brokenhearted, to preach deliverance to the captives and restoring sight to the blind, to set to liberty them that are bruised, to preach the acceptable year of the Lord." (Luke 4:18–19) The spiritual event at Golgotha indeed set at liberty our captive souls.

The comprehension of what was finished at Golgotha would help us know who we are, the reason why we are here, and where we go from here. The planet Earth is a large space without borders for all humanity. The national boundaries are artificial boundaries created by humans. We control nothing here. How can one control what he or she did not create? We have allowed most of our actions to be controlled by the Devil and his demons. The Devil became our master.

The gates of the prison are now open, and nobody can close them. It is you who must get out of that prison and seek a new life-a new spiritual frontiers in the spiritual world outside the planet Earth-that is not centered on the accumulation of earthly wealth but instead is a preparation of your soul for life with God, our Father. It is you who must vow never to go back to the prison. It is you who must use the spiritual weaponry given to you to develop your empowered spirit and silence the Devil. It is a fact that whenever we are given the chance to select the weaponry for our progress, we select the ones that would help us to enslave the disadvantaged, kidnap the innocent, embezzle public funds, put on the hypocritical crown of power and glory, and preach the Gospel without living by its percepts and divine instructions. At Golgotha, the deployment of the weaponry humans can use on earth against "the rulers of darkness of this world, and against spiritual wickedness in high places" was completed. At Golgotha, Jesus wielded forgiveness, love for mankind, and obedience to the will of His Father as weapons for the accomplishment of all the works His Father gave Him to do. We are pilgrims on this planet. It is you who must use those weapons to help you navigate your way to the Kingdom of God prepared for you at the beginning of the world.

Golgotha is the source of the perpetual light that shines in its purity upon that divine design. It was the place that carried the divine portraits of infinite love God and Jesus Christ have for humanity. Golgotha was the place that spoke of forgiveness, of sacrifice, of truth, of righteousness, and of mercy. It was the place of the infinite power that radiates forever into the human immortal spirit, awakening it from its slumbering state and setting it on fire to manifest the Father-human spirit indwelling and experience. Nobody knew, not even Peter, that at that time humanity would be celebrating and immortalizing those events as Good Friday and not as Bad Friday, but Jesus knew. He knew that those events would illuminate His Gospel that extensively revealed His Father and His message of the kingdom of God.

The jubilant outcry from Jesus, "It is finished," marked the moment in history when the glory of God was made manifest in Jesus. It was that moment in history when we as humans were guaranteed that we too will receive the glory of God through Jesus. It marked a new epoch in the human spiritual evolution when the tools for that evolutionary creative process of all human to new spiritual creatures were made permanently available and free to all humans. The weaponry deployed is to be used for the enthronement of the true God in human hearts and for the obedience of His will. On that day, the construction of the superhighway that leads to the Father was completed.

Jesus said, "Follow me." That was a humble instruction to follow Him, observe and learn how to be home with God, our Father. Only through the gate of Golgotha can one enter into the spiritual realm of Jesus and bask in the illumination of His divine glory and power. Although we may have been powerless, now you are under He who is powerful. Although we are incapable of love and forgiveness, we are loved and forgiven. The gate of Golgotha is the portal to His upper chamber, which is now open to all humanity and not just to the twelve holy men. All other gates are closed. Golgotha is the lens through which the Gospel of Jesus can be analyzed for comprehension of God's holy purposes. The "cup" Jesus drank from at Golgotha was for God's holy purposes, for the glorification of the Son of man, and for permanent glory for humanity. To study the Gospel of Jesus without understanding the spiritual events of Golgotha is to sail an uncharted sea, and to concentrate only on the external manifestations of Golgotha events is not to go to sea at all. Can one plan a fishing trip and leave home without the fishing rods and baits? Without Golgotha events, there would be no Christianity as we know it today. If Christianity is to "cast into the deep for a draw" then Christianity must assemble all the weaponry needed for that fishing.

The Jewish laws and traditions must not be allowed to interfere with the doctrines of the Father's business. Unsubstantiated utterances on the Golgotha event, dogmas, human doctrines, the proceedings of any council outside what is in the Gospel, must not be allowed to replace the truth of what was accomplished at Golgotha. Perhaps because of our spiritual blindness, Christianity must take a reverse quantum leap back to Golgotha as to get the real net to cast into the deep. For three years before the crucifixion, Jesus had tried in vain (except for the apostles and a few of His disciples) to bring humankind and God together. He had revealed the true images of God to an unbelieving audience. This generation stands at platform of a great spiritual evolution. Humanity cannot and must not fail to grasp the opportunity and act upon it. The consequences of failing to do so are unimaginable.

The crucifixion of Jesus of Nazareth left an everlasting memory of Him in our hearts. It made a divine imprint in our consciousness, awaking our slumbering human souls to seek the spirit of truth and justice. Those that have embraced that spirit of the truth are not waiting for the second coming of Jesus. They are intimately living in His presence. Paul was a living testimony to this infinite experience. The victory and glory of the crucifixion are the depth and the power of its spiritual forces on our memory of our knowledge of God and of He who came to set fire on earth: "I came to set fire on earth. What would I if it is already kindled?" (Luke 12:49)

The above metaphoric expression described why Jesus came to this world. The earth is the human soul. The fire is the Spirit of God through Jesus Christ. Jesus came to open and ignite our souls with the true spirit of God. His work would have been worthless if human souls were already spiritualized and had developed the God-human indwelling and experience. The weaponry for such accomplishment was carefully chosen: "But I have a baptism to be baptized with; and how am I straightened till it be accomplished!" (Luke 12:50) That baptism was the crucifixion of Jesus at Golgotha.

The comprehension of what was finished at Golgotha is the key to the revelation of the true meaning of the cross and its glory. Much misery has come to the world because of the incomprehensibility of what was "finished." Humanity has chosen war instead of dialog as a solution for conflicts, hatred instead of love for their enemies, division instead of tolerance, monopoly instead of sharing, propagation of tools for ignorance instead of promotion of the principles of education and more education, extreme fraud and greed instead of mercy and consideration for others, take all you can and give nothing back instead of give to them all you can, pollution of the earth's environment instead of protection and green policy for the earth.

The time has come when the glory of what was "finished" in Golgotha must manifest in our hearts and be portrayed in all our human activities. Never before in any age has the world been in such a bad shape as evidenced by nuclear proliferation and production of third-generation nuclear weapons, genocide, selfishness, moral and spiritual degradation, proliferation of evil activities, extreme fraud and greed, embezzlement, terrorism and war, monetary-driven theological doctrine proclamations, direct and indirect destructive activities, misconstrued nationalism, tribalism and pollution of the planet Earth's environment. Jesus characterized the generation of His time as an evil and wicked generation. Today He would say the same of our generation.

Christianity has put so much emphasis on the agony and sufferings of Jesus of Nazareth that it has blanketed, in essence, the iridescent rays from the cross that were meant to shine into the hearts of humanity. The portraits of the suffering of Jesus of Nazareth, has for centuries masked and delayed the revelation and the spiritual manifestations and the glory of the cross. As the mystery of Golgotha unfolded, and it is still unfolding, elements of its cosmic phenomenon, the revelation of the invisible God, the power of the glorified spirit of Christ, and the gift of the

Holy Spirit for the continuation of the evolutionary transformation of our souls for the riches and glory of God's design for all humanity all became illuminated. This is the story of the cross.

The conception that the Golgotha experience wiped away all sins of mankind is a gross injustice to what was "finished" and a hindrance to the comprehension of the blessings and the glory of the cross. One of the current theologies of the cross promised to elevate the individual to a divine status by guaranteeing authentic, divine eternal life by merely believing that the Golgotha event was for the atonement of our sins. As many still believe that all humans (including all newborns) are born in sin, it was easy for the atonement theory to find its abode in human hearts. These misconceptions of the cross are like weeds in the garden, choking the good seeds planted by the landlord. To comprehend the mysteries of Golgotha and benefit from its blessings, we must strip from our consciousness these misconceptions and sinister designs handed down to us through centuries.

"A city set on a hill cannot be hid." (Matthew 5:14) Likewise, Golgotha is like a city set upon a hilltop. We celebrate the glory of its events every year as Good Friday with hymns, supplications, and adoration of He who built that castle on the hilltop. As the newborn searches for the mother's milk to drink for survival, likewise Christians and whoever wants to do the will of God for eternal life must go to the city set upon the hilltop to search and drink the milk of everlasting life for survival. Golgotha is the touchstone by which God through Jesus of Nazareth guaranteed the perpetual revelation of the truth for the past, present, and future generations. It bore the stamp of the Royal King upon a royal edict. There one finds the angelic spectacles to wear and the divine platform to stand on as to be able to find the truth for its own glory and for your glory. This is the glory of Golgotha!

Many people seeking the spiritual truth of what was "finished" at Golgotha surround themselves with foolish things and the cares of the world, which causes them to fail at making progress. They become like the seeds that fell on the rock or on the wayside in Jesus's parable of the sower. (Matthew 13: 31–32) This principle of hedonism is a hindrance to the ecumenical truth that was revealed at Golgotha. The inability to comprehend what was "finished" at Golgotha led many to think that Jesus failed in His aspiration to establish a kingdom of God on earth. As the Jews are still waiting for their Messiah to come and restore the glory of Israel, likewise the Christians are waiting for Jesus to come again and establish here on earth the kingdom of God. Jesus said that "My kingdom is not of this world." Establishment of another kingdom on this planet is not in the doctrine of the Father's business.

The failure to comprehend the glory and the divine instructions of the cross is portrayed, as you are my witnesses of our time, by the Israeli-Palestinian conflict, the Muslim-Christian relationship, the Iraqi and Afghanistan wars, the dictatorship in many countries (especially the developing nations), the opium-cocaine war, the tribal wars, the global piracy, the economic raiders of Africa and other developing nations and many other *Ali Baba and the Forty Thieves*-type activities. The final phase of the work that was "finished" was accomplished in Palestine. Yet today Palestine is a land where people are killed every day. It is a portrayal of ignorance of what was "finished" at Golgotha. The wickedness of man, the evils in human hearts, and the abusive acts inflicted on defenseless individuals and others were clearly demonstrated and exemplified by what the Jewish mob and the Romans inflicted on Jesus of Nazareth.

The crucifixion of Jesus of Nazareth is the authentic and divine seal and the foundation stone of His Gospel. It guaranteed the everlasting availability of that spiritual force for us to use. Golgotha was the place where Jesus illuminated the true Father-Son bondage and experience. St. Paul, who ventured into the spiritual realm of Golgotha, spoke of "the riches of the glory of this mystery." (Colossians 1:27) The experience of the outcome of what was finished at Golgotha is like the spirit of God that moves on the earth, bringing with it love, peace, justice, righteousness, tolerance, truth, forgiveness, mercy, comfort, and liberation for humanity, glory for the Son of man, and victory for God. It brought the light that illuminated the darkness of our time. It was a testimony for the existence and the imagery of God. Its bearing is heavenward, to the gate of the Father's house. What was accomplished at Golgotha is the life force of Jesus's Gospel that prepares the human spirit for restoration to the new spiritual body in preparation for the Father-human spirit bondage and experience. What was "finished" was the fulfillment of the dreams and the visions of the prophets that resulted in the transformation of the spiritual events of Golgotha to a global citadel of the infinite love of the Father and Jesus Christ that was bestowed on humanity. The depth and the power of what was "finished" at Golgotha are unimaginable. It carries with it the images of the Spirit of God and the Spirit of Jesus Christ that touched the human hearts with a flame that cannot be quenched, hence the many jubilant outbursts blessing the cross that are recorded in many Christian literatures.

What was "finished" also provided the human spirit with weaponry against the destructive illusions of worldly conquest, hypocrisy, human or national superiority, and what has been described as the destructive evil forces of this world. We fight for earthly survival and security, to be alive, to have a home on earth. However, in reality nobody survives. No, we all die because the earth is not our home. We are passing through here on earth as a phase in our creation as planned by God. We must all die in order to advance to the next phase in our evolution for the glory that awaits all humanity. We must use the spiritual weaponry that was assembled at Golgotha to awaken our soul, educate it, and set it free to seek the kingdom of God and His righteousness.

The twelve precious jewels of His kingdom (the twelve ordained apostles) who knew what was "finished" at Golgotha realized that the call to the apostolic office brought with it the zeal to spread the Gospel with unquestionable obedience to His will, presentation of themselves as living models in words and deeds, mortification of their self-will, love for their Master and His Father, reliance on their Master and on His Father for their security, zeal for the kingdom of God, and the practice of virtue, faith, hope, charity, love, mercy, and righteousness. The gift of what was "finished" at Golgotha enabled the apostles to attend the highest spiritual evolution possible on earth as evidenced by the protean miracles performed by them and by their unbreakable Father-Son-apostles bondage and experience that resulted in the holy plea from their

Master to the Father: "Father, I will that they also, whom thou, hast given me, be with me where I am; that they may behold my Glory, which thou has given me; for thou loved me before the fountain of the world." (John 17:24)

That the love wherewith thou hast loved me may be in them and me in them. —John 17:26

The history of humanity is essentially the history of God and the creation of humans in His image and likeness. For the Christians, the path to be benefactors of that destiny is through Jesus of Nazareth. For the Muslims, it is through Prophet Mohammed. For the Buddhist it is through Siddhartha Gautama. Every human group has a spiritual leader who made possible the completion of God's design for humanity.

Darkness is the absence of light. —Albert Einstein

We must all follow the light of what was finished at Golgotha to penetrate the darkness of our time. Humanity is sick at its heart. The cause of this sickness is spiritual poverty of the human souls. We are holding ourselves back from what rightly belongs to us and was given to us unconditionally by God. We live in this world with our rudimentary, unpowered human souls and have refused to make changes for the education and advancement of our souls. We have refused to activate our souls and harness their power with the unconditional gift of the Spirit of God that was given to us freely through Jesus Christ. If today the seven billion people of the world, in whatever religious category one may belong, are all like the twelve ordained apostles of Jesus Christ, the road that leads to heaven would be wide. God would have to construct more roads that lead to heaven. The celebration in heaven that would ensue would be fantastic. If the apostles can do it, why can't we do it? This is what Jesus would like us to do. This is what His Father would like us to do. The road to the Father's house is never and will never be broken down. The potholes on this road are the worldwide Ponzi schemes that have permeated all institutions and professional establishments, fraud, extreme greed, deep-rooted corruption, and moral depravity, all of which are now accepted ways of living for many people. This treatise is an introductory guide for all who, like the prodigal son, wish to repent and embrace what God had planned for humanity.

The methodology for complete human spiritual evolution in this, our earthly phase of our creation, was revealed and the spiritual tools for its accomplishment were given to humanity. God's task for the provision of the spiritual tools to humanity that would enable Him to complete His plan for humanity by the gift of His Spirit through Jesus Christ ended at Golgotha. Jesus's task for the same purposes by the gift of His Spirit from the Father and His task that silenced the gods and goddess of many nations and enthrone His Father as the Lord of all Spirits ended. Jesus's task for the perpetual continuation of the Father's business through the gift of His Spirit that the Father will send as the Holy Ghost also ended. Our colossal task had just begun. It is you who must open the manual of the spiritual weaponry and practice with the weapons for victory that is not the defeat of "the enemy" but for the glory that awaits all humanity. It is you who must open that book of truth and justice and look at it in all its spiritual forms. It is you who must worship God in truth and in spirit. You must obey God's divine commandments and the laws in that book. That book is the Gospel of Jesus Christ. It is you who must act as a living model in words and deeds and teach humanity how to use the spiritual weaponry. It is you, bruised, brokenhearted, but freed from captivity, who must vow never to go back to that prison. It is you who must use the spirit of the Father, a gift to us through Christ, to silence your acquired evil spirit from the Devil.

You cannot accomplish all the colossal tasks by yourself because there are many obstacles that would discourage you. Jesus metaphorically represented these obstacles in His Gospel as tares in the field where the landlord planted the good seeds. Today these obstacles present themselves as human greed, injustice, savagery, racism, and many evil deeds humans heap on one another. It is you who must partner with the appointed Executioner of the Father's business to help in the accomplishment of your task for your glory. It is you who must take frequent spiritual and physical pilgrimages to the holy Golgotha to give glory to the Father and His son Jesus Christ. It is you who must empower and equip your soul for your colossal task. Then you would presume that you are doing your duty that your task would end soon, but I would say to you that your task had just begun on earth and would continue in the next spiritual realm, "Let Thy will be done on earth as in heaven." — Matthew 6:10

But God forbid that I should glory, save in the cross of our Lord Jesus Christ, by whom the world is crucified unto me, and I unto the world. —Galatians 6:14

Rumination

The key to the whole mystery of the Father's business and why Jesus came to earth to execute it is a fuller understanding of some of His utterances that referred to His crucifixion and death. The timed spiritual events assured that today we speak of the glory of the cross, eternal life by Jesus, the power of Jesus Christ, the gift of the Holy Ghost, and the power and glory of God, His Father. The planned return of Jesus to the Father led to His glorification. The will of Jesus and that of His Father was done. The divine plan of God for eternal life and for the continuation of what God had designed for humanity was executed with precision. Many of the spiritual events at Golgotha were examples of His Father's business that showed Jesus's divine instructions for our glory are practical and can be done. Some of the spiritual tools given to us for eternal life by Jesus preceded His death. What looked like a humiliating, catastrophic event at Golgotha was indeed a well-organized hermeneutical spiritual event that brought joy to Jesus, victory for His Father, and blessings to humanity. It silenced many gods and goddess and enthroned the Father as the universal supreme God.

The part God played at Golgotha is part of the inscrutable mysteries of Golgotha and the glory of the cross. As I searched the Gospel of Jesus and meditated on the events at Golgotha, it become obvious to me that the Golgotha events were not only how Jesus revealed His true nature and the power of the Father He presented to humanity but also the way to return home to His glory. Those events became the perpetual light, shining on the divine laws and the spiritual tools in the Gospel that the prodigal sons must use as guide to return to the Father. At Golgotha, Jesus gave a practical demonstration on how to obey those divine laws. This is one of the glorious achievements of the cross. The glory and the blessing of the cross is the continuation of the gift of the Holy Spirit bestowed on us by His Father through the risen Christ, to perpetually shine in our hearts and bring to our memory all the words and deeds of Jesus. One must look behind the doors of the cross to hear the voice of Jesus Christ and see the iridescent light of spirituality from heaven. That light that was not from the moon or sun blinded Paul on his way to Damascus. The voice behind the cross also spoke to Him. Paul became the agent of that Spirit. Enjoy the blessings and the glory of the cross.

19

CHRISTOLOGY OF THE CROSS

All things are delivered unto me of my Father. And no man knows
the Son but the Father, neither knows any man of the Father
save the Son and to whomsoever the Son would reveal Him.
—MATTHEW 11:27

THE TRUE KNOWLEDGE of who Jesus of Nazareth is rests in the domain of His Father. It is the prerogative of the Father to reveal Jesus as the "Christ" to whomever He wishes. The Father did that to the apostle Peter.

"You are the Christ, the Son of the living God," Simon Peter said to Jesus. Jesus answered, "Blessed art thou Simon BarJona for flesh and blood had not revealed it unto you, but my Father who is in heaven." (Matthew 16:17)

We don't know how God revealed it to Peter before the event at Golgotha. Our interest here is to find out what being the "Christ" means to Jesus of Nazareth and to us in this 21st century. If it has something to do with the cross, then we must go to Golgotha and look again at the spiritual events. The chief priests had mocked Him with the scribes and elders and said, "If he be the King of Israel, let him now come down from the cross and we will believe Him." But Jesus did not come down from the cross.

Two of my patients believed the living Christ accompanied them to the hospital on the day of their surgery. "Why didn't you bring a family member?" I asked the first patient.

"I did," she replied.

"Who?" I inquired, seeing no one at her side.

"Jesus Christ."

Similarly, a second patient insisted that somebody came with her on the day of her surgery, although she appeared to be alone. When asked who accompanied her, she also replied, "Jesus Christ."

Christology is the study of the meaning of Christ. The Christians believe that Jesus of Nazareth is the Christ and their Christological philology centers on His words and deeds in Palestine and on His perceived presence since He ascended to heaven. My two patients and many others believe in the living Jesus Christ who guides all their activities. They see in Jesus a Christ who is a companion whom they trust. Many of my patients also found in Jesus a Christ who heals them. For the Christians, the word "Christ" is the symbol of infinite power that binds all God-human spiritual experiences. It expresses itself in terminologies such as faith in Christ, hope in Christ, the Messiah, Son of God, Son of the Blessed, a new Creature in Christ, obedience and suffering of Christ's mercies, wisdom of Christ, humilities and weakness of Christ, love and peace of Christ, the glory and triumph of Christ, salvation in Christ, redemption and reconciliation in Christ, forgiveness/justification in Christ, the blessings and the promises of Christ, and so forth and so on.

It speaks of absolute trust in this Christ and manifests itself in truth, love, righteousness, mercy, forgiveness, compassion, charity, and the revelation of God's plan. It transcends and rides above all the Mosaic laws and commandments. It prides itself in the divine "Father-Son bondage and experience, as expressed by Jesus: "my Father and I are one." It portrays itself as a symbol of ultimate authority and power both on earth and in heaven. That power transcends far beyond human experience as expressed metaphorically by Jesus of Nazareth Himself: "I am the Way, the Truth and the Life"; "I am the Good Shepherd"; "I am the door of the sheep"; "I am the light of the world"; "I am the Bread of Life"; "I am the true vine"; "I am the Resurrection and the Life"

The glory and symbolism of the cross would have no spiritual significance if we fail to comprehend the true meaning of the "Christ" as portrayed by what Jesus of Nazareth accomplished at Golgotha. By His works, many symbolic and metaphoric expressions, and the spiritual events at Golgotha, Jesus revealed the true meaning of the word Christ. This revelation was made possible by the events that Jesus "finished" at Golgotha. Golgotha is the spindle on which Christianity spins. Take the spindle out, and then there will be no Christianity, no Christian Redeemer, and no Jesus as the Christ or Son of God. Without Golgotha, the star of Jesus of Nazareth would reside among those of the other prophets who came before and after Him. The spiritual events at Golgotha brought with them the universal divine presence of Jesus as the Christ in many hearts. It formed the touchstone on which one can look at the "Christ" aspect in Jesus of Nazareth.

The Christology of the cross that I have introduced looks at the Father's business, the spiritual events at Golgotha, Jesus's inward aim, His intention, and His driving force that made Him insist He must go to Jerusalem to drink from the "cup" His Father gave Him. Without the accomplishment of the predetermined events that were "finished" at Golgotha, the realization of all the specified goals in the Father's business would not have been possible.

Today more than one billion people live with less than $1 a day, no, I would say, a dime a day. Millions of children and the elderly die every day of preventable diseases: malnutrition, infectious diseases (HIV, malaria), contaminated drinking water, and exposure to adverse conditions of weather. Without your honest desire to help, of what use is it to preach to them of the title "Christ" means to Jesus, the righteousness of Christ, the doctrine of the Trinity, the future work of Christ, the Messianic offices of Christ, the Old Testament predictions of Christ, Immanuel the Christ, the glory of Christ, the atonement of Christ, the Salvation and redemption brought by Christ, and so on and so forth? Of what good would the terminology "Christ" be if it is relegated to the divine and not connected to all human activities?

Perhaps it is by divine selection or random event that a child is born into a rich or poor family. The child has no control of those phenomena. Likewise, many that are born into various religious groups tend to belong to the same religious faith as their parents. The newborn child has no control over his or her nationality or ethnicity. Jesus had given this instruction: "suffer not the little children (irrespective of their cultures, religion, nationality or ethnicity inside all religious or social status) to come to me, for such is the kingdom of God." (Matthew 19:14)

Humanity is under tremendous pressure by both visible and invisible forces. More than ninety percent of the evils perpetuated on earth are by humans. The mighty nations and major religious groups initiated many of the major wars. The "Christ" of the cross and the Father He presented have no enemies and do not belong to any religious group. Father "makes the sun to shine on the evil and on the good; and the rain to fall on the just and the unjust." (Matthew 5:45)

Any new Christological philology (whether it relates to the Messiah whom the majority of the Jews are still expecting, or Jesus of Nazareth, the Christian Christ and Messiah, whom the Christians anticipate will return, or any other divine being that may surface in the future) must reveal the true God and His plan for humanity. It must provide the answer to the perplexing questions of who we are and why we are here on this planet. It must reveal in unequivocal terms our endless relationship with the infinite God. It must give guidance to human life and activities, both in health and sickness. It must find the common ground for the unity of all humans irrespective of their cultures, nationality, or religion. It must manifest itself in fellowship of humankind and the universal love that extends to the enemy. It must direct humanity on how to serve God, the Father of Christ. The new Christological philology must direct us on how to access our inherited spirituality, how to tap into our spiritual ability, how to develop it from this rudimentary stage, and how to advance and manifest it, propelling all our spiritual emancipations heavenward.

The "Christ" as revealed by Jesus of Nazareth is not just for the Christians. The Christ is for "whosoever" will do the will of the Father. The time has come when any new Christological philology must transcend beyond super nationalism or super individualism or being confined to one religion. The comprehension of the spiritual illumination of the cross and the vision of Jesus's divinity are made possible by gazing upon the contents of the Father's business and the specter of Jesus's divine mission.

What is the meaning of Christ? To understand the meaning of Christ one must first understand where and how those terminologies originated. There is no one record of the word "Christ" in the Old Testament literature. The terminologies must have been introduced when the Babylonians invaded Palestine before the birth of Jesus. Since the Romans landed, the people of Israel looked forward to the Deliverer, a Savior to save the people from the Romans and establish an everlasting kingdom for the Jews, the "chosen" people of God. Simon Peter was not the first one to use the term Christ to address Jesus. When Jesus started His mission, both terminologies were in common use as evidenced by the following reference: "as the people were in expectation and all men mused in their hearts of John, whether he was the Christ or not." (Luke 3:15) The early Christians were not the first to use the word "Messiah" to address Jesus, as shown by what Andrew said to his brother Simon Peter, immediately after the baptism of Jesus: "We have found the Messiah, which is, being interpreted, the Christ." (John 1:41) Perhaps, the Christians, adopted what Andrew said to his brother, Simon Peter that Messiah when interpreted is the same as Christ. The Christians now proclaim Jesus Christ as their Messiah. Jesus did not reveal to anyone that He was the Messiah.

The question of being the Christ and the Son of God persisted throughout His mission, popping up like obstacles in the *Super Mario Brothers* game. It followed Him to Golgotha, where the true meaning of this transcendent cosmic symbol "Christ" was spiritually revealed. The spiritual experiences at Golgotha formed an everlasting mirror reflecting the images of the revealed Christ. For this reason, I have used the term "Christology of the Cross" in the philology discussion of the word Christ.

The meaning of Christ changes with time, space, and culture. To the Jews, the birth of Jesus was portrayed by the angel as the arrival of the Christ: "behold. I bring you good tidings of great joy, which shall be to all people. For unto you are born this day in the city of David, a Saviour which is Christ the Lord." (Luke 2:10–11) In addition, to "all who look for redemption in Jerusalem" this Savior would be "A light to lighten the Gentiles and the glory of the people Israel." (Luke 2:31) For the Jews, Christ is the promised Deliverer; the Savior with divine power, the promised Messiah will fight for them, defend them, restore the lost glory of Israel, and establish a spiritual kingdom for them on earth. For the Christians, redemption depends on the Christ, the Messiah with divine power who was crucified on the cross, died, and rose from the dead on the third day. Like the Jews, the Christians believe that this Christ will come again to establish a spiritual kingdom for them on earth.

The origin of the Christian perception of Jesus as the Christ started at Caesar Philippi when Simon Peter said to Jesus, "Thou art the Christ." However, how did Jesus see Himself as the perceived Christ of His time? Did Jesus think at that time that He was the Christ, the expected Messiah, or did He think that He was a divine authority bigger than the human conception of Christ or the Messiah? The truth on this matter is simply that we do not know. The truth is that Jesus of Nazareth revealed very little about Himself. It is for this reason that I have concentrated my efforts on the Christology of He who came to this world, was condemned to death by His own people, allowed the Romans to crucify Him, and died on the cross.

Hebraic Christology (*Christology of the heavenly sign*)

The Hebraic Christology demanded a sign from heaven for them to believe that Jesus of Nazareth was the Christ, the Son of God. "Master, we would like a sign from you," demanded the scribes and the Pharisees. The New Testament record is riddled with records where the Jews demanded a miraculous heavenly sign from Jesus to prove that He was the Christ, the Son of God. The Hebraic Christology of the heavenly sign looked at the possibility of the Christ in Jesus of Nazareth. In a retrospective analysis, it looked at the various spiritual phases represented by the laws and the prophets. It looked at the protean Messianic prophecies from the time of Abraham, Moses, and the prophets and concluded that Jesus of Nazareth was not the Christ or the Messiah. It is not possible to discuss all the Christological philology in literature, but as the word Christ originated from the Jews, it is reasonable to consider the Hebraic Christology as the prologue of all Christology.

The Hebraic Christology looked forward to the time when God revealed to them by Moses, would fulfill His promise by sending down the "Son of man," the "Christ" also called the Messiah, who would liberate them from their enemies, establish the kingdom of God on earth, and restore the glory to Israel. It projected an apocalyptic Kingdom, as revealed by their Prophets where the Son of man is the King and the Lord. The Hebraic Christology was also the first to introduce to the world the concept of a divine being: the "Son of man." In many instances in the Gospel literature, Jesus used the terminology to refer to Himself, touching in essence the vision of the prophet Daniel: "You'll see the Son of man sitting in His glory at the right hand of God." However, without the sign from heaven, many of the Jews did not believe Jesus of Nazareth was the "Son of man" (portrayed and referred to) in the book of Daniel. However, the title "Son of man" used by Jesus has no connection to the prophetic 'Son of man' revealed in the Jewish literature by Daniel and others.

The great Hebraic Christological expectation was summarized in the conversation of two men with the resurrected Jesus on their way to Damascus. They did not know that the stranger in their midst was the resurrected Jesus and said, "But we trusted that it had been he which should have redeemed Israel." (Luke 24:21) However, Jesus did not redeem or liberate the Jews from the Romans. He did not restore the glory to Israel. He did not gather the elect together in the holy city Jerusalem to liberate them from their enemies and restore the kingdom to Israel. Today Israel is still fighting with their enemies. Many still hope that one day the holy one, called Christ, the Messiah, will come.

The Jewish expectation of "Christ" was given transcendent and apocalyptic dimensions at the time of Jesus of Nazareth. The expected Christ was viewed as not only a Liberator and a Redeemer but has many other protean missions for the nation of Israel. The Hebraic Christology philology centered on when God would fulfill His plan to bring the promised seed of Abraham, 'the Jewish Christ' to the nation of Israel. The Christ would not only redeem Israel but also move the entire nation to the everlasting kingdom of God in the new heaven and the new earth as was prophesied in the book of Isaiah. (Isaiah 65:17–19, 21–25)

Any benefit of this plan of God for other nations must be through the nation of Israel and its people, who consider themselves to be the chosen people of God. The Hebraic Christology was super nationalistic. The God of Israel is the Architect of their exclusive grand plan, and had promised He would send a Deliverer to save them. It portrayed this God as a merciful, loving God but also a punitive and vengeful God who favors Israel but punished their enemies. It portrays God as exhibiting favoritism: a God who gave to Israel the Promised Land and encouraged them to drive away the natives of that land. The planet Earth is for all humankind and for God's holy purpose. If God told you to come and live in my house, it does not mean that I must be driven away from my house. But God's intention is that we should live together in peace and in unity. When the Palestinians and the Jews realize this and love one another, there will be lasting peace in Palestine!

The Hebraic Christology looked at Gethsemane as a place where Jesus of Nazareth was sweating profusely, afraid and unwilling to complete His mission. It portrayed the act of Judas Iscariot as not only treason but a betrayal of Jesus of Nazareth, telling the whole world that Jesus of Nazareth was not the Christ. They knew that nobody can betray Christ. Hebraic Christology reiterated the fact that Jesus did not give to the Jews any heavenly sign to prove that He was the Christ and that the resurrection was not a sign from heaven that proved Jesus was the Christ. It portrayed the event at Golgotha as a disgrace and the resurrection of

Jesus was not a true event, stating that His disciples stole the body. To the Jews, Jesus of Nazareth failed to bring glory and salvation to Israel. Many of the Jews are still waiting for their Christ, the Messiah, who will not only redeem Israel but restore its glory even in this troubled world.

Many of the Jews rejected Jesus of Nazareth because He did not fulfill the Messianic expectations and His doctrines did not conform to the doctrines of Moses, which are the foundation of the Jewish faith. The Jewish Christology philology looked at the period when the expected Messiah would restore Jerusalem as the capital of the new earthly kingdom. The expected new Christ would establish the best-equipped army in the world so that no nation would do to them again what the Germans and Romans did to the Jews in the past. The result of such an endeavor, as we see it, would be countless wars even up to now. It has led to many misconceptions that have plagued humanity: the idea of a superior race, super nations, privileged individualism, divine favoritism, irrationalism, injustice, and hypocrisy.

Any true Christological philology must elucidate a true conception of God, human life, and our current world. It must reveal what God's love is: giving not receiving; service to others and to God; the care of the common man; love for the poor, the elderly, and the enemy; the right to allow poor nations to use their natural resources for development; justice and mercy for the defected; forgiveness of all debts of poor nations; support for poor nations; elimination of hunger and preventable diseases all over the world; empathy for our enemies; protection of the earth and environment; development of our spirituality; doing His will on earth as it is done in heaven; and obedience of His holy commands. Any Christological philology must reveal tools for the accomplishment of all of the above.

The Hebraic Christology in its quest for 'a sign from heaven' failed to keep the holy commandments and the will of God, the Father of Jesus Christ. Any new Christological philology must revisit those Holy Commandments and the will of the Father revealed to mankind by Christ. The ultimate purpose of any Christological study is to illuminate our understanding and experience of our spiritual evolution. If Christianity is to help humanity in this spiritual evolution, then Christianity must reveal to the world the true meaning of 'Christ'. It must present to the world the real Christ, not the Jewish 'Christ' for the real 'Christ' is not a Jew. Christ is a universal divine Being of no nationality, who directs humans to God and provided us with the weaponry for Father- human bondage and experience.

The Doctrinal Christology: the Christology of Jesus's Deity

The doctrinal Christology viewed Jesus of Nazareth not only as the Christ, the only begotten Son of God, but also as God. It related the crucifixion of Jesus of Nazareth not only as an atonement for our sins but also as an event that brought redemption, forgiveness of sins, and salvation. By the blood of Jesus of Nazareth that was shed on the cross, all who believe that he is the Son of God and the Christ are saved and will also inherit the kingdom of God that Jesus will establish on earth when He returns again. And all who do not believe that He is the Christ will be subjected to shame and everlasting contempt in Hell.

A crude survey of the Christian group showed that some believe that Jesus of Nazareth was a man with human nature, but after His death and resurrection, He became the Christ. One-third believe that He was both man and divine even before His death and resurrection. Another group believes in His immaculate conception in the Virgin Mary, and Jesus of Nazareth was God that lived among us at one stage in human history. A minority group believes that at His baptism, He became the Christ. All these beliefs were highlighted in various conventions by the early Christians: the Council of Nicaea in AD 325, the council that was convened by the Emperor Constantine; the Council of Constantinople in AD 381, convened by Emperor Theodosius; Council of Laodicea in AD 303; the Council of Ephesus in AD 431; and the Council of Chalcedon AD 451.

The Christians have portrayed this Christ as one who fulfilled all the prophetic predictions of the son of Man, the Suffering Servant in the Old Testament literature, and the Messiah in the Jewish literature, using in essence some of the Hebraic Christological platform as its foundation. The believers in the Christology of Jesus's deity tried to make "disciples of all nations" by introducing human doctrines and dogmas to prove that Jesus is not only the Christ but also God. They spread the words of the Gospel by various peaceful and non-peaceful methods: missionary works, holy wars, inquisitions, miracles, mesmerisms, hypocrisy, born-again philosophy, Catholicism, evangelism, Protestantism, Jehovah witnessing, Jewish Orthodoxy, composition of hymns of praise for Jesus and His Father our God, doxology poems, erection of magnificent places of worship, establishment of numerous institutions for religious study where people will learn how to "make disciples of all nations."

Members, who view the Christology of Jesus of Nazareth as sine qua non for Jesus's deity, look for the second coming of Jesus when he will establish His kingdom on earth. All who do not believe in Jesus as the Christ, the only begotten Son of God, will be excluded from membership of that kingdom. The Catholics, if they get into that kingdom first, will not allow the Protestants or any other group not authorized by their leaders to go in. Not only will they be excluded from the kingdom, the nonbelievers will be burning in fire and brimstone. In this regard, the Jews who also look for the establishment of the kingdom of God on this earth are better than the Catholics because at least they would allow the Gentiles to be servants in that new kingdom.

We all know that since the existence of humans, even today, we encounter many people of other religions (even the group we call heathens) whose moral and ethical characters are beyond reproach. They all believe in God. Many of them don't need Jesus or Mohammad or Buddha to illuminate their inherited spirit of truth in them. They spontaneously manifest it for the good of humanity, fulfilling their earthly duty. They embrace compassion as their greatest gift and hypocrisy as the greatest force of evil. At the same time, we have encountered many that believe that Jesus is the Son of God, the Christ, who wait patiently for the second coming of Jesus Christ but make no preparation for it. While they wait, they take money from people to pray for them. They sell bottles of holy water, even though they know that no earthly water is holy. They talk of compassion but their hearts are far from it. Hypocrisy is their greatest ally. They cannot wait for the second coming of Christ when according to their doctrine; Jesus would judge the living and the dead. They judge now and condemn all who did not believe in Jesus as the Christ, the only Son of God. Viewed this way, the doctrinal Christology of Jesus's deity led in the past to division among its members, to holy wars; inquisitions; exploitations; and "making disciples of all nations" by encouraging the poor, the widows, and the elderly to contribute to their church. With such a view, the future of humanity holds nothing but further conflicts, religious wars, anti-secularization efforts, division among all religions, more hypocrisy, more exploitations of the poor nations, more refugee camps, and stagnation of human spiritual evolution.

What we are doing today—international conflicts, rich nations exploiting the poor nations; glorification of the principle "take all you can, give nothing back," terrorism—reflects gross misconception of the meaning of the word "Christ." This misconception has led to the inability to explain and comprehend the true value of what was "finished" in Golgotha. If Christianity is to shed light upon this darkness of our time, then Christianity must reveal to mankind the true meaning of Christ and connect it with the objectives and goals of the Father's business. As the cross was placed on the trajectory of that Father's business, Christianity must look at the cross in any interpretation of the meaning of Christ. It must allow the heavenly light from the cross to shine into the hearts of all humans in its true spiritual form. The heavenly light originated from God, the Father.

Christology of the Cross

The Christology of the cross looked at the spiritual events of what was accomplished at Golgotha. The Jews are still waiting for their Christ, the Messiah to come. The Christians looked at all the Old Testament prophesies of His preexistence, His birth, His mission, His sufferings during His trials, His death and resurrection, and His second coming to establish the kingdom of God on earth and came to the conclusion that Jesus is the Christ, the expected Messiah. To the Christians, all the requirements for Jesus to be considered as the Christ, the Messiah, were fulfilled in Jesus.

Jesus hid Himself inside the work He did, what was executed at Golgotha, and what manifested subsequently. Jesus said that when He is lifted up on the cross, we will know who He is. The crown jewel of the manifesto of the Christology of the Cross rests, therefore, on the spiritual events at Golgotha, what was reveled on Easter morning and what manifested on the day of Pentecost and in the Greco-Roman Empire, three centuries after the death of Jesus Christ. I considered it appropriate to term this philology the "Christology of the Cross" on the ground that everything we need to know about Christ originated from Golgotha, where Jesus was crucified. Jesus was eager to go to Jerusalem. It was in Golgotha that Jesus captured the hearts of humanity. The Christology of the Cross also carries with it the light of the truth from the spiritual events at Golgotha, illuminating His Gospel, revealing its mysteries sporadically to generations, and making it comprehensible. To understand the meaning of "Christ" one must understand the Gospel of Jesus of Nazareth and what was accomplished at Golgotha.

The true meaning of the word Christ does not depend on the prophetic utterances of the Old Testament. Those prophetic utterances pointed to the Messiah the Jews are still expecting. The true meaning of Christ does not depend on many of the titles we have given to Jesus. It does not depend on the edicts of the Council of Nicaea (325 CE) or that of the Council of Chalcedon (451 CE). We cannot find the Christ behind those frontiers. The word Christ has its own wisdom and transcendental experience that is rooted in the duty the Father assigned to Jesus that was accomplished at Golgotha and in the bondage and experience Jesus had with the Father. Of all the divine authorities in heaven, the most trusted divine agent was given that colossal task to come down to this planet for the Father's business that ended with the spiritual events at Golgotha. To understand the meaning of Christ, you must comprehend the driving force that made Jesus insist that He must go to Jerusalem in the last days of His mission despite the fact He knew

He was going to be crucified. What was that driving force? The driving force was the commitment He made to His Father to finish what He came to the world to accomplish.

Golgotha was the powerhouse that provided the perpetual light for the illumination of what is Christ to Jesus and to us in this 21st century. Jesus's commitment to the Father was fulfilled at Golgotha: to demonstrate the words of God; reveal the Father; silence the enemies of His Father; and guide humanity in their journey to seek bondage with the Father. The command for all of Jesus's activities came from God. Jesus's activities centered on God and on His design for humanity and our future. The Christology of the Cross looked at Jesus of Nazareth and His influence of human spirits, the *modus operandi* He used to revealed Himself and God's plan to all humans. It explored the graded planned spiritual evolution of the human soul in its journey to eternal life. It took as its banner the supreme symbol "Christ." And used it as a lens to search the Gospel of Jesus of Nazareth with the light from Golgotha for the revelation of who is Jesus, the nature of His Father and what human life is all about. What it found was a Supreme Being who revealed the truth, the mysteries, and images of God and man. It found a supreme Being who is concerned with the improvement of all human activities, awakening the "kingdom of God within" the human souls. It encountered a Supreme Being who provided tools to whoever would like to use them for the advancement of their spiritual evolution in the knowledge of God and His plan. It found a Comforter and a Liberator of the bruised and the brokenhearted and a divine Master who empowers the spiritualization of human souls. It found a Supreme Being who functioned as a trusted companion for many of my patients and a guide for the physicians and surgeons in the treatment of these patients. It found that whoever will help eliminate hunger, control preventable diseases, prevent conditions that make people migrate to refugee camps, stop all killings, treat all children of the world as the same, and prevent rigging of elections (whether by carrying away illegally the ballot boxes or by dimple ballots or bribing people to vote for them) that the same is a companion and friend of this supreme Being.

"Whosoever shall give to drink unto one of these little ones a cup of cold water only in the name of a disciple, verily I say unto you, he shall in no way lose his reward." (Matthew 10:42) The philology of the Christology of the Cross found a Supreme Being who did not enter into Jerusalem to demonstrate to the Jews that he is the expected Messiah or promised the establishment of any kingdom on the planet Earth. It found a compassionate supreme Being, who was buffeted, scourged, humiliated, condemned to death by His own people, and crucified by the Romans, yet He asked His Father to forgive all of them: "Father, forgive them, they know not what they do."

The Christology of the cross looked at the current age (pre-Advent period) as a preparatory one when humanity must advance spirituality by opening their hearts to the iridescent heavenly light that was made manifest at Golgotha.

This Christology of the Cross looked at this pre-Advent period when Christianity and humankind must "launch out into the deep and let down for a draw," making disciples of all nations with compassion, love, justice, forgiveness, empathy, and goodwill. It looked at this period when we must give all to humanity and to God.

This is the period when the Father seeks people to worship Him not at Jerusalem or in the mountains (shrines, temples, churches, and etcetera) but to worship Him in truth and righteousness in the temple of the truth, erected for Him at Golgotha by Jesus Christ. It looked at this period when humanity must use the spiritual tools and build spiritual wealth and wisdom. It looked at this period when all Christians and non-Christians will join hand in hand to prepare and behave as the angels do in heaven, by opening their hearts to one another, encouraging all to know God and bask in His image. The Christological philology of the cross looks at the Advent not as a period when Jesus would come back to establish His kingdom on Earth but as a stage in human spiritual evolution when what was revealed at Golgotha would be fully manifested. That would be the time when God would accomplish His plan for humanity. It would be preceded by a time when all the evils of the world would be cured not by brute force or intimidation or by taking other nations natural resources, but by a change in the heart of each individual all over the world, when everyone that is of the truth will hear His voice: love one another and extend that love to the enemy.

After diligent exploration of the spiritual events at Golgotha and what manifested thereafter, I found a supreme spiritual Being, who promised His apostles that His Father would send the Holy Ghost in His name to them. That omniscient spiritual Being was sure that His Father would send that Spirit. On the fiftieth day after His ascension to heaven, that promise was fulfilled by His Father on the day of Pentecost. The fulfillment of that promise provided mankind with the proof of the existence of His Father and the divine origin of the words and works of Jesus. It gave us the confidence to believe that the title "Christ" revealed by the Father to Peter on who Jesus is was authentic.

I found a supreme spiritual Being whose power and authority transcended far above the Messiah that the Jews are still waiting to come. I found a supreme spiritual Being, who is being resurrected in the hearts of humankind everyday and yet many Christians are still waiting for Him to come again. I found a spiritual Being, who would continue to spiritualize, protect and save our souls for what His Father planned for mankind. I found a supreme spiritual Being, who with unflinching obedience to the will of His Father, fought vigorously for us at Golgotha. This supreme spiritual Being is the Christ of the cross.

To this end was I born, and for unto this end came I unto the world, that I should bear witness unto the truth. Every one that is of the truth heareth my voice. —Jesus, John 18:37

I have overcome the world. —Jesus, John 16:33

20

Instructive Metaphors of the Cross

Whomsoever does not bear his cross and come after me cannot be my disciple.
—*Luke 14:27*

He that does not take his cross and follow me is not worthy of me.
—*Matthew 10:38*

Whosoever will come after me, let him deny him-
self and take up his cross and follow me.
—*Mark 8:34, Luke 9:23, Matthew 16:24*

THE INSTRUCTIVE METAPHORS of the cross have nothing to do with the physical crosses you see everywhere. Those metaphors are divine instructions crafted by Jesus, when revealed; show the inescapable prerequisites of our colossal tasks in the Father's business. Most philosophers are poets, and they use poetry to convey and also protect their messages. Likewise, artists use their painting for the same purpose. Today, we are still giving many interpretations to Mona Lisa's smile. The entire Gospel of Jesus is a book of metaphors, parables, and proverbs. As a prelude to the discussion on the human task in the Father's business, I have explored some of the instructive metaphors of the cross as to enhance the thorough understanding of our assigned duties in the Father's business.

Once upon a time, on the coast of Judea, beyond Jordan (Garza), a rich ruler, the city mayor by today's standard, asked Jesus for advice on eternal life. (Mark 10:17-22)

"Good Master, what shall I do that I may inherit eternal life?" he asked.

"You know the commandments: do not commit adultery, do not kill, do not steal, do not bear false witness, defraud not, honor your father and mother," Jesus replied.

The rich man answered, saying, "Master, all these I have observed from my youth, what lack I yet?"

Jesus knew he was a rich man with great possessions. He looked at him with compassion and love and said to him, "You lack one thing: go and sell whatsoever you have, give to the poor, and you will have treasures in heaven, and come, take up your cross and follow me." He was to follow Jesus, listen to His words, observe His works and learn what he had to do as to inherit eternal life.

Jesus did not tell the rich man about His planned events at Golgotha. The correct interpretation of instructive metaphors of the cross reveals the way to the bright inheritance as planned by God. The rich man had to follow Jesus to Golgotha for him to acquire that kingdom.

The metaphor of the cross is the lens through which Jesus's view of His Father's plan is revealed. The cross was considered the infamous stake on which the Jews were shamefully crucified by the Romans. To mention the word at all was an offense to the Jews. And to make the matter worse, they must sell everything, distribute it to the poor, and carry the ignominious cross, if literal interpretation is permitted, and follow Him to Golgotha to be crucified too. The conception of the cross, whether used metaphorically or looked upon as the spiritual events at

Golgotha, was not at that period and is not at present acceptable to many Jews as the way to their salvation.

Jesus had suggested selling everything and giving it all to the poor. Many critics have suggested we must not translate it literally—that Jesus did not mean that all rich people must sell all they have and give to the poor. The young man in the story went away sorrowful because he had great possessions. Is it possible in today's world to sell everything and give to the poor for the possession of the kingdom of God? The further discussion on the subject between Jesus and the apostles revealed something that is encouraging.

"Verily I say unto you, that a rich man shall hardly enter into the kingdom of heaven," Jesus said.

"Who then can be saved?" the disciples asked.

"With men this is impossible, but with God all things are possible," Jesus replied.

The encouraging feature of the discussion was that Jesus did not say that no rich man will enter into the kingdom of God and that with God everything is possible. Esoterically anyone can develop and manifest this invisible kingdom of God. One of the bishops in Africa came from a wealthy background, and he chose to give up all the riches of his family and the comfort of his country to be a priest and work in Africa. He did not receive a single penny from the church. His family supported him. His family could buy him the best house in any country he chose to work, but instead he lived a modest life, helping the poor with whatever he had. He was a good man, a rich man who gave up all and carried his cross to Africa and worked endlessly for the poor. To give all to the poor means also service for the poor.

I will share my experience of the bishop with you. We were all in the cathedral during one of the evening services. It was raining heavily. After his sermon, he sat down on his chair and observed a moment of silence, meditating and praying silently as his custom was. Then he stood up, moved his chair backward about four feet, and then sat back down. He had never done this before. Soon after, within seconds, the overhead light bulb shattered and the pieces fell in front of him. He was a bald-headed British missionary; if he had not moved, the pieces of glass could have traumatized his head. He subsequently became the archbishop of West Africa. This is a poor legacy for the holy man. In contrast we see many church leaders and evangelists all over the world who are multimillionaires, taking all they can from the poor and giving them back nothing.

Recently, many United States-based rich evangelists are streaming into Africa to spread the new Gospel. They declared that the deaf would hear (many had their ear drums destroyed in infancy for lack of medicines); that the blind would see (even those whose sight had been destroyed by glaucoma; that the lame would walk and jump (crippled in infancy by polio because of lack of vaccinations); that anybody sick would be healed (they don't even know why they are sick as there are no diagnostic tools); that the jobless would gain employment, and that the enemy, called the Devil, would be vanquished. They preached that the sacrifice of Jesus at Golgotha brought forgiveness and wiped away the sins of the world. To the poor Africans, those men of God, as they call themselves, preached the Gospel that people must believe in Jesus and support their mission by donating money for the spread of the Gospel. Many United States-based evangelists go to Nigeria and other sub-Saharan African countries to raise millions of dollars. So long as the local currency is supported by the oil and other mineral industries, they will continue to do so. In return they build mega churches and provide bus services to bring the villagers to the churches where they can buy the holy water and blessed cross for healing. Poor people had the equivalent of thousands of dollars stolen from their employers to give to the church. From time to time they even risk going to jail by stealing from the banks or kidnapping innocent people for money to give some to the churches.

The prophets and the prophetesses of Christ organize crusades that attract millions of worshipers for the jackpot. In the process of serving God and the poor, the preacher becomes a millionaire, buys private jets, and lives in the best homes. Is it possible for a preacher, who is the servant of Christ, to sell all he has and give to the poor? Is it even possible for him to stop taking from the poor, whether in Africa or at home? Can he really carry his cross and follow Christ—that is, can he really sacrifice and serve humanity and God, asking nothing in return?

Recently *TIME* magazine featured the persons of the year 2005. It is very interesting because they were chosen based on what they did for the poor, not only in Africa but all over the world. The *TIME* magazine (January 2006 issue) featured also other great philanthropist who also recognized that we have the poor with us always and did something to help them. I salute them. I thank them. I am sure the deeds of these humble, compassionate givers would also always be brought before God as a memorial. They had fulfilled the Master's instruction: "Whosoever shall give to drink unto one of these little ones a cup of cold water… he shall in no wise lose his reward." (Matthew 10:42) The effort to help the poor, if we are loving, sympathetic, compassionate, and caring individuals and nations, would eliminate poverty from the world. The poor represents a complex group of people from all over the world that are featured every day on television, books, and magazines, from the workers in oil and minefields and the migrant workers on the farms, to the homeless, the unemployed, and the elderly without anybody who cares for them. We see them every day.

The term "cross" used by Jesus in His discussion with the rich young ruler was purely metaphorical. The metaphor was one of discipleship and not of the horror and humiliation of crucifixion on the cross. This discipleship calls for personal sacrifice. It calls for service to humankind and to God. That was exactly what Jesus did. It calls for what we call help. For some people earthly possessions form a barrier for the successful outcome of that sacrifice. For those people the advice from Jesus is that they have to give up not only the quest for worldly things and give to charity many of their possessions but also to follow Him, observe and learn from Him how to enter into the Kingdom of God that He proclaimed.

For the philanthropists featured in *TIME* magazine and for many other rich people in other parts of the world that help the poor, their earthly possessions must enhance that personal sacrifice as demanded by Jesus. Additionally, it is prudent to uphold the principle of giving all they can and take nothing back as opposed to take all you can (their oil, gold, diamonds, rubber, platinum, good farm products) and give nothing back.

Blessed are the merciful, for they shall obtain mercy. —Jesus

What shall it profit a man if he gains the whole world and loses his soul? —Jesus. Mark 8:36

To sell everything is a figurative expression. For the philanthropist to sell everything and give it to the poor would be a disservice to the poor and the entire human race. The money will end up in private Swiss accounts or in what the Americans call off-shore accounts. The poor would be in a miserable state. The beneficiary of such an action would be the con artists who parade in various camouflaged clothing or what Christ describes as wolves in sheep's clothing. The world record shows that most of the money donated to the poor nations ended in foreign accounts of their leaders.

Jesus said to the apostles, "follow me." The twelve apostles responded to that call from their Master. It was not necessary to remind them of their personal sacrifices nor was it necessary to remind them of the tribulations and the pains of the discipleship. With love and humility the twelve humble servants accomplished their missions, promoting the understanding and worship of God through Jesus Christ. The selfless service to humanity and to God, their sacrifices, and tribulations were their cross. To follow Christ is again a figurative expression. It does not mean you have to abandon your work or profession to be a religious teacher, setting up your church or going from one city to another teaching like Jesus did. To follow Christ is to be a servant of God, seeking after God's righteousness and His kingdom and being obedient to His will and commandments. Partnership with the Father and Jesus Christ would be your reward. Jesus of Nazareth did not seek earthly kingdom or treasures. The metaphoric expressions of the cross were like a kernel hidden in a shell. That shell was broken at Golgotha, revealing its contents: love that extended to the poor, compassion, mercy, justice, forgiveness and obedience to the will and commandments of the Father, our God. The Master of divine wisdom is still calling on Whoever is ready, not just those who call themselves Christians, to "take up the cross and follow Him", to listen to His words of eternal life, observe His lifestyle and learn what to do for eternal life.

The Spiritual Cross has spoken. To bear the cross is to reject evil in all its facets and reject all that Jesus rejected. The world is not ignorant of the evil going around. To pretend we don't know what is evil is hypocrisy. The cross requires that not only must you recognize the evil forces but you too must use the spiritual weaponry displayed at Golgotha to fight against it. Jesus accomplished all His tasks without killing anyone. The Father that Jesus presented to us is not a vengeful God who delights in killing what He created and is still creating. One day humanity will wake up and ask the following questions: who is making us kill each other? Who is making us steal from each other? Who has made us children of greed and envy? Who has made us to be inhuman and stopped generosity? Who has made us to worship in temples of injustice and hatred, seeking the solitude of vainglory? Who is setting up these mouse traps for humanity? Is it humankind or some other gods?

To identify the beast and tackle it, it is not enough to sell everything and give to the poor. We must follow Jesus to Golgotha and learn from the classroom of human spiritual evolution. Some people who graduated from that school comprehend what is required for a fuller destiny for all humans: suffering, hard work, quest for righteousness, sorrow, despair, giving, not receiving, serving, not getting the best of others, loneliness, humility, forgiveness, mercy, love, complete obedience to the will of God, and the understanding that the next cycle of life is the true life. Those who are deepened by their experience rise triumphantly to glory and to that authentic life. Furthermore, to attend to this fuller destiny, you must look at the world with a different spectacle. You must want nothing, accumulate nothing. You must love the world and hope for the hopeless. You must open your heart to the iridescent heavenly rays and allow the light to shine into your inner consciousness. You must embrace that light and manifest it to humanity. Then:

Take up your Cross and follow me (to the Father). —Jesus

21

THE DIVINE TRINITY OF THE HUMAN SOULS

Behold, we have forsaken all and followed Thee; what shall have thereafter.
—MATTHEW 19:27

And every one that hath forsaken houses, or brethren, or sisters or father, or mother, or wife, or children, or land, for my name's sake, shall receive a hundredfold and shall inherit everlasting life.
—MATTHEW 19:29

THERE IS ONE and only one purpose for the earthly life of all humans. That holy purpose is to be part of the divine Trinity with God and Jesus Christ. All other purposes are of no value.

This holy purpose will not be completed on this planet Earth. It may involve our spiritual journey through other planets or spiritual kingdoms. Jesus came to activate and energize the inherited spiritual powers in humans, propelling them to higher realms that open up new purposes in life, new directions in life, new revelations of the spiritual forces and laws that influence our spirits, new spiritual superhighways to the Father, and the new consciousness of the Father-human spirit fellowship

Through obedience to the will of God, Jesus was crucified at Golgotha. If your ambition is for your soul to be saved and live in Paradise with Jesus, the Father may send you down to earth for a mission. Will you be ready to obey when you know that you will be humiliated, abused, tortured, and crucified by the people you love? The most important of all instructions from Jesus is that we must obey the will of God, both here on earth and in heaven. That divine instruction was not from the Father but from Jesus Christ, who understands His Father and how He operates.

God is not creating us to come and live in Paradise with Him and Jesus and the angels and to put on white robes and sing hosanna and alleluia day and night for them. God is not creating humans to expand His angelic army. Does God need more workers in heaven and for that reason sent Jesus to save us and bring us to Paradise to help Him? Jesus was silent on the reason why God is creating us. Jesus did not reveal openly to anyone what we will be doing in Paradise when you get there. Perhaps, if Jesus had revealed that information, people would refuse to do what He prescribed for eternal life.

The process of human creation is still an ongoing process and workers are needed at all times, even as of today, as portrayed in the parable of the laborers in the vineyard (Matthew 20:1–16) Those who make it to heaven may indeed be sent down again in human forms to help humanity in our reproductive earthly lifecycle. Jesus gave us the spiritual tools to use and educate our souls on how to obey the will of God. Oftentimes we have called on the angels to help, guide, and protect us. We see angels every day in our lives; they pose as humans, some as beggars on the street and so we do not recognize them. We search for angels in white clothes with wings. Nobody has seen such except in the movies and in dreams. When you get to heaven, you may, by obeying the will of God, be sent down to help. You too, on the next mission from heaven to this planet, must be ready to be beheaded like John the Baptist, be crucified, be brought before judges and magistrates and be cast into prison. However, the most important thing is that you will be a servant to humanity and to God. The will of God must be done. The duration of Father's business is unknown. Countless workers are needed on this planet Earth and maybe in other spiritual worlds to help Christ and His Father.

Again and again, Jesus said that the twelve apostles "are not of the world, just as I am not of the world." They suffered, were persecuted, and many of them were killed in the line of their duty for humankind and God. The seventy men Jesus sent out to spread the Good News of the kingdom of God were told to rejoice because their names were written in heaven. Do not be deceived. If you make it to heaven and, in accordance to the will of God, you may be sent down again to earth for a specific objective, you may end up in a refugee camp or in prison for the execution of that God's holy purpose.

The life of the late President Nelson Mandela of South Africa had a significant and purposeful outcome. God saw the suffering of the people of South Africa. You will notice that President Mandela's message was the same right from the beginning to the moment he took his last breath. He was imprisoned for twenty-seven years. But he liberated his people. We must not weep for him. How can you weep for him when his name was written in heaven? We must rejoice for him. The prison was the fortress the Father used to protect him until the time was fulfilled. Before he was sentenced, President Nelson Mandela was ready to die for what he believed must be done: creation of a free society for both the oppressed and the oppressors. He was a young man at that time, ready to fight and die for the salvation of his people from bondage. But the Father had other plans. The judge found no real reason to sentence the young man to death or even put him in prison. However, under divine influence, President Nelson Mandela was sentenced to serve a lifetime in prison. It was a battle between good and the evil, involving principles, dominion, and power. If President Nelson Mandela had been set free during his trial, he might have been killed soon after. The prison became the protective citadel and President Nelson's cross of suffering, righteousness, and virtue that the Father had crafted for the salvation of the people of South Africa. Victory was assured; the good triumphed over the evil. Late President Nelson Mandela was obedient to the will of God and, like Jesus Christ, drank from his 'cup.' He came out of that prison armed with a bag of spiritual tools containing tolerance, negotiation with the enemy, forgiveness, and unflinching love for his people and for all humanity. Today you are my witnesses that President Nelson Mandela when he was released from prison, not only forgave the people that put him in prison but also carried the banner of Jesus's commandment of love for one another and with that love penetrated into the frontiers of the enemy for the sake of our brothers and sisters. What a man! Are you ready, if you go to heaven, to be sent down again to suffer for God's holy purposes?

Look again at the Lord's Prayer. The first directive is that we must pray for God's will to be done on earth as it is done in heaven. If you are not ready to obey whatever may be God's will for you, whether in heaven or on earth, then I have labored in vain for the last six years to produce this treatise. But if your answer is affirmatively yes, then gather together your spiritual tools and be ready for your divine assignment in this reproductive cycle of human life. Your rewards will be fantastic.

Labor not for the meat which perisheth, but for that which endureth unto everlasting life, which the Son of man shall give unto you." —John 6:27

The truth is that the reproductive cycle of human life is a long process. It may take millions of years and God needs workers. "The harvest truly is plenteous, but the laborers are few; pray you therefore the Lord of the harvest, that He will send forth laborers into his harvest." (Matthew 9:37–38) The Lord of the harvest is His Father. The harvest is what His Father is creating: humans and all living things. He is already using humans who believe in Him for the work, but they are not enough. We must pray to God to send down more workers to help. Although you have graduated and are in heaven, you may be sent down again. You can now understand why Jesus put so much emphasis on obedience to the will of God on earth as it is done in heaven. Both the Father and Jesus

Christ are discerners of what is in our hearts. If you are not willing to obey them, they will remain hidden from you. Jesus gave one and only one commandment—"love God and love one another"—and one piece of advice—"seek after the kingdom of God and His righteousness (His will)"—as prerequisites for the promised everlasting life.

Jesus revealed many things we must do on this earth to help us get to heaven and be with Him and the Father. The evolutionary process of human life, which was created out of the infinite love of God, the Father of Christ, the Creator, catapulted the evolved spiritual man beyond everlasting existence in Paradise, beyond the obedience to the will of God, and to infinite union with the Father and Jesus Christ. This is what I call the new Trinity of the human spirit: divine bondage of the Father, Jesus Christ, and the created human spirit. Jesus knew what would be the final reward for all who had forsaken everything and had followed Him: "that they all may be one; as thou, Father art in me, and I in thee, that they also may be one in us, that the world may believe that thou hast sent me." (John 17:21) That was part of Jesus's prayer to His Father for the apostles. However, revealed in that prayer is what awaits all humanity. The divine Trinity of the human soul was echoed by one of His apostles: "That which we have seen and heard, declare us unto you, that ye also may have fellowship with us; and truly our fellowship is with the Father, and with His Son Jesus Christ." (1 John 1:3) This is the story of the terrestrial and extraterrestrial journey of the human spirit. Both the human life on earth and in heaven is bound together and cannot be broken.

The new Trinity of the human spirit does not mean that the created spiritual man is a God or that Jesus Christ is God the Father. The first time Jesus told the Jews that "the Father is in me and I in the Father," they tried to seize Him, but He escaped. In this new Trinity of the human spirit, the Father and Jesus Christ will be in the created spiritual man and the spiritual man will be in the Father and in Jesus Christ. This true divine union is our reward. The twelve holy apostles, Paul and many others already got this reward. The blending of the spirits of the twelve apostles and our spirits in the new divine Trinity was clearly outlined by Jesus: "My prayer is not for them alone. I pray also for them who will believe in me through their message; that all of them may be one, Father, just as you are in me and I am in you, may they also be in us." (John 17:20)

This inscrutable mystery of the new Trinity of the human souls with Jesus Christ and His Father was experienced by Paul even before he left the planet Earth: "It is no longer I who live, but Christ who lives in me." (Galatians. 2:2) Jesus asked, "What shall it profit a man if he gains the whole world and loses his soul?" The interpretation is self-explanatory: of what use are all the earthly wealth and power to a person if he or she fails to inherit the spiritual and everlasting glory of the divine Trinity of the soul with the Father and Jesus Christ?

I have made many references in this treatise that God, the Father is still creating us, and that this earthly phase is just a single phase in the creative cycle. We can call this phase the reproductive earthly cycle of the human life. This plan was in place before Abraham was born. Adam and Eve underwent the same process we are experiencing now. From the beginning of time, all humans, regardless of race, nationality, or social status, have had to pass through the reproductive phase. We are conceived the same way and for this reason: "at the beginning, God made them males and females." (Matthew 19:4) We will all complete this phase the same way, by death, and move on to the next phase. This cycle is irrepressible. The duration of this phase is hidden from humans. It could last from a few seconds or few days for some people. It could last for years. Perhaps, some human spirits may be given a second chance and be sent back to the reproductive phase to repeat the cycle. In the next spiritual phase, there are no marriages, no births, no million-dollar mansions, no run-down homes, no gold or silver because everything is left behind. Jesus made reference to our current and the next non-reproductive life cycle. "The children of this world marry, and are given in marriage. But they which shall be accounted worthy to obtain that world, and the resurrection from the dead, neither marry nor are given in marriage; neither can they die anymore; for they are equal unto the angels; and are the children of God, being the children of the resurrection." (Luke 20:34-36)

Our biggest problem is that we have refused to acknowledge this oneness of all humanity. The planet Earth, from the beginning, was a baby factory for what God planned. It is still a baby factory for what God is creating. If from the beginning humanity had adopted the principle that no child must be left behind, not just in education but in all aspects of life, it would not have been necessary for the Father to send Jesus. Again, Jesus, as His custom was, used metaphors and symbolic expressions to address the principle we must follow: "I tell you of the truth, unless you change and become like little children, you will never enter the kingdom of heaven. Therefore, whoever humbles himself like this child is the greatest in the kingdom of heaven. And whoever welcomes a little child like this in my name welcomes me. But if anyone causes one of these little ones who believe in me to sin, it would be better for him to have a large millstone hung around his neck and to be drowned in the depth of the sea." (Matthew 18:3–6)

Let the little children come unto me, and do not hinder them, for the kingdom of heaven belong to them. —Matthew 19:14

See that you do not look down on one of these little ones. For I tell you that their angels in heaven always see the face of my Father in heaven. —Matthew 18:10

A child is an interesting human being. Endowed with the highest power of observation, intellect, language, and skill, spiritual evolution and development in science and technology become elementary. The child is not interested in worldly possessions or power or in any form of violence. If allowed to live in his or her own world, the child would perform his or her own duty and leave the earth to be a component of the divine union. But these children are encouraged to struggle for earthly power and wealth and coached to practice hatred, discrimination, and racism. Some of them are kidnapped, abused, forced into child labors, forced to wear soldiers' uniforms to fight a war, forced to steal, and forced to live in refugee camps. In this earthly reproductive phase, humans must perform like a child, think like a child, hope like a child, believe like a child, and grow up maintaining all the qualities of a child in order to be a component in the true divine oneness with the Father and Jesus Christ. The glory of this infinite bondage with the Father and Jesus Christ belong to the following elects:

- All who promote world peace and justice and have used tolerance and negotiations instead of war to accomplish their objectives.
- All who would never take from poor nations or from the poor in their country, even though they have the power and opportunity to do so.
- All who use the proceeds from their natural resources to help the poor, educate them, provide adequate health services, alleviate their sufferings, and build an enviable infrastructure for economic growth of the nation.
- All who hate hypocrisy and greed, envy, jealousy, worship of idols, racism, and discrimination.
- All who seek the truth that Jesus revealed.
- All who have developed expressions of a pure heart and worship the Father in truth.
- All who have knowledge of the Father and Jesus Christ and use it to work for humanity.
- All who believe in Jesus Christ and His Father's plan for humanity.
- All who love mankind and are servants to humanity and to God.

You see the elects every day. You may be one of them. Ever since humans walked on earth, they have been with us. They are those who gave to humanity with no knowledge that they gave; their left hands do not know about such gifts, and their right hands have no memory of ever giving such gifts. They are the ones that saw the kingdom of God come with power before they died. God uses them as instruments for His holy designs. Jesus used them as apostles. Today, the Father and Christ still use many people to execute their will. You have read the biographies of many elects that were endowed with power from above. Some were chained or imprisoned, like the late President Nelson

Mandela, but came out and led their people to freedom. Others were murdered so that we may be free from our masters. There are those, like Mother Theresa, whose secret is simply to pray. There were also many elects who discovered the path to enlightenment and encouraged others to follow. Some were great prophets who found God's love and translated that love to their fellow humans. You do not have to go to Jerusalem or Rome to find an elect. They are seen everywhere. They are those who, with pure hearts, have maintained their sinless status by simple act of forgiveness, tolerated people of other religions, and have developed God-Jesus-human bondage and experience. The ones I know are from many parts of the world and belong to different religious sects.

The spindle of all our earthly spiritual manifestations rotates on our spiritualized immortal human soul that seeks for union with the Spirit of the Father and the glorified Spirit of Jesus Christ. The earthly manifestations of the life of that spiritualized soul are love, joy, peace, compassion, long suffering, gentleness, humility, mercy, meekness, obedience of God's holy laws, avoidance of hatred, and all things that are evil. The ignorance of the nature of human soul and God's design for humanity and what was accomplished at Golgotha are the basic causes for what could eventually destroy mankind. The human souls must be educated, not just in advances in science and technology but also in multiculturalism, religious tolerance, compassion and love for one another. Let that education evolve to the highest earthly spiritual level and carry with it, the message of what was finished at Golgotha, and proclaim it to the world. This would bring real change to other human spirits by turning the hearts of many to seek God and His righteousness.

Finally, brethren, whatever things are true, whatever things are honest, whatever things are just, whatever things are pure, whatever things are lovely, whatever things are of good report, if there be any virtue, and if there be any praise, think of these things. And the peace of God, which passeth all understanding, shall keep your heart and minds through Jesus Christ. —Paul, Philippians 4:8, 7

The jackpot of the infinite trinity of the human soul that Jesus revealed belongs to these elects. Jesus belongs to them. The Father belongs to them. By the purity of their hearts, by the rejection of all that Jesus rejected, by their refusal to serve the evil and cruel men and women in power and authority-rulers of this world-and by their obedience to the will of God, our Father, they too must rejoice, not because of what they have done for humanity, but they must rejoice because their names are written in heaven. They must rejoice because Christ has claimed their souls for the new divine Trinity of their spirits with His Father.

If a man loves me, he will keep my words; and my Father will love him, and we will come unto him, and make our abode with him. —John 14:23

Where I am going, you cannot follow me now, but you will follow afterward. —John 13:36

22

OUR COLOSSAL TASK IN THE
FATHER'S BUSINESS

*But seek first His kingdom and His righteousness and
all these things will be given to you as well.*
—MATTHEW 6:53

Be you therefore perfect even as your Father which is in heaven is perfect.
—MATTHEW 5:48

Why do you call me Lord, Lord and do not the things I say do?
—JESUS

I DON'T KNOW HOW I can express the colossal tasks for humanity that I see
before me so that you can comprehend them. The work that must be done
is real and practical. But you may say it is impossible. It is terrifying to me
too. The spiritual weaponries we need were carefully displayed and personified by Jesus at Golgotha and by His earthly lifestyle. How Jesus of Nazareth
lived His life and manifested the power of His Kingdom of God is the life
force of Christianity. We cannot and must not detach ourselves from such

a virtuous, exemplary life. We must not and cannot reject the use of the power of Jesus's Kingdom of God. There is no defense or hope for any of us—no, there is no place to hide except to emulate the examples of how Jesus lived His life. We must use His spiritual powers to develop the highest spiritual evolution for the attainment of God-human indwelling and experience, which is required for our return as a unified, indivisible family of God to the kingdom that has been prepared for us since the beginning of the world. There is one straight, but narrow way to this kingdom. Our duty is to assist each other, despite our religious, cultural, or ethnic differences, in finding our ways to this pathway to that Kingdom. We have the opportunity to join together and be one, just as it was at the beginning of time.

The earthly center of all spirituality that Jesus introduced is the human soul. That spirituality originated from heaven. Nobody can fully understand Christianity because of this single fact: what Jesus Christ brought down to the world (the words of God and what He revealed about His Father and His business) is only a fragment of the fathomless spirituality we call Christianity. Jesus spoke to the human souls and directed all His efforts to the human souls. The colossal task before us is not what the bodies have to do but what the souls must do. Jesus said that "the body profited nothing; it is the spirit that quickened." My intention in writing this section of the treatise is to outline:

1. What is our task?
2. The obstacles to our task
3. The consequences of our inability to finish our task
4. The heavenly and earthly tools Jesus Christ left for us to use for our task

What is our task?

Believe in the Gospel of Jesus Christ

Our task is simply to serve mankind and participate actively with Christ in our journey to eternal life. We must first find the road map to the Infinite Trinity of human souls with God and Jesus Christ. This map gives us directions to the Father's house. Forget about your GPS. Forget about your Google maps or MapQuest. This map designed by Christ leads us to God, our Father. The Gospel of Jesus is that map. Read it and let the light of what was released at Golgotha help you, as you walk on that pathway, to accomplish your task. "The time is fulfilled, and the Kingdom of God is at hand; repent you, and believe the gospel." (Mark 1:15 The ethics and moral observations that Jesus preached and lived by His examples, common in many religions, direct you to that narrow but straight pathway to the bondage with Jesus Christ and His Father. The power of His Kingdom of God sustains you in that journey.

As you walk on the road that leads to God, using the gospel as your guide, you must strive to be perfect. God is perfect; therefore, the created human spirit must be perfect. The lesson on perfection starts on the planet Earth. For many years, I felt that Jesus's instruction to be as perfect as the Father was impossible. As I learned about this Jesus of Nazareth and gained knowledge of His laws and commandments for God-human spirit indwelling, it became obvious to me that if it was impossible to be as perfect as the Father, then Jesus would not have given that instruction. God's spirit is divine; therefore, the spiritual human that must finally evolve at the end of human creation must be divine. How we are to live must be directed to this effort. God cannot and will not live with imperfect spirits.

Believe in Jesus Christ

The people had asked Jesus, "What shall we do, that we might work the work of God?" Jesus replied, "This is the work of God that ye believe on Him whom He had sent." (John 6:28-29) The belief in Jesus Christ played a very significant role in His ability to perform many miracles. In the performance of His miracles, Jesus always asked the person if he or she believed He was able to do that work. The philology of the belief in Jesus Christ forayed beyond His power to heal, into an untouched spiritual realm as revealed by many of His utterances:

"If any man thirst, let him come unto me and drink. He that believeth, as the Scripture hath said, out of his belly shall flow rivers of living water."—John 7:37-38

"I am the resurrection and the life; he that believeth in me, though he were dead, yet shall he live. And whosoever liveth and believeth in me shall never die."—John 1125-26

"And this is the will of Him that sent me that every one which seeth the Son, and believeth on him, may have everlasting life; and I will raise him up at the last day."—John 6:39

"I am the bread of life; he that cometh to me shall never hunger; and he that believeth on me shall never thirst."—John 6:35

For the apostles and all who believed in him, Jesus prayed to His Father, "That they all may be one; as thou, Father, art in me, and I in thee, that they also may be one in us; that the world may believe that thou hast sent me." (John 17:21)

Believe in His Father

Jesus believed in His Father and did things that always pleased Him. To love the Father, we must first love one another. To serve the Father, we must first serve humanity. Humankind created environments in which other living things are happier than we are. The dogs are happier than human beings are. The birds wake up in the morning from their nests and sing glory to their Maker who completely takes care of them for the rest of the day: "Behold, the fowls of the air, for they sow not, neither do they reap, nor gather into barns; yet your heavenly Father feedeth them." (Matthew 6:26) We enshrine and camp around many of the living things to admire their beauty and splendor. We travel to distant places to see the exotic living things. Have any of them come to see us? No. They know what we will do to them. Animals do communicate with one another. The reports of forced labor from the horses and our merciless methods of killing animals we use for food alerted the animal kingdom of the vicious ways we deal with them.

With the advances in science and technology, the high standard of our living is unprecedented when compared with the generations before us. Yet humankind is miserable. There are millions in prison and in refugee camps. We kill each other for intangible reasons. The worldwide humanitarian services are overshadowed and hampered by the evils of market capitalism and socialism, unjustified wars, racism, religious intolerance, extreme greed, the false concept of super nationalism, the ego of individualism, unprecedented unemployment, eviction of people from their homes, homelessness, and misery. After World War II, the United Nations assembly was formed to foster unity and cooperation among the nations. Today, that assemblage can be rightly called "Divided Nations" because there is no true unity, mutuality, or harmony among the majority of its members. United Nation policies that would advance civilization are influenced by politics, economic favoritism, self-preservation, religious affiliations, and hatred. Many people are working hard to save the planet Earth, but these nations have continued to produce nuclear arsenals that would completely wipe out humankind and all living things.

Humanity is growing in spiritual darkness. Plants need light to sprout and grow. We need the light that is not of the sun or the moon to grow spiritually. Humankind needs the light of what was accomplished at Golgotha for the evolution of our immortal human spirits. Humankind is suffering today because we lack that spiritual sunshine. We have material things for happiness but are not happy. It is a common knowledge that many rich people are miserable. What we need is spiritual development. Many people have concluded that God has abandoned us, that He left this planet a long time ago. However, God is with us and has never abandoned us. Human beings are the ones who have abandoned God. What is true is that humankind has refused to obey His holy commandments and completely refused to use the spiritual tools made available at Golgotha. God has not left this planet. He will not abandon what He is creating.

"Verily, verily, I say unto you, He that heareth my word, and believe on Him that sent me, hath everlasting life, and shall not come into condemnation; but is passed from death unto life."—John 5:24

Partnership with Jesus Christ in the service for mankind in our journey to eternal life

The seed that God planted in our souls sprouted and has grown. It must grow and bloom into an image in the likeness of our Creator. The harvest is ready. God is creating man in His own image and gave us unprecedented "dominion over every living thing that moves upon the earth" during this lifecycle. In this earthly reproductive cycle of the human life, we can walk on water, heal sicknesses by miracles, command the wild animals to obey our commands, and communicate directly with the Father. What shall we do to manifest these privileges? We must collaborate with Jesus to harvest what His Father had planted. "Behold, I say unto you, Lift up your eyes, and look on the fields, for they are white already to harvest. And he that reapeth receiveth wages, and gathereth fruit unto life eternal; that both he that soweth and he that reapeth may rejoice together." (John 4:35-36)

Obstacles to the Human Task

These obstacles are like potholes on the narrow pathway that leads to the Father's house. It is not good enough to recognize and walk over them. We must repair them permanently for the generations that would come after us.

False Christ and prophets

This is a major obstacle to our task. Jesus warned them, "False Christ and false prophets shall rise, and shall show signs and wonders to seduce, if it were possible even the elect." (Mark 13:22) On another instance, Jesus advised us to, "beware of false prophets which come to you in sheep's clothing, but inwardly they are ravening wolves." (Matthew 7:15) Today we see them everywhere deceiving people, selling bottled holy water, occupying chief seats in the temples, crafting human doctrines for humankind to observe and do, but they themselves as Christ observes, "will not move them with one of their fingers." (Matthew 23:4)

Jesus warned us to be aware of people who would use the information that Jesus is the Christ, to deceive us. "Many shall come in my name, saying, I am Christ; and shall deceive many." (Mark 13:6) I am not waiting for the second coming of Jesus Christ. His Spirit is with us, even as of today, watching all our activities. Jesus assured us that, "I am with you always, even unto the end of the world." (Matthew 28:20) For the people waiting for Jesus to come again, I would advise them to be on high alert. What may come could be a distraction and not a fulfillment. Jesus's advice is this: "If any man shall say to you, lo, here is Christ; or lo, he is there, believe him not. Take heed: behold, I have foretold you all things." (Mark 13:21, 23) In the execution of your colossal task, be vigilant, watch and pray.

Humankind

God uses humans to accomplish all His objectives. We are the instruments through which He hears the world, sees the world, feels the world, and executes His planned design for humanity. God manifests His divine images and power through Jesus Christ, likewise God wants to manifest Himself through us. This is how the loving and merciful God controls and rules all things. However, the greatest of the obstacles to our task is humankind. Jesus warned His apostles of this problem, "Yea, the time cometh, that whoever killeth you will think that he doeth God's service." (John 15:2)

It is impossible to educate humans on love, injustice, forgiveness, mercy, kindness, and develop the quest to live daily with God, if they have no idea of what life is all about and the value of what was "finished" in Golgotha. The obstacles to our task today, are not the Jewish priests that plotted and betrayed Jesus of Nazareth, nor the Romans that crucified Him. Today, the real obstacles to our task are people that sit in Moses's seat, robbing people in the name of Jesus Christ. They use the money collected freely in the name of Christ to enrich themselves. They are like the chief priests that Jesus encountered during His earthly mission, who were blind guides to the Jewish people. (Matthew 23:16, 24) The obstacles to our task include also, those who knowingly and intentionally paraded the cross of Jesus of Nazareth as earthly events and failed to educate the congregation on the spiritual values of what was accomplished at Golgotha. They are also like the chief priests at the time of Christ, who "shut up the kingdom of heaven against men." (Matthew 23:13) The human obstacles of our task are, "those whose action end in destruction, whose God is their belly, and whose glory is in their shame, who mind earthly things," (Paul. Philippians 3 18:19)

Temptations

The word 'temptation' immediately brings to memory the recorded temptations of Jesus and Job by the Satan. Jesus did not yield to the satanic temptation to abandon the will of His Father and His own will. When we are led into temptation, and have entered into temptation, it means: the temptation of accepting what Jesus rejected of Satan; the temptation of the use of your power and influence for self-interest; the temptation of fighting physically for people to believe in Jesus; the temptation of forcing all to obey the will of God; the temptation of passing a law for the benefit of those that contributed to your political campaign and forcing the people you govern to obey that law; the temptation of greed and injustice: the temptation of refusing to use the spiritual weaponries in the Gospel to advance you spirituality; and the temptation of taking all you can from poor nations. We must learn how Jesus survived the satanic temptation and apply the same principle.

"Learn of me..." Jesus.

Evil activities

If there were no evil, Jesus would not ask us to pray to God to deliver us from evil. The stories of Abraham/Sarah and Ishmael and his mother, Joseph and the other sons of Jacob, King David and the soldiers' wife, Emperor Nero, Ivan the terrible, Joseph Stalin, Adolf Hitler and the Slave Traders are well documented in our history books. The list is exhaustible. Today, we know what is evil. Many individuals and nations still go on to carry out such activities. We lack the guiding principles on how to avoid evil. Today's generation is evil and the future generations, unless they change, would be classified also as evil. However, living among us are many good men and women. We want that number to be the majority of the people. It has been said that the root of evil is money, greed, power, seeking abundance of possessions and fear for survival. They are just contributing factors. The real root of evil is ignorance of the knowledge of God and what Jesus accomplished in His Earthly mission.

Lack of understanding of human spirits and the intrinsic value of human life

To understand what is happening to us and how we are to live to finish our task, we must understand the God and Jesus Christ we worship. Jesus knew the language the human spirits understand and exposed the human spirit to the words of God. To follow Him is to seek exposure of your spirit to the words of God and His righteousness. The accomplishment of this requires the evolutionary process of training your spirit by the Lord of spiritual evolution: Jesus of Nazareth. His classroom is the Gospel and His life examples. His students are the human spirits. Only few have entered into that classroom. Some got lost on the way there because either they were not given the right directions or the "cares of the world" distracted them. Destructive intent, greed, malice, hatred, get-rich-fast schemes, injustice, racism, cultural genocide, unjustified medical malpractice litigations, piracy, and kidnapping of innocent people, all became hindrances to finding that classroom and being tutored by the Lord of spiritual evolution.

The list of obstacles to our task is inexcusable. The worship of gods and goddesses feature prominently. The planet Earth has a harsh environment in which we live, as evidenced by the destructive forces of earthquakes, volcanic eruptions, tornadoes, extreme flooding from rain, killer lightening, and cyclones. Many people are fearful and unhappy. Episodic joy is what is considered to be normal now in many parts of the world. Humans are besieged with many things they cannot control. The financial meltdown, foreclosures, joblessness, recession, food crisis, infectious disease epidemics, broken human relationships, genocide, wars, and nuclear proliferations are things that confront humans now. However, there is hope for the future of humankind. That imperishable future depends on our profound knowledge of the spiritual tools that

Jesus introduced to the world. However, the knowledge of these tools will not be enough. We must use them.

Knowing is not enough; we must apply. Willing is not enough; we must do. —*Goethe*

Consequences of our inability to finish our Task

The best illustration on the consequences of our inability to complete our own task was portrayed in the timeless story of the rich man and the beggar named Lazarus. It would not be prudent to write a synopsis of this story for the fear of missing essential elements that may distort Jesus's intent of the narrative.

There was a certain rich man, which was cloth in purple and fine linen, and fared sumptuously every day. And there was a certain beggar named Lazarus, which was laid at his gate, full of sores, and desiring to be fed with the crumbs which fell from the rich man's table; moreover, the dogs came and licked his sores. And it came to pass, that the beggar died, and was carried by the angels into Abraham's bosom; the rich man also died and was buried; and in hell he lifted his eyes, being in torments, and saw Abraham afar off and Lazarus in his bosom.

And he cried and said, Father Abraham, have mercy on me, and send Lazarus that he may dip his finger in water and cool my tongue; for I am tormented in this flame. But Abraham said, Son, remember that thou in thy lifetime received good things and likewise Lazarus evil things; but now he is comforted and you are tormented. And beside all this, between us and you there is a great gulf fixed; so that they which would pass from hence to you cannot; neither can they pass to us that would come from thence. Then he said, I pray thee therefore, father Abraham, that thou wouldest send him to my father's house; for I have five brethren that he may testify unto them, lest they also come into this torment. Abraham said unto him, they have Moses and the prophets; let them hear them. And he said, nay, father Abraham; but if one went unto them from the dead, they will repent. And he said unto him, if they hear not Moses and the prophets, neither will they be persuaded through one who rose from the dead. —*Luke 16:19-31.*

How we are to live for the God-human experience and indwelling is a sacred obligation for the human spirit. From my observation, human beings have persistently failed to comply with such sacred duties, seeking nothing but earthly glory for themselves. The plethora of situations that humans encounter on this planet must not be a hindrance to the sacred duties. The consequences of neglecting the sacred duties are unimaginable. "And if thy right eye offends thee, pluck it out, and cast it from thee; for it is profitable for thee that one of thy members should perish, and not thy whole body should be cast into hell. And if thy right hand offends thee, cut it off, and cast it from thee, for it is profitable for thee that one of thy members should perish, and not that thy whole body should be cast into hell." (Matthew 5:29–30)

The above figurative expression does not mean you have to destroy any part of your body. It portrays the sacrifices one has to make for the accomplishment of our task. The performance of sacred duties is the way to be on the pathway that leads to our glory. All other roads are closed. Hell for the human soul is the soul that lacks the Spirit of God by refusing to perform our task, and tormented in the remembrance if its own memoir.

Heavenly tools for our task

The Lord's Prayer
 Our Father which art in heaven, Hallowed be thy name, Thy kingdom come; thy will be done, in earth as it is in heaven. Give us our daily bread. And forgive us our debts as we forgive our debtors. And lead us not into temptation, but deliver us from evil; for thine is the kingdom, and the power, and the glory, forever. Amen.
—Matthew 6:9-13, Luke 11:2-4

When Mother Theresa was asked what had sustained her in her earthly mission? She replied, "I pray" Jesus used this tool many times. The Lord's Prayer outlines what you must do for God and for your fellow human beings. It carries with it the portrait of our omnipresent

Father. It serves as a mirror for you to see the unity of both our heavenly and earthly relatives. It brought to our consciousness this unity in all our dealings with God and our fellow humans. The profound use of 'us' and not 'I' or 'me' silenced individualism and rejuvenated unity of human commonwealth. A deeper analysis of the Lord's Prayer portrayed us, in Jesus' view, as a group who are spiritually poor, but are aware of our low level of spiritual evolutional status. The petitions in the prayer are for those who are collectively seeking, by humble means, with the help of the Father through Jesus, to improve their spiritual level. The anticipated reward would be great.

Without any hesitation or deliberation, this model infinite prayer was given to the apostles who simply asked Jesus to teach them how to pray. What followed was the best of His teachings. The instructed prayer was unprecedented and unparallel in the history of any recorded supplication to God. Embroiled and incorporated into that prayer were spiritual words of eternal life. The central beam of the iridescent heavenly light that was released from Golgotha, like the eye of the hurricane, was focused on the Lord's Prayer. That prayer is the nucleus of the Gospel.

The Lord's Prayer is a divine universal constitution. Many nations have constitutions composed mainly of human doctrines. Most of them left God out in the cold. The Lord's Prayer is the constitution, crafted by Jesus with the Spirit of God and His own Spirit inside. The Lord's Prayer is a compendium of all the essential equipment humankind must use for our task. As I searched the Gospel for the weaponry one has to use for the development and expression of the God – human habitation, it became obvious that the best weaponry was found in the Lord's Prayer. Its introduction was the most important instructions ever given to humans for our spiritual evolution.

If you are a Christian missionary planning to go to an unknown place to spread the Gospel message, but you have not raised enough money to buy a single Bible, nay not even for yourself, what would you do? If however, you were given an opportunity to print, as many copies as you want, a page out of the Gospel for distribution, what page from the Gospel would you request? The page that contains the Gospel in a nutshell, the synopsis of the Gospel would be what most people would request. That page is the one with the record of the Lord's Prayer. (Matt 6 9:13, Luke 11 2:4). The Lord's Prayer is like a bag of tools every worker needs for the accomplishment of his task. In it, one finds the doctrines of the Father's business and all the weaponries for our spiritual evolution. In it, one finds the weaponry for the earthly life and for the authentic future life. The goal for Christianity is surmised in that prayer. The essential duty of humans toward God and humanity was revealed in a nutshell in that prayer.

The Lord's Prayer is the mirror through which we see God, His Omnipresence, His Omnipotence, His Omniscience, His love, His forgiveness and mercy, His justice, His daily care of us, His protection of us and our dependence on Him. It also reveals the portrait of Jesus and the human dependence on Him, not on what we put in our mouths, but for 'the bread of life 'we ask the Father to give us daily in that Prayer. The glory of God, His design for all humans, and the essential elements for our existence and spiritual evolution were spiritually crafted in that grand Prayer.

What was 'finished' at Golgotha would be of limited value if it failed to impact in our consciousness, the perpetual remembrance of that angelic prayer. The Golgotha spiritual events carried all the elements of the Lord's Prayer for a show, and placed them conspicuously in the human consciousness for everlasting remembrance of Jesus Christ. "We have piped unto you, and you have not danced: we have mourned to you, and you have not wept...." (Luke 7:32f.) This is our only opportunity to prove Jesus wrong. He has given us this prayer; we must not behave like our fore fathers and the people of His time. We hear the music clearly and we will dance and rejoice for the spiritual gift of this prayer. We will mourn for our low level of our spiritually. This prayer would be our comfort and we pledge to use it as spiritual tool from heaven to improve our evolutional spiritual status. The Lord's Prayer revealed what is required of us for perfection.

The Lord's Prayer also carries with it the portrait of humanity, our weaknesses, our dependency on the Father and on Jesus, and our intrinsic capability to love and forgive one another. The Master of wisdom, without your knowing it, has, through this prayer, accomplished part of His mission for humanity. You have pledged, through that prayer, to love God, to love Jesus and to love one another. You have pledged without realizing it, to fulfill Jesus' two great commandments. To seek to do the will of God as is done in heaven, is your pledge to love and obey Him. To seek to forgive those that trespass against you without any qualification is the pledge to love your fellow humans. To ask God to give us our daily bread is you bold request to love Jesus who portrayed Himself as the bread of life. The petitions using 'us' instead of 'I' or 'me' are an expression of your intrinsic love for humanity that you do not even know you possess. The Lord's Prayer is the way to regain your pre-existent angelic attributes with perfection in God-Jesus-human bondage and expression, just like the way it was from the beginning.

The apostrophe 'Our Father' reveals God as a Universal Father. He is no longer just the Father of Jesus, or the Jews or the Christians. He is the Father of all irrespective of your nationality, gender, race or culture. The moment you decide to pray to God implies your desire to have access to this Father in heaven. Many people are sure, God would hear their prayer. You don't need to pay anybody to pray for you. If you did that, please request a refund. When you pray, His Spirit is there with you if you have created the right environment for that to happen. You do not need to go to Jerusalem to pray. Jesus told the Samaritan woman; "Woman, believe me, the hour cometh, when you shall neither in this mountain, nor yet at Jerusalem, worship the Father. But the hour cometh and now is, when the worshippers shall worship the Father in spirit and in truth; for the Father seeks such to worship Him." (John 4:21, 23.)

The Lord's Prayer that many think is a 'common' prayer is not so. It carries with it the triad of infinite faith: infinite love for God, infinite love for Jesus, and infinite love for all humanity. On this infinite faith, rest all things that are eternal and external. The infinite faith as reveled in the Lord's Prayer is the *modus operandi* through which God speaks and control all things. Believe in God and in His power to grant you all your petitions. Do not ask Him to save a terminal cancer patient from death. Rather ask Him to make the transition of that patient to His Kingdom, to be peaceful and painless. The Lord's Prayer provided the weaponry for the realization and expression of the will of God that was proclaimed as a constant reminder of our duty to God and to humanity. The promised reward is also awesome. "And all things whatsoever ye shall ask in prayer believing, ye shall receive." (Matthew 21:22)

Moral and Ethical tools for our Task

The earthly weaponry for victory comes in many forms. Many nations have organized their military into multiple divisions: the infantry, the air force, the navy, the marines, and Intel under one military commander with the head of the Joint Chiefs of Staff as the second in command. In America, the headquarters for military operations is the Pentagon. This arrangement varies in many nations, but the basic infrastructure is the same. They all have at their disposal the military arsenal for victory. Likewise, Jesus of Nazareth provided to all humanity (whoever would like to use it) all the tools that are needed for victory but for a different victory: eternal life of the resurrected human souls that manifested in the divine Trinity with the Spirit if Christ and His Father, as I have outlined throughout this treatise.

As portrayed in many movies and in real life, combatants were allowed to choose the weapon of their choice for combat. Likewise, all humans have the freewill to choose his or her weaponry for the spiritual victory. Military blunders and inability to use the weapons properly can and have resulted in defeat and death of the soldiers. Likewise, the inability to use the tools assembled by Jesus of Nazareth can lead to spiritual blindness, inability to find the way to God, inability to develop and manifest the images of God, inability to know even what the will of God is, inability to love one another and inability to be a component of the divine Trinity. The end result is spiritual death of the human soul and rejection by God. The twelve blessed holy men that I have frequently called the twelve merchants of Light or the twelve precious jewels of His kingdom selected their weaponry very well. They selected weaponry for loyalty, obedience, devotion, service, unselfishness, justice, peace, compassion, and love that extended to the enemies who pursued them from one city to another and in the end killed all of them, except John. They did not fight back with physical swords. The weaponry they selected guaranteed victory, and today we are the beneficiaries of their labor.

Paul had a glimpse of the spiritual arsenals for victory as shown by his letter to the Ephesians: "Wherefore take unto you the whole armor of God that you may be able to withstand in the evil day, and having done all, to stand. Stand therefore, having your loins girt about with truth, and having on the breastplate of righteousness; and your feet shod with the preparation of the gospel of peace, above all, taking the shield of faith, wherewith you shall be able quench all the fiery darts of the wicked, and take the helmet of salvation, and the sword of the Spirit, which is the word of God." (Ephesians 6:13–17)

There are many things in the Gospel of Jesus of Nazareth that are still beyond our comprehension but are revealed to different generations, as the Father considers appropriate. We must stop now to take a survey of what is displayed in the storage (Gospel of Jesus of Nazareth) that we must use as a guide to live like God planned for us and how we are to live in order to guarantee spiritual victory. I must advise you that in looking at the display there is nothing in it that will help you to be a millionaire or help you build your dream house. There is nothing there that will make any nation the master of the universe or any leader the custodian of the world.

Today, we want earthly possessions, power, and an earthly kingdom—all the things Jesus rejected. A survey of some of the moral and ethical weapons that we can choose from to use is:

The Weaponry of Love
A new commandment I give you; Love one another. As I have loved you, so you must love one another. —John 13:34

Love your enemies, do good to them who hate you; bless them that curse you, and pray for them which despitefully use you. —Luke 6:27

The human soul first must learn how to use its most potent weapons: love that extended to the enemy that Jesus used during His mission was epitomized at Golgotha. To have knowledge of the spiritual tools is not enough. We must apply them and practice with them for the perfection of our souls to help God accomplish His task for the glory that awaits all humanity. The future of humanity must be built on this vision. Jesus's commandments of love, forgiveness, and obedience to the will of God are reflections of His own identity: a humble servant in love with humanity and His Father.

Jesus was a humble Lord among both friends and enemies. He was a Lord who sought no fame or earthly glory. He was the Son of God who forgot self and rejected all earthly powers. He was the Christ who in order to execute that service sought nothing but absolute obedience to the will of His Father. Jesus said, "Learn of Me. I am meek and humble." We must learn from Jesus what our duty is to man: the unconditional love of one another. For our duty to God, we must "seek the kingdom of God and His righteousness (His will)." Jesus executed the Father's business as if everything depended on Him. We too must work and execute our part of the Father's business as if everything depended on us. What Jesus accomplished at Golgotha would be of no value if we fail to comprehend those spiritual events and apply them in the spiritual evolution of our human souls.

Love for one another, even for the enemy, is the most potent spiritual weapon ever offered to humanity. However, many people and nations of the world never use this weapon. Two thousand years ago, Jesus constructed that commandment of love that extended to the enemy in Palestine. On many occasions, humans have picked up this weapon only to cast it away. Look at Palestine today where this precious weaponry was crafted; many attempts were made to solve the conflicts in that region, but none succeeded. They have continued to fight, and the conflict will continue until they love their neighbors. Jesus knew this perpetual conflict was going to happen and gave them the only solution: "love thy neighbor" and the commandments "love one another" and "love your enemies." There is no other solution. They have tried war; it did not work. They have tried keeping their opponents in prison camps; it did not work. They have tried United Nation mediation; it did not work. Today as I was writing this section, the news broke that Israel and Syria were holding a meeting aimed at resolving their conflicts by peaceful means. Will it work? No, because they still hate each other. The Hamas and the Israeli have agreed to stop fighting and seek peace. Will they succeed? The answer is no for this simple reason: the two brothers hate each other. The descendants of Ishmael and Isaac hate one another. The element of love is not there. It is my hope that the future generations in that region decide to solve the conflict with this priceless weapon of love that costs nothing. They must add this weaponry to whatever other methods they use in solving this perpetual problem and put a smile on the faces of the spirits of Abraham, Isaac, Ishmael, Esau, and Jacob.

Jesus of Nazareth laid the foundation stone of love as directed by God. This is the tool for victory. Weapons of mass destruction are not the tools for victory. Human beings have built up so much destructive weaponry that it would be impossible to get rid of it all without destroying the entire planet Earth and its habitants.

Human love is very peculiar. It is variable and most of the time unsustainable. Many people have written textbooks and dissertations on love. We do not need to do that. The basic principle of love is simple: "to do unto others as we will like them to do unto us." It is what God would like us to do. It is what Jesus who gave us that commandment would like us to do. It is what we must do. It is the way to God. The world is in a mess today because we have not tried this weaponry. It was in a mess yesterday and will be tomorrow if we do not try this weaponry. We must add a weapon to whatever else we are using today. With that as the objective and knowing fully that God cannot and will not release us from that responsibility, we must use that tool in solving conflicts.

For almost three years, Jesus of Nazareth went around Palestine demonstrating these many aspects of His love and God's love. We must emulate those examples. The way to show love is not to seek revenge. The simple act of not seeking revenge or justice for a wrong done to us is love. That is what God wants us to do and that is what He does.

Revenge has led to many wars. We sought revenge after the Sept. 11, 2001, terror attack involving the Twin Towers in New York. It is true that many innocent people were killed. However, by seeking revenge, we lost men and many innocent women, and children—from Iraqi, Afghan, and coalition forces. We knew of the collateral damage, yet we embarked on seeking revenge. Many spiritual leaders, who would have brought forward the weaponry of love that extended to the enemy, gave their blessing for the war. Many of them, as they gathered with the military leaders in the big Cathedral in Washington, said nothing as if they never knew about the existence of this weaponry that was crafted in Palestine. I have to reiterate that whatever weaponry we have for resolving conflicts, like dialogues and negotiations, we must add the weaponry of true love: "love your enemies, do good to them that hate you, Bless them that curse you, and pray for them which despitefully use you." (Luke 6:27–2). To love God, you must first love your fellow human beings, even your enemies. As Jesus loved His enemies, you too must love your enemies. To love Jesus, you must first love your fellow humans. If you do not love the human being whom you can see, how then can you love God whom you cannot see? The journey to God starts with the journey to your fellow humans. All other roads to the Father, to Jesus, and to the angels are closed. If you have obeyed this commandment, you will be on the right path to the Father that will lead you to experience the ecstasy of the spirituality that Jesus Christ introduced to the world.

The Weaponry of Compassion

In my observation, humans all over the world have bottled up the spirit of compassion in a genie jar. It takes catastrophic events like Hurricane Katrina, tsunamis, the Burma cyclones, and destructive earthquakes to release that spirit. After such events, it goes back to the same jar. Humans are very compassionate when such events occur, revealing in essence what spirit they are made of. The question is why don't we manifest this spirit every day? We are capable, but we do not. The wisdom of Jesus Christ was revealed in that timeless story of the Good Samaritan. (Luke 10:30)_The compassionate spirit of the Good Samaritan never went back to the genie bottle after taking care of the injured stranger. He did not just walk away as we do after our initial support of catastrophic victims from the man who was robbed. The Good Samaritan gave more money to take care of him and then promised to come back and pledge more support. Once that spirit of compassion came out, the Good Samaritan took the genie bottle and cast it into the bottomless pit. We too must do the same. To the Good Samaritan, the injured man was a child of God worth being cared for and loved. He did not ask for his nationality, religion, or race. Today many people would suggest that the Good Samaritan was an angel, that humans are incapable of such compassion. The truth is that there are some Good Samaritans among us. The world needs everybody to be a Good Samaritan...

Weaponry of Repentance

The supreme purpose of human life is to be a participant in the Father's business. The effulgence of our souls, when developed and activated, enjoys the infinite experience with God. As narrated in the Gospel, the Prodigal son remembered that experience and decided to return home to the Father. The first step he took in this process was a change of heart: repentance. The record in the Gospel of Mark revealed that Jesus started His earthly ministry with the call for repentance: "The time is fulfilled, and the kingdom of God is at hand; Repent ye, and believe in the Gospel." (Mark 1:15) The imprints of the doctrines of repentance with the supported parables are all in the Gospel of Jesus.

The Weaponry of Forgiveness

The plea to "Forgive us our trespasses as we forgive others who trespass against us" is the only petition in the angelic prayer that was followed later by an explanatory note as was written: "For if you forgive men when they sin against you, your heavenly Father will also forgive you. But if you do not forgive men their sins, your Father will not forgive your sins" (Matthew 6:14-15) A deeper revelation of 'those who trespass against us' and our expected responses are alarming. "But I tell you who hear me, Love your enemies, do good to those who hate you, bless those that curse you, pray to those who mistreat you. If someone strikes you on one cheek, turn to him the other also. If someone takes your cloak, do not stop him from taking your tunic." (Luke 6 27-29) Jesus' instruction is that we must not only forgive those who trespass against us, but we must also show love and empathy. Why? The answer is simple: this is what we must do as we seek God human bondage and experience. God would forgive all our sins if we forgive those that trespass against us. Peter had asked Jesus, "Lord, how often shall my brother sin against me, and I forgive him? As many as seven times?" Jesus replied to Peter that he must forgive, not seven times but seventy times seven. (Matthew 18:21-22) The spiritual Cross would lose its heavenly luminous rays and would not find any heart to awaken for the Father – human experience if it had failed to forgive. When Jesus was on the cross, Jesus had asked His Father, "Father, forgive them for they do not know what they do."

The weaponry of forgiveness is one of the most important of all the spiritual weapons. It carries in its flagship the elements of loving one another, kindness, mercy in victory, self-denial, mortification of your appetite for worldly things, compassion, charity, sympathy, love, multicultural respect, and tolerance of all religions. It is displayed in the spiritual storehouse on a tripod of anti-racism, anti-hatred, and anti-wickedness.

Forgiveness was very important to Jesus. This is one of the deep mysteries of His personality. Where did He get that experience of forgiveness? It must be from the Father: "Verily, verily, I say unto you, The Son can do nothing of himself, but what he sees the Father do for what things soever He doeth, these also doeth the Son likewise. For the Father loveth the Son, and showeth him all things that Himself doeth; and will show Him greater works than these, that you may marvel." (John 5:19–20)

We must invite the Spirits of the Father and Jesus to come into our hearts so that we too may have this experience of forgiveness, compassion, repentance and love that extended to the enemy. I must warn you that that experience carry with it great responsibilities and sacrifices. You will be sacrificed according to the courage and purity of your heart. However, let that experience be the weaponry you must use to resist the evil that is always in human form. It eats and drinks like us, moves like us, wears clothes like us, sleeps like us, walks like us, functions physiologically like us, and has friends like us. However, when it strikes, innocent victims are sent to their graves or refugee camps. Unsuspecting victims are kidnapped, many are rendered homeless, the poor are exploited, banks are raided, and lifetime savings and pensions are wiped out. Young men and women are deployed to fight this evil. However, your spiritual weaponry of forgiveness is the only effective tool against this monster. God has used it successfully. Jesus learned from the Father and used it for victory. We too must use it to fight this horrendous evil. Do we have any other choice? The answer is no, except if we want to be "delivered to the tormentors" until our hearts are broken and until we forgive our fellow humans their trespasses. People never truly become great until, with purity of heart, he or she forgives all who trespass against him or her. That is the supreme test. Those who are deepened by the experience of forgiveness rise triumphant to an infinite union with the Father and the Spirit of Jesus. For the consecration of that divine intimacy, it would not be necessary for Jesus to wash your feet with water. With His help, and you would not have done it without Him, you have carried with you the spiritual fire of forgiveness to His tabernacle, ready for the holy global banquet and rightly called "the child of God." This is salvation! This is the life Jesus came to give you and give it to you abundantly.

The evil-driven and fear-stricken world in which we live today, the unabated strife and competition for power and wealth, the massive buildup of destructive weaponry, the violence against one another, marginalization, human trafficking and slavery, genocide, rigged elections, and the enslavement of women, children, and the weak show that we are ignorant of what was finished at Golgotha. It carries with it the hallmark of the poverty of our human souls. Like a plague, evil has spread all over the planet. What must we do?

The time has come when we must realize that human lives are more important than minerals, oil, money, power, or conquest; that virtue is not hedonism but rather a way of life toward authentic life. The beatitudes and the sermon on the mount, as outlined in the Gospel, does not lead to earthliness but a heavenly state of perfected happiness and blessedness through the education of our souls. Jesus's message is divine in its origin and ecumenical in its dispensation of the message of the words of God.

Come unto me, all ye that labor and are heavy laden, and I will give you rest. Take my yoke upon you, and learn of me, for I am meek and lowly in heart, and ye shall find rest unto your souls. For my yoke is easy and my burden is light.
—Matthew 11:28–30

I must confess that the yoke cast upon us is not easy. However, with His help, the burden would be light. To learn from Jesus is to learn humility, compassion, mercy, meekness, gentility, and unquestioned obedience and to be a tireless servant of God but above all to rely on God for all things. We have depicted the life of Jesus as the image of divine essence and as the effulgence of the glory and wisdom of God. The truth is that all of Jesus's characteristics were what He wants us to emulate so that we too may manifest the image of God and allow the Spirit of God to find its abode in our hearts. We must follow Jesus to God. Jesus's way to God was uncharted and freely chosen. Jesus said, "Learn of me."

To learn how Jesus developed the infinite God-Jesus experience, we must trust in God and in His powers. We must love God and all humans. We must practice self-denial or mortification of our appetites for earthly things like those that the twelve apostles did. We must want nothing, seek nothing, and depend on nothing earthly. We must be patient in tribulation; and trust in nothing but the righteousness of God and His love and plan for us. We must strive with all out heart and soul to practice mercy, forgiveness, love, justice, being nonjudgmental, purity of heart, integrity, incorruptibility, honesty, and above all humility, and we must subject ourselves to the will of God like Jesus did. To be humble is to share with the poor and have goodwill toward all people because it is the right thing to do. Jesus and His Father would do the same.

Love is forgiveness even before hearing "I am sorry, please forgive me" from whoever offended you. To love one another is to take Jesus's yoke upon us; to be a servant for humanity and God; to be one who is willing to do His will, love the world, hope for the hopeless, show compassion for all who are suffering, and love our neighbors as we have loved ourselves. This is how we must live.

"Blessed is that servant, whom his lord, when he comes shall find him or her, a faithful and wise servant." —Matthew 24:46

EPILOGUE

"IT IS FINISHED" No, it is not over yet. What happened in Jerusalem and at Golgotha had an end. However, the manifestations continue. The Father and Jesus positioned themselves to draw people of all nations to enter into the temple the Jesus built without hands on the human hearts, made possible by the spiritual events at Golgotha. The gates are open and people of all ages to worship the Father and Jesus Christ in spirit and in truth. They will continue to do so to the end of time. Jesus and His Father had planted, "the mustard seed, which indeed is the least of all seeds; but when it is grown, it is the greatest among herbs, and becameth a tree, so that the birds of the air come and lodge in the branches thereof." (Matthew 13:31-32) Humankind in this current age and in future, will continue to lodge under the shadow of it.

The earthly history of humanity is essentially the history of human creation and the promised God-human indwelling and experience: the true divine Trinity of the human soul with the Father and Jesus Christ. This is the epicenter of the Christian religion. That divine Trinity of the human souls with the Father and Jesus Christ is the spiritual bond that unites all human souls. Christ Himself predicted this: "If I be lifted up from the earth, I will draw all men unto me." Under the divine influence of the invisible Father, Jesus was lifted up from the earth to the cross. He will draw all people to God to be under one fold and one divine Lord who reigns and controls all things.

The spindle of our Christian spirituality rotates on the infinite bond of our spiritualized immortal human soul with the Spirit of the Father and the glorified Spirit of Jesus Christ. The earthly manifestations of the life of that soul is love, joy, peace, compassion, long suffering, gentleness, humility, meekness, obedience of God's holy laws, avoidance of all things that are evil. The ignorance of the nature of human soul and God's design for humanity and what was accomplished at Golgotha are the basic causes for what could eventually precipitate our downfall The human souls must be educated, not just in advances in science and technology but also in multiculturalism, religious tolerance, compassion and love for one another.

Finally, brethren, whatever things are true, whatever things are honest, whatever things are just, whatever things are pure, whatever things are lovely, whatever things are of good report, if there be any virtue, and if there be any praise, think of these things. And the peace of God, which passeth all understanding, shall keep your heart and minds through Jesus Christ. —Paul, Philippians 4:8,7

Our souls are in deep sleep mode. They are like inert objects or what Michelangelo described as "an angel in the stone."

I saw an angel in the stone, and I carved to set it free. —Michelangelo

We must strive to awaken them with the spiritual power of Jesus that was released at Golgotha, to set them free, to seek for the truth and manifest it. Humankind has closed its hearts to the Spirit of the Father, which is trying to express itself through us. Today, the road to harvest what was planted at Golgotha is filled with potholes. We must start repairing them, so that we can get to Golgotha, to find the truth of what was accomplished. The inscriptions on the fourteen Stations of the Cross that are now displayed on the wall of our religious institutions must be replaced with inscriptions of the laws of the Father and the two great commandments of Jesus Christ. Jesus instructed us not to weep for Him but to rejoice. We must rejoice for what He did for humanity and the victory He won for His Father. The glorified Spirit of Jesus is hedged in at Golgotha by human doctrines and dogmas. We must take the fence down, to set the Spirit of Christ free, to find its abode in human hearts. The entrance to the holy Golgotha or what we may call the door of the cross is blocked by mammon and the cares of this world. "No man can serve two masters; for either he will hate the one and love the other; or else he will hold to the one, and despise the other. Ye cannot serve God and mammon." (Matthew 6:24, Luke 16:13)

We must remove the blockade that was placed at the entrance by mammon, so that humankind could enter to serve God and see the blessings and the glory of the cross. Humankind, as our custom is, by much questionable rhetoric on why Jesus was crucified and died, had erected a shield that prevented the iridescent heavenly rays of the spiritual light from Golgotha to shine on the Gospel of Jesus. We must take that shield off, so that the light from Golgotha that is not from the sun or moon will shine on His Gospel to reveal its messages in its true spiritual form. We have displayed the wooden, plastic, and metallic crosses in all Christian institutions, in our homes, and carried them with us wherever we go. We must transform all of them into spiritual crosses, carry the memory of what was finished at Golgotha in our hearts, to educate, illuminate and activate our immature souls, and help prepare them for the glory that awaits humanity. This generation, as the generation before us, has turned off the light of life from Golgotha, and we are drifting like sheep without a shepherd. We must call upon the Good Shepherd to give us that light of life, rekindle that light in our hearts, and direct us to the path of the truth.

Truth is elusive, it is like a butterfly. You have to search for it. —Veda

The truth is indeed elusive. However, I hope that this treatise will guide you to the temple of the truth built by Jesus for His Father so that you may find the truth and bask in the light from the Spirit that built the temple. Golgotha is the classroom where the divine master, Jesus Christ, taught the mystery of life. It was the place where Jesus revealed Himself and the divine origin of His words and works. It was the place where the authentic imagery of God, our Father and the proof of His existence were revealed. Through the spiritual events at Golgotha, God bestowed His best blessings to all humanity. All who believe in Jesus and wish to follow Him must take up the cross and enter the temple at Golgotha that Jesus built without hands for the Father, our God.

It is you who must walk through the narrow but straight path that leads to the temple. It is you who must enter into that temple to be educated on the knowledge of God and learn how to do the will of God as it is done in heaven. It is you whom God is creating that must bond with Him. It is you the prisoner, released from the shackles of the mammon, saved and protected by Jesus Christ from the influence of the Roman gods and goddesses and other gods that must be united with Him to receive the gift of the living waters of everlasting life: "whosoever drinketh of the water that I shall give him, shall never thirst; but the water that I shall give him shall be in him a well of water springing up into everlasting life." (John 4:14) The Spirit of His Father, the Lord of Lords, the owner of the temple, whose Spirit is in the temple, says come to me and abide in me. The glorified Spirit of the risen Jesus Christ says, come into the temple I built for my Father and learn about me, for as I have revealed the vision of my Father that you may have knowledge of Him and I too will reveal to you who I am.

The temple of the truth built for the Father by Jesus without human hands, is in your heart. *"Know you not that ye are the temple of God, and that the Spirit of God dwells in you."* (1 Corinthians 3:16) The foundation of that temple is the fathomless, boundless love of the Father and Jesus Christ that is limitless. Inside the Holy of the Holies of that temple, you will not find any gold and silver or any graven images to worship or to offer sacrifices. Again, all you will find is a glimpse of the iridescent light of the spirituality that Jesus introduced to the world and the infinite love of the Father for humanity. This temple of God is invisible. However, some people see this temple in the hearts of people in refugee camps, defeated enemies, the poor, the just and the unjust, the good and the bad and have clothed themselves with the garments of love, compassion, and forgiveness, mercy and have entered and worshipped in that temple. They are the exemplary Christians

Let Thy will be done on earth as in heaven. —Matthew 6:10

Afterwards

Pentecost-the Sign from Heaven

But the Comforter, which is the Holy Ghost, whom the Father
will send in my name, he shall teach you all things, and bring
to your remembrance, whatsoever I have said unto you."
—John 14:26

The Jews had demanded a heavenly sign from Jesus to prove Himself the Christ, the Son of the Blessed. They wanted to "see, and know, and consider, and understand together, that the hand of the Lord hath done this, and the Holy One of Israel hath created it." (Isaiah 4:20) Jesus knew what He would do. He gave different responses to the demand for a sign from heaven whenever that question surfaced. Jesus maintained His policy of silence and secrecy on how the sign would manifest. To the public, Jesus maintained that they would see "signs and wonders as to believe." (John 4:48) However, when in private with His apostles, Jesus repeatedly promised that He would send the Holy Ghost to them. The apostles did not know how that Spirit would come or how it would affect their lives and those who believe in Jesus. The everlasting sign from heaven must be given as His Father designed it.

Timing was very important in the execution of the Father's business. The crucifixion of Jesus was carried out during the week of the

Passover feast. The Father and Jesus Christ wanted the people who came to Jerusalem from many parts of the world to witness that event. The sign from heaven must also be given at a time when people from many parts of the world would come again to Jerusalem for an occasion to witness the glorious event. The Father and His Son waited until the time was fulfilled. The Pentecost feast, a festival of thanks for the harvest, and remembered as the time when the Law was given to the Israelites on Sinai was celebrated on the fiftieth day from the Passover feast. Jesus had told His apostles not to leave Jerusalem. The resurrection of Jesus was a prelude to His demonstration of the sign from heaven that the Jews demanded from Him to prove His divinity and the divine origin of His work.

Nevertheless, I tell you the truth; it is expedient for you that I go away; for if I go not away, the Comforter will not come unto you; but if I depart, I will send him unto you. —John 14:7

The Holy Ghost came on the day of Pentecost. "And when the day of the Pentecost was fully come, they (the apostles) were all with one accord in one place. And suddenly there came a sound from heaven as of a rushing mighty wind, and it filled the entire house where they were sitting. And there appeared unto them cloven tongues like as of fire, and it filled the entire house where they were sitting. And there appeared unto them cloven tongues like as of fire, and it sat upon each of them. And they were filled with the Holy Ghost, and began to speak with other tongues, as the Spirit gave them utterance." (Acts 2:1-4)

That glorified Spirit of Christ that would guide the human soul in all its future evolutionary processes was released in full power on the day of Pentecost. "Verily I say unto you, that there be some of them that stand here, which shall not taste death, till they have seen the kingdom of God come with power." (Mark 9:1) That power manifested again as was demonstrated by the apostles on the day of Pentecost.

The apostles did not know where the power that sat upon them came from, but they knew it came from their Master, who was crucified, died, rose from the dead and ascended to heaven. That Spirit remained in them and guided them in all they did for their Master and for humanity. On the day of Pentecost, the apostles saw the sign from heaven. The Jews and the people from other nations, who were present at Jerusalem, witnessed the manifestations of the sign from heaven and were amazed. They knew that a spectacular event had occurred. "Now when this was noised abroad, the multitude (Jews, devout men, out of every nation under heaven) came together, and was confounded, because that every man heard them speak in his own language. And they were all amazed and marveled, saying one to another, Behold, are not all these which speak Galileans? And how hear we every man in our own tongue, were in we were born?" (Acts 2:5-8)

Jesus Christ and His Father, kept their promise. "But wait for the promise of the Father, which ye heard of me. For John truly baptized with water, but ye shall be baptized with the Holy Ghost not many days hence." (Acts 1:4-5) On the day of Pentecost, when the Spirit of the risen Jesus manifested again, the apostles received the promised power. That sign from heaven, as requested by the Jews, was divulged not just to the apostles and the Jews but also to the world. The Jews of Jesus's time, who were able to "discern the face of the sky; but cannot discern the signs of the times," (Matthew 16:3) again were not able to discern, that what happened to the apostles on the day of Pentecost, was the long-awaited sign from heaven that they demanded from Jesus to prove that that He is the Christ, the Son of the Blessed.

For many centuries, many Christians perceived that the resurrection of Jesus was the sign from heaven. The manner in which the Spirit that came upon the apostles, the immediate and the subsequent manifestations of its power, even as of today, bear witness that the promise of the Father, was the sign from heaven. It was an event that empowered the souls of the apostles and since then, had continued to empower the souls of all that believe in Jesus Christ and His Father. It gave humankind confidence that when we pray, that we have direct access to the glorified Spirit of Christ and His Father. Its conception was spiritual. Its dispensation was from heaven. It opened a door for all who are able to receive that glorified Spirit of Jesus that came back on the day of Pentecost, to enter and see what had been hidden from wise men and the Prophets, but revealed only to the apostles. Its manifestations since that Spirit was endowed to humankind on the day of Pentecost have been spectacular and extraordinary.

Many who truly received that Spirit have manifested the glory and the blessings of the Holy Ghost. Because of the manifestations of the power of Spirit that came, Paul, who also was given his own sign from heaven, in the presence of witnesses, and subsequently received his own gift of the Spirit, declared, "Jesus to be the Son of God, with power according to the Spirit of Holiness, by the resurrection from the dead." (Romans 1:4) The gift of the spirit of God through Christ cannot be purchased with money. Simon the magician thought that he could buy it with money, but Peter rebuked him; "Thy money perish with thee, because thou hast thought that the gift of God may be purchased with money." (Acts of the Apostles 8:20)

The authenticity and the divine origin of Jesus's words and deeds were validated by the gift of the promised Holy Ghost from heaven. On the day of the Pentecost, there were one hundred and twenty people who believed in Jesus Christ. Today, there are more than two billion Christians! The Spiritual Cross is still revealing some of its mysteries and would continue to do so to the end of time. That gift of the Holy Ghost will live in our hearts forever. It would accomplish and manifest all the divine imprints it carries along with it. With its power, we can imitate the apostles. If we obey all the commandments of Jesus Christ, we will, like the apostles on the day of Pentecost, obtain the gift of this living water that will help us understand and remind us of the teachings of Christ and allow us to be benefactors of what was accomplished at Golgotha.

The life of Jesus Christ is now our life to live as He did. The love He bestowed on us is now our own love to show the world by loving one another. The "cup" the Father gave Him is now our cup. We must drink from our cup by seeking after the kingdom of God and His righteousness and by implementing our own task in the Father's business. The cross of mercy, love for the Father and humanity, forgiveness, and obedience to the will of the Father that Jesus carried to Golgotha is now our cross to carry. We must carry our own cross and ride in our own chariot to eternal life with the glorified Spirit of Jesus Christ. The Father-Jesus bondage and experience is now the bondage we must seek for our glory and to be a component of that divine union. His Father's business that Jesus referred to when He was twelve years of age is now our business that we must carry on to the end of time. The leaven that the woman took and hid in three measures of meals until all are leavened is now ready for consumption. Enjoy this bread from God, given to humanity through Jesus.

My Father gives you the true bread from heaven. For the bread of God is He who came from heaven and gives life unto the world. —John 6:32-33

This bread was fully leavened and baked at Golgotha. We must eat it every day to speed up the spiritual evolution of our souls and be participants of the great spiritual evolution designed by the Father for our glory.

Never give in; never give in nothing, great or small, large or petty. Never give in, except to convictions of honor and good sense. Never give in to force. Never yield to apparently overwhelming might of the enemy. —Winston Churchill, 1941

Never allow any other spirit to direct your soul. The Father and Jesus Christ control eternal life and those spiritual gifts are given to whomever they want. Never allow any human being to act as an intermediary for you in the process of your journey to eternal life. Jesus gave humanity the greatest liberty. Celebrate the glory of that freedom every day by obedience to the will of God and the commands of Jesus Christ. Seek after the divine Trinity of your soul with the Father and Jesus Christ with all your might and with all your strength. Give to humanity and never stop giving until your bones feel the pain of giving. Carry with you the precious bag of the spiritual tools-love that extended to the enemy, forgiveness, mercy, compassion, obedience to the will of the Father and the commandments of Christ-from Golgotha to help you in this endeavor.

"I have yet many things to say unto you, but you cannot hear them now." (John 16:12)

Jesus still has many things to reveal to us. His policy of secrecy and silence as directed by the Father and His refusal to fully reveal Himself still persists. It would seem that this policy made the interpretation of who Jesus is and what He accomplished in Jerusalem and at Golgotha imperceptible and elusive. But Jesus told His apostles that "there is nothing covered that shall not be revealed; and hid, that shall not be known." (Matthew 10:26)

We have looked behind the veil of the cross. Today we have some knowledge of who Jesus is and the objectives of the Father's business. However, the cross is still holding back many things. As they manifest (it may take centuries), many things will be revealed to humanity and their interpretations will be perceptible at the time determined by God who reigns and control all things.

Today the glorified Spirit of Christ is still using the same tools He used at Golgotha to tackle obstacles to the Father's business. He will continue to execute the Father's business with the manifesto of His crucifixion, death, and resurrection, bearing with it His potent weapons of love, forgiveness, and unblemished obedience to the will of God until all that the Father has created participate in the divine Trinity of the human souls with Him and His Father and are subject to God. Jesus had said, "I have overcome the world." However, along the way for this promised glorious end in the execution of the unstoppable Father's business, more gods and goddesses would be silenced, more temples would be cleansed, and more fig trees would be cursed for not bearing fruits. As it was in the past and as it is today and will be tomorrow, the "axe is laid unto the root of the trees; every tree, therefore, which bringeth not forth good fruit, is hewn down, and cast into fire." (Luke 3:9)

The Father's business is still going on. It is like, "the seed which a man cast into the ground, and should sleep, and rise night and day, and the seed should spring and grow up, he knoweth not how. For the earth bringeth forth fruit of herself; first the blade, then the ear, after that the full corn in the ear. But when the fruit is brought forth, immediately he putteth in the sickle, because the harvest is come." (Mark 4:26-29" The growth of the Father's business is irrepressible. It will increase and expand worldwide, bearing with it the flagship of the cross, decorated with the everlasting words of God, the Father, introduced to humanity by Jesus Christ. Allow Jesus to resurrect in your heart and feel His presence. Jesus opened a spiritual door for all mankind. That door leads to the spiritual world of His Father, who reigns and controls all things, both in heaven and on earth. Do not be afraid to enter to know what is behind it. Enter with your sickle, for the harvest is plenteous. Be a participant in the Father's business in preparation for the glory that awaits all human souls. May your immortal spirit shine like the early morning star in the firmament of the everlasting Kingdom of His Father, our God.

It Is Finished.

BIBLIOGRAPHY

Adams, Marilyn M. *Horrendous Evils and the Goodness of God*. Ithaca: Cornell UP, 1999.

Anderson, Hugh, ed. *Jesus*. Englewood Cliffs: Prentice-Hall, Inc., 1967.

Aulen, Gustaf. *Dag Hammarskjold's White Book*. Philadelphia: Fortress Press, 1969.

Barclay, William. *Jesus as They Saw Him*. Grand Rapids: William B. Eerdmans Company, 1962.

Bornkamm, Günther. *Jesus of Nazareth*. Trans. Irene McLuskey and Fraser McLuskey. Minneapolis: Fortress P, 1995.

Brown, Raymond E. *The Death of the Messiah*. Vol. 2. New York: Doubleday, 1994.

Burton, Trochmorton Jr. *Gospel Parallels*. Nashville: Thomas Nelson Publishers, 1979.

Carus, Paul. *The Gospel of Buddha*. Chicago: Carus Company, 2004.

Cooper, Terry D. *Dimensions of Evil*. Minneapolis: Fortress P, 2007.

Davies, Oliver, trans. *Eckhart: Selected Writings*. London: Penguin Books, 1994.

Emerson, Harry Fosdick. *The Man from Nazareth*. New York: Harper and Brothers, 1949.

Enumah, Festus. MD. *The Innocent Blood and Judas Iscariot*. Guardian Books: Canada, 2002.

Fallows, Samuel Rt. Rev. *Bible Encyclopedia and Scriptural Dictionary*. Chicago: The Howard-Severance Company, 1907.

Forde, Gerhard. *On Being a Theologian of the Cross*. Grand Rapids: William B. Eerdmans Comp., 1997.

Goguel, Maurice. *Jesus and the Origin of Christianity*. Vols. 1 & 2. New York: Harper Torchbooks, 1960.

Gordon, D. Kaufman. *In Face of Mystery*. Cambridge: Harvard University Press, 1995.

Häring, Bernard. *The Law of Christ*. Trans. Edwin G. Kaiser. Westminster: The Newman P, 1963.

Harnack, Adolf. *What is Christianity?* New York: Harper & Brothers Publishers, 1957.

Hengel, Martin. *Crucifixion*. Philadelphia: Fortress P, 1977.

Hick, John. *Death and Eternal Life*. Louisville: Westminster/John Knox P, 1994.

Hoenig, Sidney B. *The Great Sanhedrin*. Philadelphia: Bloch Publishing Co. 1953.

The Holy Bible, Original King James Version. Gordonsville: Dugan Publishers Inc., 1985.

Jeremias, Joachim. *Jerusalem in Time of Jesus*. Philadelphia: Fortress Press, 1969.

Kittay, Eva F. *Metaphor*. Oxford: Clarendon P, 1989.

Lakoff, George, and Mark Johnson. *Metaphors We Live By*. Chicago: University of Chicago P, 1980.

Lockyer, Herbert. *All the Messiah Prophecies of the Bible*. Grand Rapids: Zondervan Publishing House, 1960.

McInerny, D. Q. *Being Logical*. New York: Random House, 2004.

Meeks, Wayne A., ed. *The Writings of St. Paul*. New York: W. W. Norton & Company, Inc., 1972.

Nelson-Pallmeyer. *Jesus against Christianity*. Harrisburg, Penn.: Trinity Press International, 2001.

Pelikan, Jaroslav. *Jesus Through the Centuries*. New York: Harper & Row, 1985.

Richards, Lawrence O. *The Word Bible Handbook*. Waco: Word, Inc., 1982.

Sanday, William. *The International Critical Commentary on the Holy Scripture of the Old and New Testaments*. New York: Charles Scribners Sons, 1920.

Schillebeeckx, Edward. *Jesus: An experiment in Christology.* New York: Seabury, 1979.

Sheen, Fulton J. *Life of Christ.* New York: Image Books Doubleday. 1958.

Simkhovitch, Vladimir. *Toward the Understanding of Jesus.* New York: The MacMillan Company, 1925.

Stott, John. *The Cross of Christ.* Downers Grove: InterVarsity P, 1986.

Townshend, George. *The Heart of the Gospel.* London: Templar Printing Works, 1939.

Toynbee, Arnold. *The Crucible of Christianity.* New York: The World Publishing Company, 1969.

Wilson, Ian. *Jesus: The Evidence.* New York: Harper Collins Publishers, 1984.

Wood, et al. *Immanuel Kant: Religion within the Boundaries of Mere Reason And Other Writings.* Cambridge: Cambridge UP, 1998.

Dr. Festus Enumah has arranged for part of his share of the proceeds from all his books to be donated to Samuel A. Enumah Africancer Foundation, www.africancer.org, a public, charitable nonprofit 501(c) (3) corporation registered in the state of Georgia, USA. The objective of the foundation is to help develop and build the infrastructure in sub-Saharan Africa for cancer control services, focusing on cancer education, prevention, early detection and treatment. The aim of the foundation is to help reduce the deaths from cancer and improve cancer patients' quality of life.

ABOUT THE AUTHOR

DR. FESTUS ENUMAH was born in Nigeria, on January 21, 1943. He graduated from the University of Ibadan Medical School in Nigeria, and completed his internship and residency in general surgery at Cook County Hospital, Chicago, Illinois. He subsequently went to M. D. Anderson Cancer Center in Houston, Texas, where he successfully completed a fellowship in thoracic surgical oncology. He is board certified by the American Board of Surgery and the Royal College of Physicians and Surgeons of Canada.

He is married to Lois Bronersky-Enumah, who is also a board certified family physician. They live in Columbus, Georgia and have four children. Dr. Enumah is the Founder and the President of Samuel A. Enumah Africancer Foundation. His first book, *The Innocent Blood and Judas Iscariot,* was published in 2002. The First Edition of his second book, *The Father's Business and the Spiritual Cross,* was published in 2014

www.ingramcontent.com/pod-product-compliance
Lightning Source LLC
Chambersburg PA
CBHW031829090426
42741CB00005B/178